Second Home

Second Home

A Day in the Life of a Model Early Childhood Program

Claire Copenhagen Bainer **+** *Liisa Hale*

Redleaf Press
www.redleafpress.org
800-423-8309

Published by Redleaf Press
a division of Resources for Child Caring
10 Yorkton Court
St. Paul, MN 55117
Visit us online at www.redleafpress.org.

First edition 2007
Cover design by Cathy Spengler
Cover photographs by Ray Enriquez
Interior typeset in Mercury and designed by Cathy Spengler
Interior photos by Ray Enriquez
Printed in the United States of America
14 13 12 11 10 09 08 07   1 2 3 4 5 6 7 8

On the *Second Home* DVD, recitation of lines from the poem "On the Ning Nang Nong" from *Silly Verse for
Kids* by Spike Milligan (London: Puffin Books, 1970). Used with permission from Spike Milligan Productions
Limited.

Principles in Appendix B are excerpted from Janet Gonzalez-Mena and Dianne Widmeyer Eyer, *Infants, Toddlers and Caregivers,* 5th edition (New York: McGraw-Hill, 2000), 4–21. © 2000 by the McGraw-Hill Compa-
nies, Inc. Reprinted with permission from McGraw-Hill.

Redleaf Press books are available at a special discount when purchased in bulk for special premiums and sales
promotions. For details, contact the sales manager at 800-423-8309.

Library of Congress Cataloging-in-Publication Data

Bainer, Claire Copenhagen, 1951-
    Second home : a day in the life of a model early childhood program / Claire Copenhagen Bainer and Liisa Hale.
      — 1st ed.
      p. cm.
    Includes bibliographical references and index.
    ISBN 978-1-929610-92-1
    1. Child care—California—Oakland—Case studies. 2. Early childhood education—California—
Oakland—Case studies. I. Hale, Liisa, 1953- II. Title.
    HQ778.67.O25B35 2006
    362.71'20973—dc22

                                        2006100565

Printed on acid-free paper.

Second Home

FOREWORD

It is well known that the United States lags behind other industrial countries as well as many developing nations in providing comprehensive support for families with young children, such as paid parental leave and accessible, high-quality early care and education services. Public policy in this arena is all too often characterized by inadequate funding and piecemeal program development. Policy tends to focus on either the needs of only a small portion of low-income parents who work, while ignoring the developmental needs of their children, or on the educational needs of older preschoolers for half a day, with inadequate attention to the needs of their families for full-day services, not to mention inadequate or nonexistent programs for younger children. As a consequence of such policies, most center-based early childhood programs do not serve children until they are two-and-a-half or three years old, often offering an educational focus without sufficient hours of coverage, and many full-day programs offer coverage without an enriched curriculum. And despite the low pay of staff, many programs are too expensive for most families.

In this climate of inadequate support, programs that take a comprehensive approach to meeting the need for sensitive, loving care and education of the babies, toddlers, and preschoolers of working families are too often the exception. As a result, much has been written about how parents and children alike feel the pressures of a hurried and demanding existence, but very little has been written about how early childhood programs can—and do—serve as supportive "second homes" for such families. Building an environment that helps families construct and sustain a healthy approach to life, that educates children and adults, and that serves as an exemplary model of early childhood practice has been the life work of authors Claire Copenhagen Bainer and Liisa Hale at BlueSkies for Children. Documenting both the dimensions and the value of that environment for other early childhood professionals is clearly and carefully accomplished in this book.

In *Second Home*, Claire and Liisa present a vibrant picture of children moving through their ten-hour days within a loving, well-designed, and creative program that serves infants, toddlers, and preschoolers. The foundation of the program is the application of long-respected and current research on child development, including a multidisciplinary approach to teaching and caring for youngsters and conscientious attention to the needs of the adults in those youngsters' lives, particularly their parents.

BlueSkies serves an economically and ethnically diverse population in an urban area, financially maintained by parent tuition, low-income state vouchers, and private scholarship funding. The center expands and enhances traditional early education best practices by individualizing, honing, and constantly reflecting on the changing needs and life patterns of its families and staff. The joy of the book is discovering that the center takes a "head-on" approach to full-day early care and education for babies through prekindergarteners, not by debating its generic merits but by working to make it the best and most fitting environment for today's families. Accepting as a given that parents need certain services and support has freed the staff to appreciate their profession and create ways and tactics to better do their work.

Second Home can be used as an overview of what the authors call a "hybrid approach" to child care, or as a text for learning about specific age groups and developmental stages. By clearly explaining theoretical concepts and illustrating them with real-life vignettes, the text is appropriate for students and new staff as well as experienced teachers and providers, and is great material for staff meetings and training. Parents, too, will enjoy reading about what their kids and teachers experience every day, and why teachers "do what they do"—in fact, some of the material in the book was originally developed to help parents understand the program at BlueSkies. One can only imagine the shift in public policy if legislators and others making decisions about early care and education read this book as well!

Like Claire and Liisa, we have dedicated our lifework to trying to secure high-quality early care and education that addresses the needs of all families and children. We began as classroom teachers and directors, but left the classroom to concentrate on trying to improve early care and education services by improving early care and education jobs. Our work centers on comprehensive policy development and systems change through advocating for more accessible, relevant professional development and better compensation for the early care and education workforce. In many ways our efforts have gone hand in hand with those of Claire and Liisa, with our modest successes helping to support staff training and supervision as well as access to higher education for those pursuing early childhood careers. But in the desert that is our current system, we often find it hard to point to what we are working toward. At BlueSkies, they have realized the vision of what we need for children and families and have invited teachers at their center and others of us in the community to experience that vision as well. With this book, they have thrown open the doors to their "second home" even wider, inviting readers to enter a program that incorporates the wealth of scientific, theoretical, and practical knowledge about children and their needs with the realities of day-to-day existence for most families. Their hospitality is truly a gift and is greatly appreciated.

——RORY DARRAH, EARLY CARE AND EDUCATION DIRECTOR (RETIRED),
ALAMEDA COUNTY FIRST FIVE

——MARCY WHITEBOOK, PHD, DIRECTOR AND SENIOR RESEARCHER,
CENTER FOR THE STUDY OF CHILD CARE EMPLOYMENT,
UNIVERSITY OF CALIFORNIA AT BERKELEY

The scenes described in this book emerge from life at BlueSkies for Children (BlueSkies), formerly Association of Children's Services (AOCS), a private, nonprofit child care center located since 1983 in Oakland, California. A group of retiring educators, who in the 1950s and 1960s had stayed home with their children while their children were young, realized that the lives of their grandchildren would be radically different from the lives of their own children: their grandchildren's generation would be largely raised in child care. In response, they gathered their collective experience, education, and wisdom and began creating a new hybrid child care program that fully integrates care and education. The authors of this book have been managing BlueSkies since 1995, and Claire continues to offer her thirty years of classroom experience to the children and teachers at BlueSkies for part of each day.

BlueSkies operates from 7:30 AM to 6:00 PM Monday through Friday, fifty-one weeks per year. There are usually about twenty-six teachers on staff and eighty-five children in six classrooms. Half the children are between two months and thirty-six months old, necessitating low child-to-teacher ratios, and there is often a "morning" and an "afternoon" teacher covering the same position. Some teachers are decades-long employees, while others are beginners with minimal experience. Some teachers have a bachelor's degree or both a bachelor's and master's degree, while others have only a few college units in early childhood—most are somewhere in between. Support staff provide daily housekeeping in the classrooms and prepare meals and snacks appropriate to every level of development.

From the beginning, BlueSkies has acknowledged that caring for young children also requires caring for adults. For teachers and administrative staff, parent conferences, seminars, and casual drop-in counseling are key to maintaining healthy relationships in the child care center. Also, since 1987, BlueSkies has taught on-site early care and education (ECE) classes for teachers from hundreds of child care centers, allowing them to experience in person what they've read about or heard lectures about. For example, when adult students study the development of one-year-olds, they observe in the Wobbly Walker classroom (ages thirteen months to twenty-four months), where instructors can point out how the classroom practice incorporates and reflects academic theory.

Seeking to extend its reach to teachers beyond the Oakland/East Bay area, BlueSkies began producing teacher training videos, and now is publishing this book. The attached DVD includes age-specific vignettes that were filmed at BlueSkies (see appendix A for author commentaries on the vignettes), along with the video *Beyond the Curriculum,* which was filmed at BlueSkies in 2003, when it was still AOCS. *Beyond the Curriculum* provides a comprehensive overview of the program and serves as an introduction to the relationship-based teaching practices used at BlueSkies.

Referring to BlueSkies as a "model early childhood program" reflects the intentionality and thoughtfulness that have informed its approach, rather than implying that BlueSkies offers the single best way to care for children. There are many wonderful child care programs for young children; BlueSkies provides one model, the result of years of thought and purpose on the part of a few professional, committed people.

We use the term *teacher* throughout this book to refer to child care professionals in all settings—providers in child care centers and Head Start programs, as well as accredited preschool teachers—in order to acknowledge and emphasize that quality caregiving and early childhood education are synonymous. We use the term *parent* to refer to all primary caretakers—biological and adoptive parents, extended family members, or appointed legal guardians—who are responsible for *parenting* a child.

When we refer to individual children, we have tried to alternate pronouns between *he* and *she*. When we refer to teachers, however, we have used the pronoun *she* exclusively, not to disregard the superb male teachers who are out there, but rather for simplicity's sake, since the vast majority of early childhood teachers are female.

ACKNOWLEDGMENTS

Many people deserve thanks for their support and insights. First and foremost, thanks to the children, families, and teachers at BlueSkies for Children, both past and present, who were the models and inspiration for much of what we wrote. Thanks to Anne Copenhagen, Claire's mother, who founded the school on principles of quality, who gave us the opportunity to run and grow it, and who continues to share her vision for young children. Thanks to the steadfast support of the BlueSkies board of directors, whose members understand the importance of this project. Special thanks to friend and colleague Gail Myers Enriquez for her contributions on kindergarten readiness and literacy, and to Ray, her husband, whose skill and artistry with the video camera make the DVD a pleasure to watch. Thanks also to Sid Farrar at Redleaf Press, who encouraged us to share our work.

We are grateful to the teachers who developed the values that inform our teaching: Dr. Elinor Griffin of the Griffin School in Berkeley, California; Frances Ruth Armstrong, child development professor at Mills College in Oakland, California; and Janet Gonzalez-Mena, author and teacher. Each of us has been shaped, too, by the experience of parenting, so we thank our children, who taught us about ourselves and who helped us become better teachers both to children and to parents. We have also benefited from our fortunate location in Alameda County, where we work with people who are setting national standards for visionary planning in the area of high-quality early care and education for all: infants through preschool, in full-day or part-day programs.

The New Extended Family: An Overview of the Hybrid Child Care Model

Over the course of their childhood, children today spend up to 12,000 hours in child care outside their home—more total hours than they will spend in elementary, junior high, and high school combined (Greenman 1998). Child care programs are reinventing themselves in response to that fact. Children attending child care centers, Head Start programs, or state-funded preschools on a part-day basis—typically three hours per day during the school year—are in those settings for 500 to 1,000 total hours, depending on whether they attend for one or two years. Clearly, children experience different kinds of lives: children in year-round, ten-hour-per-day programs are living virtually all of every weekday in a child care setting, whereas children in three-hour-per-day programs spend considerably more time at home with a relative or caregiver.

The debate over the past four decades about whether children should be raised at home or in child care is now beside the point. Loving parents may both need to work in order to meet the high cost of living, or both partners may want to continue in careers they love, even as they raise a family, knowing that by leading whole, well-rounded lives they can give their children the gift of emotionally healthy parents. Families headed by a single parent or by kinship caregivers need time to care for their own needs as well as the needs of a small child. Each unique situation brings unique requirements for child care. The bottom line is that parents *are* working out of the home and children *are* spending long days, weeks, and years in child care settings. Child care is here to stay for many children from many different walks of life and many different circumstances. Wealthy families, middle-income families, and families living in poverty all use child care for their children. Children developing typically and those whose development is not following a typical trajectory are in child care settings. Middle-income parents stretch to afford care for their children because they know, as many studies show, that quality child care is good for children and that the quality of care is linked to educated caregivers. It is human nature to want what's best for our children.

Instead of debating whether care in the home or out of the home is best for children, the focus should be on identifying and providing quality child care programs for children who will be in group care. Studies show that although children who complete certain kindergarten readiness programs do well when they start school, they end up falling behind by the third grade. Children from other kindergarten readiness programs show less dramatic gains in kindergarten but dramatically better long-term school and life success. It's important to know what makes the difference. No child will thrive in an "institutional" setting for ten hours a day. It's also true that the child care experience and the elementary school experience should be very different, as the needs and developmental abilities of children at different ages are so different. The challenge is to reinvent child care so that the long hours away from parent figures and out of the home environment are meaningful, rich, and sustaining, giving every child a wonderful experience in the first years of life.

Applying Research to Quality Care

Much is known about what young children need to live and thrive. Great thinkers have studied and written about human development, the ages and stages of growth, and changes in a child's ability to comprehend and adapt as different levels of understanding correspond with the brain's growth and development during the first five years of life. Psychological studies and research on infant attachment and mental health give insight into the reciprocity between a caregiver and infant and the infant's ability to process and regulate, not only through its nervous system but through its entire being. Occupational therapists, physical therapists, and those who work with the body teach early care and education specialists about physical development. Studies in sensory integration and brain development show how a small child tries to regulate the amount of stimulation he receives and how overstimulation is hard on the development of the nervous system. Theories of mental health systems bring forward the importance of the dynamic that works among all these systems as they come together and play out in the structure of families and in the culture of the child care center.

Although much research is being done on what it means to be a developing human being, this research often reflects only the narrow area of the researcher's interest. Early care and education specialists have the responsibility to draw from research in other fields, to understand and to think clearly and deeply about what is now known about the needs of young children and how to meet those needs, so that all children can thrive, regardless of the care setting they are in. All the related fields of human development inform how the child care environment should look and feel to a young child. A calm, quiet, restful space is actually a more stimulating learning environment than a brightly colored, busy classroom, which is often pictured as the ideal preschool setting. In the busy classroom, the young child must learn to block out input before she can effectively take in important data from the world around her.

Early childhood pioneers such as Harriet Johnson and Maria Montessori thought carefully about how to enrich not only the school experiences but also the home experiences of young children participating in part-day nursery-school programs. Today, directors and providers in full-day child care programs must think equally carefully about how to enrich the child care and preschool experiences of children who are home for only a small part of the day.

Combining the academic knowledge of the early care and education field with the reality of the lives of today's young families can result in high-quality, sustainable learning and a wonderful support system for families. It was not so long ago that zoologists realized that the animals they cared for would thrive if their habitat better met the needs of their species. Zoologists studied everything known about the needs and preferences of each species: physical space needs; whether or not the species is social, and if so, how to create an optimal social group; what foods support growth; how the animal prefers to receive foods; and so on. Bears needed caves where they could hibernate, and water buffalo needed pools of water to stand in, so zoos were remodeled to provide individual species with what they needed to live and thrive in captivity. Similarly, early care and education providers, teachers, and specialists need to ask what a human child needs in order to live and thrive. Teachers and centers are expanding their imaginations to develop child care settings that show a real understanding of how to care for young children so the children will thrive.

Supporting Learning and Development on Many Levels

Anthropological studies document the evolution of human beings in small multigenerational communities of forty to fifty people who lived and worked together. Their continued existence rested on mutual support and the interdependent needs that brought them together as a society. They helped each other, took care of each other, and created language to communicate and connect with each other. They were also connected to the world around them, as their existence was dependent on understanding the rhythm of the earth, the migration of game, and the cycles of plant growth. Although most of the world's societies have relatively quickly evolved beyond small, earth-connected tribes of people, individual human beings do not evolve as quickly. Organically, the people who lived in those small communities thousands of years ago were at about the same stage of evolution as the people who live in New York City today. That means the things children need to become whole, healthy, productive adults are in fact very similar to what their ancestors needed thousands of years ago, even though many children today live in a crowded, busy, social world full of fast-moving vehicles and electronic gadgets. Children grow to be smart, kind, thoughtful, creative, disciplined, productive people when they feel, from the beginning, loved, safe, and cared for in a world that offers both stimulation and calm, both surprise and predictability, as well as secure, loving connections.

The age-old question of nature versus nurture has become obsolete, reflecting a simplistic understanding of the way human beings take in information. It is now known that learning occurs in the brain in a proximal zone of development: while a child appears to be focused on learning one task, he may in fact be learning other things as well. Information comes into the brain in many ways. In the mind, the ability to receive and organize is regulated by the way sensory input is managed. The brain grows with use and responds to repetition; new experiences initially attract the brain's attention by their novelty, then become familiar, and ultimately become internal and habitual. Creating a new child care setting that will support the complex and complicated way young children learn requires intentional thought and must include the breadth of information available from the many fields that study the growth and learning of young children.

Psychologist Abraham Maslow's hierarchy of human needs informs and expands on the responsibilities of the full-day child care teacher. Physiological needs are at the base level: human survival requires food, shelter, warmth, and so on. A level of security follows, then love, affection, and community; respect for oneself and others; and finally, self-actualization. Optimal development occurs when all these needs are met. Each level is attainable only after the more basic needs before it have been fulfilled. Clearly, children who spend most of their waking hours in child care need far more than food and safety in order to thrive.

Meeting Multiple Needs in Different Settings

While there is of course some overlap, the following chart, which is from an earlier era, shows a young child's needs for optimal growth, along with where those needs are expected to be met under the "traditional" part-day model of child care or preschool.

Needs of a Whole, Healthy Preschooler	Met at Part-day Preschool or at Home?
Attached relationship with an adult	Home
Human touch, intimacy	Home
Caring and nurturance (loving support)	Home
Empathy and understanding (reflection)	Home
Challenging motor-development activities	Preschool
Security, ease	Home
Social connection with peers, friends	Preschool
Mystery, joy, beauty	Home
Cognitive/intellectual awareness	Preschool
Change and unpredictability	Home
Opportunities to explore and experiment	Preschool

Today, children in a quality child care setting need to receive all of the "home" experiences listed in the chart both at home *and* in their child care setting. And, since this chart describes a preschool experience only for three- and four-year-olds in an earlier era, it does not even consider infants and toddlers, who in those days had no formal experiences outside the home. Child care is reinvented and redefined when the needs of the working family *and* the needs of the young child are met, when all that is known about the human mind and about what children need is incorporated into the care offered to children and their families. In the past, three-hour programs viewed issues such as attachment and trust as skills a young child developed from an attached relationship with a parent, skills that could then be transferred to the child's relationship with her teacher. A child in a part-day program who goes home for lunch and a nap and who spends most of his day with a parent does not require the same level of teacher attachment as a child in a ten-hour program. But neither infants entering care at the age of two or three months nor toddlers can be expected to have developed a strong enough parent attachment to easily transfer it to a teacher. A teacher in a full-day program must develop the ability to form attachments with young children by making full use of information from studies on infant mental health and by developing a sensitivity about gaze and touch in order to build a secondary attachment that will support the baby and the family. In a three-hour program, teachers don't have to take on as many of a parent's nurturing roles as they do in a full-day program, since, for example, no lunch is served and there is no naptime. Part-day teachers also don't have to pace themselves for an eight-hour day working with children, nor do they have to think about what to do to help a tired toddler at 4:30 in the afternoon or how to toilet train a toddler.

Achieving Predictability and Consistency in Quality Programs

No teacher could ever replace a parent; a parent's level of intimacy and emotional engagement will always be much deeper than that of the teacher. Attachment with a teacher is more about predictability and the level of safety the child feels. A good full-day program must make it safe for children to explore the world around them, not just physically but emotionally: safe to get into trouble, safe to get mad, safe to try new things, safe to take a break and rest in the sunshine, safe to understand one's feelings, and safe to learn how to manage oneself in relationships with others. A child must trust that she can express her full self and still be accepted and supported. In a full-day program, the deep yet objective attachment of teacher to child, along with consistent teaching, creates for the children a feeling of safety. A parent's activities and a teacher's activities may become blended unless conscious thought, academic rigor, and creativity come together to redefine the role of the child care teacher.

It is challenging to engage and sustain teachers who understand the complexity and importance of consistency in supporting children's healthy development. For example, it can be difficult to achieve consistency in full-day care, where rooms are commonly staffed by two shifts of teachers who take vacations throughout the year. In a part-day program, on the other hand, it's common for a few teachers to cover the entire half-day, and to vacation when the program is closed for holidays or summer break. Creating a center culture that offers children a consistent philosophical approach as they are cared for throughout the day is made more difficult when teachers bring into their classrooms diverse cultural beliefs about child rearing. Recognizing and working with these challenges are key steps toward creating quality child care.

CONSISTENCY IN PHILOSOPHY AND TEACHING STYLE

In a small family, most of the rules and information about life come from one or two adults. A child in such a family quickly learns to "read" those adults, who usually have closely aligned philosophical approaches. A child in group care has many more adults interacting with him; if he has to spend a lot of time understanding their meanings and motives, he'll have no time left to devote to his own growth! Thus, a quality setting ensures that teachers are thoroughly grounded in a common philosophy and teaching style. In such a setting, the teachers all

- learn to use positive language with the children, even if they themselves were spoken to harshly as children;
- learn to set firm but friendly limits, even if they themselves were raised permissively;
- agree to common procedures for various activities, so that children hear the same instructions from all teachers.

This continuity helps children understand their world and it supports children's cognitive and language development.

Growing up in a home, or in a tribe, children know what to expect of all the adults. At a school where there is a focus on the importance of consistency, all teachers will have agreed on the way they will talk to the children. For example, whenever a child attempts to climb on a table, the teachers will say something similar, such as "Keep your feet on the floor" or "Here's a place to climb over here." If a child begins to run in the classroom, a teacher will say, "Use your walking feet." If a child throws sand, a teacher will say, "Keep the sand down." If a child starts yelling at another child, a teacher will remind him, "Use a talking voice." Throughout each day, children receive messages about what they can do and how they can do what they want in an acceptable way. A teacher's ability to convey optimism in her language helps children develop optimism in themselves, for they will then trust that they are good learners and will do better the next time a similar situation comes up. Making negative statements such as "Get down!" "Stop running!" "Don't throw that sand!" or "Stop yelling!" conveys a message that the child is not doing what he *should* do, and the child will therefore likely stop listening to the teacher's comments.

Teachers match their expectations to a child's development, so that a child never feels more is being asked of her than she can manage. The unique, positive, constructive stance of the early care and education teacher builds an ambience for the child's day; it is the teacher's goal to communicate to the child over and over and in every circumstance that she believes the child is a wonderful human being who is doing his best and is capable of learning and managing his world. Teachers develop a kind of "ECE speak" as they learn to turn negative statements into positive ones, and to coach a child to be the best person he can be.

The Importance of Fulfilled Teachers

Teachers in full-day programs need deeper nurturing than teachers in part-day programs. Teachers working forty hour weeks need to replenish themselves while on the job so that they can keep giving of themselves to the children. The pleasure of watching and guiding the emerging development of the human beings in their care is enhanced when teachers are given the opportunity to grow professionally and to intellectualize their teaching and learning every day. Fulfilled teachers believe in their work, trust each other to contribute thoughtfully to the community, and trust their ability to guide and support the self-righting nature of child development. Teachers who are stressed and unfulfilled cannot give children the optimistic, trusting environment that will enable them to feel safe and be able to grow.

Parents who entrust most of their children's waking hours to a child care center must likewise trust that the teachers are educated and thoughtful in their work, and are putting the children's best interests at the forefront of their planning. Parents learn to trust teachers by developing their own attached relationships with them. Ellen Galinsky's phrase "the new extended family" describes this model of relationship-based care for the entire family. Whereas part-day nursery schools developed around a young child's need for enriched group experiences outside the home, quality child care settings today need to serve the entire family. They need to allow parents to go to work or school each day with the knowledge that their children are having a wonderful experience—not the same experience they might have at home, perhaps, but one that is rich, nurturing, developmentally appropriate, and sustaining. During the first days of transition into child care, when a parent watches the teachers' interactions with all the children in the group as well as with her own treasured child, the teachers begin to earn that parent's trust by responding respectfully, thoughtfully, and appropriately to the children's needs. When a parent's natural inclination to be distressed about leaving her baby with strangers for the first time is met with compassionate support from the teacher, more trust is built. Over time, a teacher's opportunity to build trust with parents is much more limited than her opportunity to build trust with the children, so the teacher should make the most of every opportunity to help parents understand that she is an educated, thoughtful, caring partner working to sustain and support a healthy family dynamic.

Quality child care settings give children the message that they can be themselves, accepted as they are but also challenged to grow at a pace that is right for them. In spending days with teachers who understand child development, children learn that the world will support their efforts to succeed. The teacher works within the child's development to help establish constructive habits, patterns of self-management, and social interaction that will serve him throughout life. The teacher holds a common goal in her mind, toward which each individual child can move in process with the other individuals in the group. While responding to each child's unique developmental process, the teacher also guides. She holds the expectation that each child will mature and develop when given the tools to do so.

When there are difficulties in a classroom, the teacher's response is based on three key assumptions:

1. The child has formed a trusting relationship with the teacher.
2. The child is not able (rather than not willing) to conform to expectations in the current situation.
3. The teacher is responsible for making the classroom work for the children.

A relationship with the teacher provides an incentive for the child to moderate his behavior because he cares about what is important to that teacher. If such a relationship has not yet been formed, the teacher does not expect the child to be as able to self-manage, and she puts a priority on building that relationship. The teacher also truly believes that a child who makes a social mistake has made a mistake and needs more coaching and support to do better the next time. Some aspect of the situation, either internal to the child or part of the external environment, interferes with his ability to manage what the other children can manage.

Most of all, the teacher believes it is her job to adapt the classroom, teaching practices, routines, or schedules to best support the needs of the children. Operating on these beliefs, the teacher accepts responsibility for using all her education, skill, analysis, and ingenuity to create a day that works for the children.

An Extended Home

The new child care serves not just as an extended family for children, it also serves as an extended home. While the relationships among children, teachers, and parents are paramount, the physical space is also important to consider. Children whose lives are largely lived in a child care facility need to experience all the warmth and interest of a home while in that facility. In most homes, rooms are painted different colors and the functional furnishings are augmented with knickknacks, photos, plants, art, family treasures, and so forth. Classrooms in child care centers also need diverse adornment. Each classroom should feel unique, just as the rooms of a home are unique. The learning experience in the child care center is holistic; the message a child receives from growing up in a child care setting where the environment is varied is that the world is interesting, fun, and full of things to think about and learn about. In contrast to children in full-day child care, elementary school children are in a school setting for less than half their waking hours; the focus of their learning is intellectual development. The elementary school environment is also very focused on intellectual stimulation, and on teacher-directed learning.

ENVIRONMENTS THAT NURTURE AND SUPPORT GROWTH

In a child care setting, children need to see beauty around them, interesting artwork on the walls, growing things in the rooms, a variety of fabrics in the play areas, vases of flowers, and so forth. Children's bodies are growing and their minds are organizing themselves; they need room for quiet and for peaceful solitude. The child care environment should support a child's ability to slow down and just be. It is in quiet that new thoughts arise and creative ideas bubble up. Building quiet into a child care environment and establishing a daily pace for children that supports it is vital. In creating a learning environment that supports the wholeness of what it is to be human, a new concept of child care takes form.

Most homes are organized and orderly. Teachers step back and look at their classroom, their work area, and the children's living space, taking notice if hundreds of play materials are jammed too tightly on the shelves or if children's artwork hangs from every surface. Such situations are overstimulating and are not conducive to providing a quality learning space. Teachers also review furniture placement, making sure play spaces are protected from traffic and that children can move around comfortably. It doesn't take a deep understanding of the needs of human beings and their development to imagine what impact long days in cramped or cluttered spaces can have on a developing human.

An infant room must have soft fabric elements, even though such elements will require washing. If everything in a room can be sprayed or wiped, the room will fail to meet the tactile needs of infants. And spaces for children should be kept small, more like a room in a home than like an elementary school classroom.

An outdoor play space offering exposure to the natural world augments the indoor space. Fresh air and a place for noise to escape shifts the classroom dynamic, refreshing children and teachers alike during a long child care day. Nature brings unpredictability and wonder to children's experiences. The weather changes, the seasons change, plants and animals grow and change. One day there is a bug under a rock or a snail on a leaf; the next day there is not. One day there are fluffy clouds in the sky; the next day the sky is dark and full of rain. While the teacher can plan a science curriculum, there is no curriculum so interesting as that which children discover in the course of outdoor play. The support and sustaining qualities of nature can be intentionally brought into the classroom as well—autumn leaves in the fall, flower blossoms in the spring, and rich loamy soil to dig in during any season all bring the human connection to the earth to the children and support their feeling of belonging.

A DIFFERENT PACE

The pace of life for children is different in full-day settings than in part-day settings. Children in part-day programs may to some extent be there for excitement in an otherwise quiet day. They have only a few hours to play with the toys, make friends, and learn to get along in a group. Part-day programs commonly operate on a school-year calendar, closing for a few weeks in winter and spring, and for several months in summer, resulting in about 500 classroom hours per year. Contrast that with over 2,500 annual enrollment hours for a child who attends full-day child care fifty-two hours per week, fifty-one weeks of the year. The child in a full-day program spends five times as many hours there as a child in a part-day program. If a full-day program offered the same stimulating schedule as a part-day program but for five times as many hours, a child would become overwhelmed and exhausted. Such a child would have lots of time to play, lots of time to be with friends, and lots of time to learn about being in a group. But a child needs time to pace herself more than she needs a flurry of activity over a few hours. She needs to know that during her long days in a group, she will always be able to find a quiet corner where she can play alone, just as she might at home. As she begins learning about the reciprocity of friendship, she needs to know that the teacher will respect her need to play with just one other friend, as she might at home. She needs to know that the teacher will help her learn to build rhythm into her days, by balancing activities and creating a predictable schedule, just as she might experience at home.

Life itself becomes a major part of the full-day curriculum. Along with playing with toys, a child's basic body and self-care functions are activities through which relationships are built. Unlike a parent at home, the teacher in a child care setting is never in a hurry to run to the store, start the laundry, or pick up a sibling at school; she is in the classroom to meet children's needs. Ideally, if a toddler wants to sit and work at putting on his own shoes for thirty minutes, the teacher can let him, since that activity is every bit as challenging as putting together a puzzle. The teacher in a part-day program might worry that a child who spends extended time putting on shoes is missing out on chances to play with other children, but in the full-day setting the child has plenty of other time for play.

Full-day children learning to use the toilet have their own baskets of clothes handy, so they can quickly change if they have an accident. A child who loves clothing may spend a lot of time changing from one outfit to another just because he enjoys it. Children learning to serve themselves at lunch are given dishes they can manage, such as a two-cup pitcher to pour from rather than a half-gallon milk carton. Children set the table and then clear dishes after they eat, and they prepare snacks for themselves as they are able. These are all examples of how the pace of the program slows, balancing home and school experiences throughout the day.

AN INCLUSIVE FAMILY

Every type of family constellation participates in the child care center. Children with parents of different race or ethnicity and children with different cultures and belief structures come into the program. There are children with physical challenges growing right alongside children being raised by single or same-sex parents, aunts or grandmothers; and children from more typical family structures. All children love their families and are proud of them, which is important to their healthy development. This love is unconditional, regardless of circumstances. When the teacher and the school set a standard that is open and inclusive, all children and families feel respected, cared for, and accepted as they are.

Classrooms are stocked with books about all kinds of families, affirming for the children that who they are and how they look can be found in the stories they read. Seeing Chinese writing helps with the concept of reading even if the primary language in the school in English, because if the child has a grandma who reads the Chinese newspaper at home, the characters have the same meaning to the child as our English letters. Similarly, putting African gourds in the dollhouse will have meaning if there is a child in the group who has family members who cook with gourds and if the teachers show all the children how to cook with gourds.

Young children first need to play with and learn about real things from their own experiences. Later, the teacher can introduce difference, but for the difference to be valuable, it must link with the real and known. To a young child, a wheelchair is not very different from a stroller unless the child understands how important a wheelchair is to someone she loves who cannot get around without it. When a toy wheelchair is introduced in the doll corner, children will play with it as a stroller unless they have an understanding of the difference between a stroller and a wheelchair. Thoughtful teachers keep these subtleties in mind as they introduce new and different objects to the classroom; a wheelbarrow in the play yard in a farming community will have a very different meaning and value from the same wheelbarrow in the play yard at a city school. While a wheelbarrow, a wheelchair, Chinese writing, and a cooking gourd are very different objects, they all need meaning to be valuable learning toys for young children, whose understanding of the world is so concrete and literal.

When developing an open and inclusive curriculum for the children, one that represents diversity and multiculturalism, it's important to shift away from adult thinking. Adult thinking has been influenced by years of experience, so it can be challenging to put that aside and experience the world as a baby does, without thinking in words, or to recall what it's like to react impulsively, without thinking about good or bad consequences. Standing in the child's world, thinking with the child's mind, and keeping pace with the child's life experience are not easy accomplishments for adults, but they do inform adults about how to understand the child and meet her needs. It's easy for adults to think that children understand more about the world than they actually do, because children learn language from adults and use the same inflection and tone as adults do when they speak, even though they may actually have no idea what they're saying.

An astute mother shared a conversation she had with her three-year-old on the way to school one day:

We were coming down the hill into town and Russell, strapped in the backseat in his car seat, said, "Mom, I see a bad guy! He's over there hiding in the bushes. He's a black guy! He's peeking in the window of that house. Now he's looking in the other window!" I was so distressed. My mind was going all over the place wondering: Should I stop? What should I do? What is he seeing? Why did my child automatically think a "black guy" was a bad guy? Just as I was looking for a place to pull over and turn around and talk to him so I could get some more information, he said, "Yep, he's black all over and has a waggy tail and says woof!"

The mother realized that *her* mind had jumped to all kinds of conclusions that had nothing to do with what her child was thinking, and she realized that if she had responded, she would have been completely out of attunement. It is this lack of attunement that makes adults laugh at children's misunderstandings—something teachers are careful not to do. Children perceive and discuss difference in accordance with their developmental ability to take in and process information. When children are interested in sorting (by about their fourth year), they sort everything. They will sort people by color, size, shape, and gender. The experience has very little to do with anything but sorting, even though it may look like race awareness; depending on the child, he or she may or may not have an understanding of racial differences (as in the scene between Anne and Bea's grandma found in chapter 7). Adults think carefully about their reactions because children pick up on the emotion behind words or actions before they listen to or even care about the words. Helping parents understand this point and respond appropriately builds the parent-child relationship and can set in place and strengthen trusting family relationships.

A child care center can give children the opportunity to learn about and enjoy all kinds of people with many different needs. Children with special needs are carefully enfolded into the group, with a thoughtful eye toward what is in the child's best interest. Children with processing issues need environments that are quiet, orderly, and predictable. Young children with Asperger's syndrome need a more rigid classroom structure in order to manage in their mind the chaos that is inevitably created by so many unpredictable children. The needs of children with hearing, vision, or mobility impairment must be met in special ways so they, too, can experience the world as an interesting, joyful place to be. The child care center director and teachers must ensure that all the children in their setting get what they need. This may include helping a family to find more appropriate placement for a child when the center cannot provide what he needs, and recognizing that meeting each child's needs means that one or two children cannot require all of the teacher's attention. If there are children who require a high level of support, the center has an obligation to make adjustments until all children are receiving what they need.

The Hybrid Setting as a Second Home

The new hybrid child care, which mixes the best of a thoughtful child development center with the nurturing support of a home, truly is a haven for children. The following story illustrates how nicely the concept supports a child.

One night as mom is settling three-year-old Ruth in bed, Ruth confides, "I was mad at naptime today."

Mom asks, "Why were you mad?"

Ruth says, "I didn't want to take a nap."

"What did your teacher do when you didn't want to take a nap?" inquires Mom.

Ruth answers, "She patted my back and I yelled and I kicked my feet. I made a lot of noise while the other kids were trying to go to sleep."

Mom asks, "And did your teacher get mad?"

Ruth bursts into laughter at such a question and answers, "Teachers don't get mad!" in the tone that implies "You must not know anything."

Mom can't resist asking, "Do mommies and daddies get mad?"

Ruth's eyes get big as she says, with the certainty born of experience, "Oh yes, they get mad!"

What a wonderful thing it is for children to have such confidence that they can be as aggravating as they can be, and their teachers will go right on giving them loving support and guidance so they won't need to act that way! What a gift to parents it is to know that their children are held in the care of teachers who can maintain a professional stance in the face of their children's tantrums!

The child care center that successfully creates the new extended family creates a culture of gentle caring and guidance for everyone: parents, staff, and children. Just as in a family home, day in and day out everyone counts, everyone plays an important role, and everyone speaks kindly to one another, assists one another when needed, offers positive suggestions, and accepts one another's strengths as well as their need to grow in some areas. The utopian world that is modeled for young children in such a setting becomes the child's expected model for the world. Though, of course, the "real world" lacks some of these qualities, teachers who convince each child to expect utopia are setting the stage for a world in which children will use their power to make it so.

Incorporating the best qualities of a loving, supportive, attuned home with the enrichment and wisdom of a wonderful early education setting, the hybrid child care setting is described in the chapters that follow. Teachers in this hybrid program teach thoughtfully and intentionally. They are aware that since the human mind is always learning, all hours of the day are equally valuable: what happens at ten o'clock in the morning is as valuable as what happens at five o'clock at night. They recognize that each experience builds the proximal zones of learning, whether that learning is about mommy, how to manage feelings, how to be in a relationship, about oneself, what is allowed, when it's good to get help, how to count, how to wait, or how to start and how to stop an activity. These teachers respect the way a child spends her time throughout the day. They meet the needs of the whole child, developing the mind, body, and soul in a full-day, year-round child care program.

The EVOLUTION *of* EARLY CARE *and* EDUCATION

1

Helen, Ruben, and Leon come into the big block area first thing in the morning, Leon talking about what they can build. Helen carries her 3-D paper art project in her hands, which is what she really wants to talk about. While Ruben stands and chats with her, Leon gets started finding the biggest blocks and standing them on end to form a perimeter to the structure. Soon Ruben finds the building looks more interesting than chatting with Helen, so he joins Leon. Having lost her audience, Helen loses interest, but the boys negotiate with her to leave her art project on the windowsill where they can admire it while they build. Soon the entire block area is encircled with big blocks. Matthew asks if he can join the block play, suggesting hopefully that he can add another layer of blocks to make the walls higher. After quick consultation, Leon and Ruben say he can to join them, but they don't want higher walls, as they're ready to put some boards across the top.

The teacher opens a door so they can fetch the 4-foot boards that advanced block builders use to make a roof.

As the first boards are laid on top, it becomes apparent that the distance from side to side is much longer than the boards, so that when one end rests on the wall, the other end falls to the floor. Ruben and Leon begin to lay a few boards slightly at a diagonal at the corners, where they can be supported on both ends, but they work hesitantly, as they puzzle over how to make a roof out of boards that are too short. Matthew sizes up the situation and, without asking permission, begins to construct an equally high wall down the center of the structure and to lay boards from each side to the center. The other two boys happily join in, and together the three boys quickly finish the roof. Ruben then suggests they hang blankets off the roof, an idea the others enthusiastically endorse. Unfortunately, one of the walls is right in front of the chest of drawers holding the blankets, making it inaccessible. After some failed attempts, the children decide they can nudge the block wall a few inches inward, just enough so that by slithering around the end of the chest of drawers it is possible to reach inside the drawer and fish out a few blankets.

The teacher watches this problem solving with satisfaction, observing that these preschoolers, who will be going to kindergarten in a few months, have been independently solving both physical and social problems throughout the past hour. They successfully negotiated social interaction among themselves, with the original artist, and when allowing a third child to join their play. They encountered unexpected problems in their building, but had enough practice to know that one problem does not require abandoning a whole plan, as younger children often believe. These preschoolers have learned to be flexible enough and "big" enough in their thinking to be able to shift plans a bit as needed in pursuit of their goal.

From Theory to Practice

The children in the previous illustration have learned to manage their play independently through their teacher's understanding of their developmental needs. The teacher's education in the field of early care and education included the study of many theories, all of which shaped the classroom in which the children play. Arnold Gesell charted the range of typical development in children. Jean Piaget and Lev Vygotsky showed that children construct their own learning through a sequence of hands-on experiences. Erik Erikson recognized that children's emotional development must be honored and equally supported along with that of the brain and the body. John Dewey illustrated how children gain social skills through their play. B. F. Skinner theorized that responses to behavior can shape future behaviors. Friedrich Froebel gave us unit blocks, which Patty Smith Hill, a pioneering kindergarten and nursery school teacher, transformed into large building blocks. Child-sized room furnishings with supplies readily accessed by children are legacies of Maria Montessori. And so on. The rich heritage of theory and science concerning the development of young children supports the experience of every child in quality child care programs today.

Theories about the education and development of children younger than five years, which form the roots of early care and education, first began to emerge in the middle of the nineteenth century. By the turn to the twentieth century, this new field was attracting some of the brightest and best minds in the academic world, drawing men and women from the fields of psychology, medicine and nursing, and education. Over the past 150 years, early care and education studies have grown more and more technical, yet it's interesting to see how much of the "scientific proof" of the past fifty years explains only why observations documented one hundred years ago are true. Each of the theorists mentioned above merits in-depth study. The following sketches are provided not as a comprehensive introduction to their work, but simply to demonstrate the breadth of thought that has shaped today's early childhood classroom. A very accessible and more comprehensive introduction to early childhood theorists is Carol Garhart Mooney's *Theories of Childhood* (2000).

THE FATHER OF KINDERGARTEN

Friedrich Froebel (1782–1852), known as the father of kindergarten, invented the concept of open-ended building blocks based on a mathematical unit. While his carefully thought-out blocks were the direct antecedent of the unit blocks that exist in every quality early childhood classroom today, his interest was in creating open-ended play materials

that developed creativity and symbolic thinking. The blocks were given to children to handle and experience, with the idea that the blocks would ultimately stimulate imagination and symbolic thinking. Froebel labeled as "gifts" specially designed toys such as these blocks. Froebel believed that children would learn through playing with carefully selected materials, and that flexible thinking is developed through inspiring the imagination (in play, the block symbolizes the road or fence).

EXPERIENCE IS THE BEST TEACHER

John Dewey (1859–1952) began his career as a philosopher, but later turned to educational reform, having been influenced by the field of psychology and his interest in social issues. Dewey recognized that the social milieu was changing for young children, and he saw that social change without change to the education system would mean that children would not be well prepared for the world. Among his vast contributions to the field of child development are the notions that children's interests will lead them to learn, that children learn through experience as well as instruction, that teachers must lead children to understand social interaction as well as subject matter, and that school life must connect with children's home life. The concept of the teacher as an experienced guide who assists children in their learning explorations, and the idea that children are human beings in their own right also came from Dewey, and describe the philosophy practiced by the teachers in this book.

MIND, BODY, SPIRIT

Rudolf Steiner (1861–1925), a philosopher and great thinker, studied child development with particular focus on the imitative nature of learning. He created the Waldorf schools after World War I, developing a curriculum designed to put an end to war; toward that end, he emphasized the need to surround young children with a positive environment that presents them with the best models. Until age seven (Erikson's "age of reason"), direct instruction at Waldorf schools centers around household activities rather than academic skills, emulating the sorts of activities that might engage a young child at home. Steiner studied temperaments and was interested in educating the mind, body, and spirit of the child. To help children with their learning, he also devised eurhythmy (a movement and dance system), and he studied the effect of food on the body and how food

influences behavior. Like Froebel's "gifts," Steiner's Waldorf schools and methods continue to elicit interest around the world.

ENVIRONMENT AS TEACHER

Maria Montessori (1870–1952) is survived by an international movement bearing her name and is perhaps the person most associated with preschool learning. Originally trained as a physician, she is known for her innovative concepts of education that allowed children the opportunity to live in a thoughtfully prepared classroom environment and to work with specialized materials. Like Steiner, Montessori believed that environment was "the third teacher in the room" and that by providing an environment that was beautiful, orderly, and child-sized, children would naturally internalize and appreciate beauty and order. She held great respect for the abilities of young children, and emphasized the teacher's role as an observer and facilitator who should allow children long uninterrupted periods of play with quality materials. These aspects of Montessori's thought permeate every quality classroom for young children today, whether or not Montessori is acknowledged in the program's name. Maria Montessori was nominated three times for the Nobel Peace Prize (in 1949, 1950, and 1951), a recognition of the impact her work has had on young children throughout the world.

PIONEERS OF COGNITION AND LEARNING

Jean Piaget (1896–1980), a biologist, began to study the process of children's learning at the same time Arnold Gesell was studying the process of growth. Piaget developed the theory that children learn through the interaction of their own actions with their environment—a perspective on the value of self-directed learning that others before him had also advocated. He contributed a predictable course of development of cognitive understanding to the field, and connected levels of cognitive development to emotional development (for example, the notion that separation anxiety in toddlers results from their new understanding of object permanence).

Lev Vygotsky (1896–1934), a high school teacher who became interested in learning theory, studied and expanded on the work of Piaget and Montessori to describe the transitional moments when a child is ready to grasp a new concept. His theories of the "zone of proximal development" and "scaffolding" describe the point at which, having formed the foundations needed

to understand a concept, a child is ripe to receive the teacher's instruction. Montessori's influence on Vygotsky is seen in the importance he places on teacher observation, which is what informs the teacher that the time is right for her participation in the child's learning process.

TRAILBLAZING THEORISTS

Arnold Gesell (1880–1961) and Emmi Pikler (1902–1964) were medical doctors drawn to investigate child growth and development. Gesell's research resulted in the first set of developmental norms for children. Along with his research came an understanding that human development follows a predictable course and that cognitive, social, emotional, and physical development are interrelated processes. Gesell's Child Guidance Nursery School at Yale University was among the first to instruct teachers how to work with young children in group situations and to teach to the unique needs of the preschool child. Pikler, through her work with orphaned children in Hungary after World War II, developed some of the first insights into how infants and toddlers could have their needs met in healthy, normal ways while living in institutionalized group care.

Psychologists, from Sigmund Freud (1856–1939) and Carl Jung (1875–1961) to Erik Erikson (1903–1994), have contributed to the understanding of the whole child that is today incorporated in the early childhood classroom. Margaret Ribble (1907–1993), John Bowlby (1907–1990), and Daniel Stern (birth year unknown) all studied babies and established the body of knowledge that focuses on the importance of attachment theory, the very foundation of all child care work with infants and toddlers. Erikson's work at the University of Chicago, in particular, is key to understanding the processes that form foundations for mental health in young children, how development builds on previous stages, and how those foundations (or lack thereof) affect an adult's mental health.

LABORATORY SCHOOLS

Lucy Sprague Mitchell (1878–1967) and Harriet Johnson (died 1934), founder and director, respectively, of the Bank Street School in New York in the 1920s, were inspired by Dewey and Froebel to set up programs for young children in which the children could learn to think for themselves rather than be dictated to in the traditional educational method. In the words of William Butler Yeats, Mitchell and Johnson believed "Education

should not be the filling of a pail, but the lighting of a fire." At about the same time that the Bank Street School was being formed, Mills College in California, under the direction of Lovisa Wagner, established the first college laboratory nursery school west of the Mississippi. And in the Midwest, Patty Smith Hill organized a multidisciplinary group of educators and researchers into a group that later became the National Association for the Education of Young Children (NAEYC), the foremost advocate for quality early childhood education in the country today. In Italy, Loris Malaguzzi (1896–1934) began to work with parents to create the Reggio Emilia model, which, among other things, connected the school experience into the community in which families live. Each of these people took the work of earlier theorists and translated it into holistic curriculums that supported all aspects of a young child's development.

A Continually Evolving Multidimensional Field

Because people join the study from many different fields and points of reference, the field of early care and education, like a lake fed by many streams, can seem to have no history or continuity. A psychologist, physician, or educator whose interest has been caught by the development and learning of young children may delve into the subject with no background or orientation to the field at all. The miracle and complexity of human development and the dynamics of human learning that form the study of child development and early education are so multidimensional that early care and education can be approached from many directions and studied through many lenses.

Researchers, philosophers, and practitioners in the 1950s built on basic theories and established philosophy. Teachers like Barbara Biber and Lilian Katz spoke and wrote about their work in the classroom, just as Maria Montessori did in her day. Psychologists and researchers like Jack Shonkoff and Bruno Bettelheim and physicians like T. Berry Brazelton and Benjamin Spock also contributed research, observations, and theories. David Elkind and James L. Hymes Jr. philosophized, just as Steiner and many others had before them. The question remained the same: How do caring adults create experiences for young children that help children learn, grow, and experience their world in the most positive, constructive

way possible, so that they will grow to become whole, happy, valuable citizens?

Today, early childhood classrooms are classified under many names and curricular models. They may be described as Montessori, High Scope, developmental, Waldorf, play-based, Head Start, state preschool, self-initiated, holistic, teacher-directed, instructional daycare, child care, or child-centered programs. They may be federally supported, state-subsidized, faith-based, nonprofit, for-profit, full-day, part-day, year-round, or part-year programs. Whatever it is named and whatever curricular model or calendar it follows, each of these schools can trace elements of its practice back to the great thinkers who shaped the field of early childhood. This complexity and breadth are what make the field unique, incorporating learning theory, developmental theory, physical development, psychology, anthropology, sociology, parenting, and mental health under one umbrella. The human organism is very complex, so it naturally follows that developing a foundation for the human child is also enormously complex.

In the same way that a child's learning, growth, and development are a holistic process, so is the study of that learning, growth, and development. A physician may become interested in the physical development of the brain, while a psychologist follows an interest in the process of memory. A speech therapist may study the way language organizes thought and is presented as words, while a mental health professional looks for lingual expressions of antisocial behavior. Each of these professionals may end up in the field of child development. The breadth of study is reflected by the number of early childhood theorists who began studying in one field and then ended up in another! One modern theorist on human development is Daniel Goleman, whose concept of *emotional intelligence* has inspired new insights into human behavior over the last decade; *emotional intelligence* refers to the holistic nature of intelligence, the very heart of early education dogma.

Understanding the theory and philosophy behind the field of early care and education creates a foundation for quality programs. Such an understanding allows the ECE specialist to discern which, if any, of the new theories and research are relevant to the goals of the field. Especially today—as the field becomes more and more political and driven by funding or by sound-bite policy—early childhood educators and parents can protect the unique learning needs of the young child only if they understand the issues. In the early theories, there is a great accumulation of wisdom about how children learn most constructively, and about what adults can do to best foster that learning. These theories have grown, evolved, and adjusted to the changing times as they continue to profess fundamental and basic truths about young children. A society that focuses on, values, and cherishes its young children will become strong, humane, and productive. Goals for a child's future must connect to the care that child is given today. The primary big-picture goal is, of course, a whole, healthy child who grows up to be productive, responsible, and happy. Parents and early childhood education teachers are thus the guardians of childhood.

Teachers Bring the Theories to Life

We earlier introduced the hybrid concept of child care, which blends the richness of quality educational and social experiences with an emotionally supportive "home" life. This concept evolved from the theories of the early childhood pioneers, beginning over 150 years ago with Froebel. Teachers today have the groundwork of these great thinkers to build on. They know their teaching must remain flexible in order to meet the unique needs of each child, as Dewey maintained over one hundred years ago. Understanding the theories and principles of child development allows teachers to respond appropriately to the challenges of children and society. It helps teachers keep their vision on the bigger picture unfolding each day, as they set up their classroom and help the children. While a teacher works individually with each child, she at the same time creates the culture of the group and of the school. An understanding of the underlying theory and philosophy of the early childhood field gives her a vision of the greater good her individual work can have on society. The difference between prescribed curriculum and curriculum based on principles is illustrated in the following experience.

One teacher asked another for help with her daily circle time, feeling that she needed new strategies to get children to sit quietly and behave. The mentor observed the circle and then asked a surprising question:

Why did the teacher have one circle time with twenty children ages two to five years? The teacher had never really thought about it—the program had always had circle time before the children went home: they needed to listen to stories so they would be ready for kindergarten, they needed to share, and so forth. The mentor continued to ask about the teacher's goals for the children. Then the mentor asked the teacher to think about child development. How do children construct knowledge? Can two-year-olds sit and listen in the same way four-year-olds can? What does it mean to be ready for kindergarten? Are children likely to learn to enjoy literacy experiences when they are nagged to sit and be still? Can the children who do sit still and listen enjoy hearing stories that are being constantly interrupted, as the teacher directs others to behave?

Slowly the teacher began to realize that she was providing an activity simply because it was expected, rather than honoring the truths she knew about children's learning and development. She and the mentor began to brainstorm other ways the children could be given opportunities to develop a love of stories, an understanding of literacy, and the capacity to be competent and welcome members of a group. The teacher developed a plan to embed literacy opportunities in other areas of the program, rather than depending exclusively on circle time for literacy.

The teacher moved her assistant from the job of managing children in the circle to overseeing free play in another part of the room. She began to invite children to join the circle, rather than commanding them to join. She realized that children who came to the circle by choice had a far more satisfying experience there, and that a child's choice to join the circle or not gave her an indication of that child's readiness for kindergarten. Children who chose not to sit in the group were usually ones who were not yet getting ready for kindergarten; they were either younger children or children who were socially immature. She came to see that silly and disruptive behavior could be an expression of a child's desire to be part of a group. The teacher decided that before sitting and listening to a story, an activity such as singing could help children release their excitement at being together in a group, and that they were then better able to sit and be quiet.

Sometimes children needed more help to join the group, and some-times they needed more time before they were interested in conforming to the needs of a group. By trusting development theories, she could see that the social drive that encourages children to restrain their impulses also helps them want to be part of a social group. Over time, she saw how the option of free-choice play during circle time did not draw children away from the circle, as she had initially feared, but instead worked in the opposite direction: as children matured and wanted to be part of the circle, they developed enough incentive to control their behavior so that they could ultimately succeed.

"A teacher needs to be a person so secure within herself that she can function with principles rather than prescriptions, that she can exert authority without requiring submission, that she can work experimentally but not at random, and that she can admit mistakes without feeling humiliated." wrote Barbara Biber (1948). In the above example, the mentor helped a teacher reconnect to her philosophical roots, enabling her to function with principles rather than prescriptions.

Reinventing Early Care and Education

The hybrid school described in this book was developed by teachers who were trained at a part-day nursery school but found themselves running programs that served families needing full-day child care. As James L. Hymes Jr. wrote: "Every day care center, whether it knows it or not, is a school. The choice is never between custodial care and education. The choice is between unplanned and planned education, between conscious and unconscious education, between bad education and good education" (1968). Rather than choosing to offer a quality part-day preschool program filled out with "babysitting" for the rest of the day, or choosing to do a quality part-day program for three times as many hours of the day, these hybrid-school teachers developed another option, an option that was true to what they knew about young children. They knew they didn't need to invent everything themselves; they simply needed to reinvent the delivery system, based on tried-and-true principles. As these teachers reinvented

child care, they recognized the need to factor in more input from the fields of mental health, cultural competence, anthropology, and sociology, in response to the vastly increased time children were spending in child care, coupled with the commensurate reduction in hours spent at home.

This reinvention process began at the core, as the teachers considered the key attributes of human development: the needs of whole, healthy young children. As already outlined in the introduction, these needs are:

- Attached relationship with an adult
- Human touch, intimacy
- Caring and nurturance (loving support)
- Empathy and understanding (reflection)
- Challenging motor-development activities
- Security, ease
- Social connection with peers, friends
- Mystery, joy, beauty
- Cognitive/intellectual awareness
- Change and unpredictability
- Opportunities to explore and experiment

Young children, like adults, need to feel respected for who they are (see appendix B, "A Philosophy of Respect: Ten Principles of Caregiving"). Child development follows an organic predictable path, and that path needs to be respected and supported just as the organic trajectory of growth in every organism on the planet must be protected, supported, and respected. Children build knowledge through their individual experiences of the world. Those experiences must be carefully managed if children are to grow healthy and whole, physically and emotionally. Without such experience, it's difficult for children to learn about who they are, how to solve problems, how to get themselves out of trouble, or how to make a new friend. A program that factors human needs into every hour of the children's day will most certainly support children's needs.

TEACHING AND LEARNING ARE ORGANIC PROCESSES

What does the early childhood teacher teach? This is a trick question, of course, implying there is an easy answer, a simple formula for working with young children. The answer, however, is as complex as a human child. Through thought and reflection on her own life experience, her careful work with children, and her education, a teacher brings to quality early care and education programs tools that can build the foundation for children to understand themselves and the world around them. Once a secure relationship is established between a teacher and the children in her group, the children can reach out from a safe, predictable, understandable world to explore and learn. Teachers with a sound foundation in early childhood education understand how profoundly organic and interconnected human life and development are. They know that "teaching" children to walk or to read or to share before all the organic connections are in place developmentally is in fact disabling rather than enabling, leading to negative consequences in the child's development.

While learning can be disrupted and redirected quite easily, any disruption occurs at the expense of a natural, organic developmental trajectory. There is an organic process unfolding in each child, and it is the job of the teacher to support that process by keeping attuned to each child as an individual. If development is disrupted—for example, through direct interference (inappropriate teaching) or through psychological stressors such as divorce, death of a parent, abuse, or neglect—it can be repaired using play therapy and special therapeutic exercises.

Learning builds on actual experiences. Viewing a picture of a rope or holding a toy molded-plastic rope, for example, does not give a child the same amount of information about rope that comes from playing with a short length of real rope. In addition, human beings learn best with and from other people. Mechanical games that talk, sing, and light up; computers; and television cannot replace the connection formed when a loving parent reads stories to a child, or when a child helps a parent mend a fence or clean the dishes. Such relationships and human-to-human interactions build psychological connections that mold a child's personality and the way he relates to the world.

RELATIONSHIPS ARE THE FOUNDATION FOR CURRICULUM

These principles of childhood have nothing to do with curriculum. Curriculum is separate from the relationships children build with their teachers and the concepts children develop of themselves as learners. If children do not develop strong relationships and self-concepts, curriculum will not have a foundation on which to build. Programs driven by accountability standards are particularly prone to confuse curriculum with the essential

qualities of early care and education. It requires sophisticated thinking to integrate the requirements of curriculum (which may be based more in public policy than in child development) with the needs and learning styles of young children.

For example, if a curriculum requires that children learn to count to ten, it would seem on the surface that teaching a child a sequence of vocabulary words—one, two, three, and so on—would be the easy and effective approach to accomplish that goal. However, the early childhood educator knows that simply reciting words by rote is not meaningful education; what a child really needs is to understand the *concept* of, for example, "one" as "one object," to understand that the number seven comes after six because it has one more, and to understand that the number five comes before six because it has one less. To do that, a child needs

- to be ready to learn, which includes
  a. knowing and trusting the adults with him to respect him and help him when he needs help, and to support him when he doesn't;
  b. knowing what is expected of him (by experiencing consistency and predictability);
  c. knowing what to expect of those around him (by understanding the culture of the classroom and center).
- the right materials with which to construct knowledge, allowing him
  a. to play frequently with items that can be counted, such as food, friends, shoes, napkins, sandbox toys, and money;
  b. to observe others counting and sorting;
  c. to develop an understanding of one-to-one correspondence.

Thus the early childhood educator looks at curriculum through the lens of her knowledge and experience with young children as learners. Rather than superficially teaching superficial knowledge, she works to authentically teach children authentic information, with the realization that knowledge will follow. Within that process, she knows that she herself is a key ingredient.

Building a Community That Meets Each Child's Needs

All over America, child care programs are evolving and changing, growing or shrinking. Social and economic trends affect the number of children staying home versus the number attending child care, and as a result, child care programs expand, contract, or adjust services to meet the needs of their community. Program structures also change as trends and communities change, and they are often targeted at specific populations of children. For example:

- Programs designed to assist children at or below poverty have unique goals and expectations.
- Programs for teen parents focus on parenting and marriage skills.
- Bilingual programs help children get ready for kindergarten-learning in a new language.
- Programs for children in respite and foster care actively teach attachment and relationships.
- Programs for children with atypical development may practice more assertive teaching to support children's developmental progress.
- Programs for middle-class children may focus on providing a relaxing environment to counter stress at home created by busy working parents trying to fit everything in.

In every child care setting, it's important that each child be treated as an individual, complex being, instead of as a "needy child," an "unattached child," an "easy child," an "ESL child," or a "special needs child." Every child from every circumstance can learn and benefit from group care. Children thrive when given a life of their own at school, and the opportunity to experience a caring, objective relationship with a teacher.

Young children may have differing needs due to the variety of circumstances they have experienced, but they generally have a rather limited repertoire of behaviors. For example, neglected children may behave in similar ways to overindulged children. And all children understand how it feels to be distressed and to want their parents nearby. Teachers deal with such feelings and needs over and over again throughout the course of their work with children.

Each child care community builds its own culture. Each facility, teaching staff, group of parents, and classroom of children comes with unique strengths and challenges. With a thorough understanding of the principles, theories, and science that underlie quality care, teachers and directors can support the strengths and meet the challenges of their own child care community. The deep and strong roots of the field of early care and education will continue to support the growth of young children, the adults who care for them, and the society for which those children will one day be responsible.

Reinventing child care to create a caring community for young children and families requires thought, commitment, and discipline. In order to visualize the ideal, the dream of what child care should look like, start by looking at knowledge-based beliefs about what a developing child needs. These beliefs guide the development of philosophy and practice, as demonstrated in the chart on the facing page.

We believe . . .	So, we . . .
We believe children should expect the world to be a beautiful and interesting place.	**So, we** create yards full of natural materials and growing things, and classrooms that invite exploration appropriate to a child's level of development.
We believe people want to be friendly and kind.	**So, we** encourage teachers and support staff to speak to children in a kind and respectful manner.
We believe all children want to please the people they live and work with.	**So, we** help children know that when something goes wrong, it's a mistake, and a teacher will help them to ensure it won't happen again.
We believe learning and growth occur in calm, pleasant surroundings	**So, we** arrange our day with consistent routines and rules, so that children know what to expect and how to manage themselves. We structure the program to support a child's growth from group to group, with the security and freedom that predictability and continuity bring.
We believe all children deserve thoughtful, respectful care.	**So, we** welcome families who reflect the world we live in. We understand that growing up among a wide variety of people, families, abilities, and life circumstance is the way to build open, loving hearts and minds.
We believe development naturally unfolds when given a nurturing, supportive, and interesting environment.	**So, we** accept each child as a being with unique strengths and needs, and we plan a curriculum that supports growth in all areas of development.
We believe it is an honor and a responsibility to be part of the formation of a young family.	**So, we** offer support and services to parents and caregivers, above and beyond being available from 7:30 AM to 6:00 PM year-round.
We believe healthy meals, peaceful naps, vigorous play, and time for quiet contribute to the wholeness of a child's development.	**So, we** prepare wholesome food on-site that is appropriate to each age; we help children get the sleep they need; and we provide play choices that meet their needs.

PREMOBILE INFANTS

2

DEVELOPMENTAL AGE RANGE

0–16 months

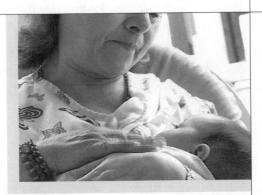

I n the infant room, babies follow their own schedules—napping, eating, and playing according to their internal clock as they learn to organize themselves. This pleasant room feels just right for babies: the light is soft, the colors are muted, and the room is clean and comfortable. Near the window, a mattress for nonmobile babies provides a pleasant spot for sunbathing. Sturdy low shelves offer a nice place to practice pulling up, and are organized so children can find what they like. Low baskets are strategically placed—one holds cloth books; another contains a few nesting bowls for the babies to explore.

It's 10:30 AM, and the older babies are beginning to get tired and hungry. Some are eating in high chairs. As they finish eating, they are changed, given a bottle, and put down to nap. Teacher Serena rocks a sleepy baby as other babies play nearby. Matthew is on his back, working on rolling over. Ling Ling is scooting on her tummy, reaching

A classroom of attuned teachers and infants

for a soft ball—each time her hand swipes the ball, it moves just inches out of her reach. Near a low shelf, LaVan positions himself to pull up. Babies babble and make baby noises. The room feels peaceful and calm as the babies play and explore, each at her own pace, watching each other and watching Serena as she smiles at them and makes eye contact while she rocks.

Darlyn, a five-month-old who has been in group care for almost a month, lies on her tummy on the rug. She kicks her feet, waves her arms, and makes noises that are neither totally content nor distressed. Serena watches as Darlyn rears up, bracing her arms; one arm jerks a bit more than the other, and the weight shift of her head starts to roll her over onto her back. Her head touches the wooden ramp in the middle of the floor, and Darlyn rocks back to her tummy. Now her babbling sounds are fussier. Another thrust of her arms throws her onto her back. The clunk of her head increases her noises of discontent, and Serena rises from the rocking chair with a sleepy baby in her arms, moves closer to Darlyn, pulls the ramp farther away from her, and sets a soft toy down near Darlyn's hand. Darlyn grasps the toy and starts to chew and suck on it.

Teacher Joya comes from the kitchen and speaks to Darlyn: "Darlyn, your lunch is ready in the kitchen. Are you ready to go eat?" Darlyn kicks her feet and drops the toy. As Joya stoops to pick up Darlyn, she says, " I think you're getting ready for lunch too, LaVan. I'll get Darlyn set and I'll be right back to get you."

Joya carries Darlyn facing away from her toward the kitchen, and they walk to the high chair. Joya places Darlyn in the chair and puts her bib on the tray. Darlyn grabs the bib and pushes it back and forth on the tray, all the while looking at the child sitting near her. Joya gets Darlyn's food and puts her bib on her. Darlyn kicks her feet and babbles. She is alert, engaged, and relaxed.

Not long ago, Darlyn was struggling to calm herself at school. Now she waits patiently for her food and reacts in a reasonable manner even when she clunks her head. Her behavior is organized and she is relaxed, knowing her teacher will meet her needs.

"When she started school, she wasn't sure that the teachers were going to meet her needs as well as her parents had, and she cried a lot," explains Serena. "I knew that she needed me to be very consistently

attentive and available, responding to every request she made. That's how new babies learn to trust the teachers. As soon as they trust me, they can relax. I'd seen Darlyn calm herself with her mother when she was transitioning, so I knew she could do it. She just needed to learn that her needs would be met at school as well. I've learned that the process of attachment is key in forming the basis for future relationships."

A Classroom Attuned to Infants

It is through thoughtful responses and everyday routines and activities that the goals listed below will be met. Building a relationship—with infants, parents, or even coworkers—is a process supported or derailed by each interaction.

GOALS FOR INFANTS

Every day in every action, teachers in the infant room are guided by these goals:

- Connection: form a trusting, reciprocal relationship with the infants.
- Comfort: provide a regulated internal schedule (for napping, eating, elimination).
- Pleasure: help infants develop muscle control and a sense of cause and effect. Provide plenty of sensory experiences.
- Joy: provide a responsive environment that projects the feeling that the world is a good place to live.

A teacher's ability to stay aligned with her goals influences the way she plans her day and the children's day. The following vignette takes us back to the beginning of the day in our infant room, and illustrates how these goals and the teachers' actions come together to create smart, responsive caregiving.

The day begins

Serena, one of the newer teachers, hears whistling as she enters the kitchen, hangs up her coat, and stows her purse. She smiles. Joya, one of the more experienced teachers, is here already, busy cutting bananas and organizing breakfast for the infants who will soon arrive. Serena puts on her apron, washes her hands, and begins taking bottles out of the cupboard. She remembers what kind of nipple each baby likes as she prepares the bottles. Anything she can do to make the babies comfortable and happy during their long day away from mom and dad will help them feel competent, safe, and ready to explore the world they live in.

"Joya," asks Serena, "do you remember where we stored the little wooden tunnel we use on the porch? Jimmy is becoming such a competent crawler that I'd like to give him a new challenge today. It took him so long to be interested in moving that I'd like to expand the pleasure he feels now that he's got his chubby little body going. Annie would like it too, because she's just trying to pull herself up and it has those nice places to hold onto on its sides."

Joya tells Serena where to find the tunnel. As Serena gets the tunnel, Joya exclaims, "I love these warm summer days! It's the perfect time to let the infants experiment with drinking water from an open cup. It doesn't matter if they get a little wet and they enjoy feeling the warm air on their bodies without too many clothes to slow them down! Playing outside in the fresh air keeps the germs down too."

Serena sets up the tunnel on the porch. She brings out the other porch toys: a basket of cloth books, some small balls that are easy for the babies to hold, and a few toys to bang on. She spreads a thick comforter down for the nonmobile babies, and sets out a pitcher of water and small cups with which the infants can practice drinking.

Serena goes back inside. She puts a clean basket of pacifiers on a convenient shelf, checks to be sure all the infant charts are ready for parents to write notes on as they arrive, changes the sheet on the big mattress, brings clean chewable toys from the kitchen, and sets out an empty basket to receive toys that will need washing after babies mouth them. She then fills the pocket of her apron with tissues for the inevitable

runny noses. Serena wants the room and the equipment to feel homey and to be as clean and fresh as possible.

Serena hears Mrs. Jones coming down the walk; her seven-month-old, Gillian, is always the first one here, at 7:00 AM, and the last one picked up, at 6:00 PM. Serena comments to Joya, "You know, I used to feel sorry for babies whose moms left them here for such a long day, but I don't feel that way anymore. Getting to know Mrs. Jones has helped me see how much she cares about Gillian. She wants her to get wonderful care during the day, and she needs to earn a good living so she can help support her family. And I've realized that by doing my job well, Gillian will have a great experience at school, with people who care about her, so her development can stay on target and she can have a great relationship with her family. It's been exciting for me to see how we can really work as a team of teachers and parents to support the children."

"Good morning, Mrs. Jones! Hi, Gilly!" says Serena. "How was Gilly's night? I saw on her chart that she was fussy and drooling a lot yesterday afternoon." Mrs. Jones responds, "I think she has a tooth coming in . . . let's show Serena that little bump under your gum, Gilly." Gilly clamps her mouth closed and turns her face away. "Well, she had a good night's sleep, but she may need a cold teether to chew on today. I hope that tooth coming in doesn't make her too uncomfortable." Serena says, "I wondered about a tooth, with all that drooling! I'm sure I'll see that sore bump later, won't I, Gilly? We'll do our best to keep you comfortable, won't we? I'm glad you all got a good night's sleep! Are you ready to come in and have some breakfast, Gilly?" Serena holds out her arms, and Gilly turns her face into her mother's shoulder. "Oh, you're not quite ready yet, are you? I see you turning your face away. I'll just go put the cereal in a bowl for you while you and your mom get ready to say good-bye."

Serena walks to the high chair with a bowl of rice cereal and a piece of banana, noticing Gillian's interest in the process. "Gillian, now it looks like you're ready for some breakfast! Should we say bye-bye to mommy?" Gillian leans away from her mom and reaches her hands out to Serena, who holds her and says, "Bye-bye, mommy!" until Mrs. Jones is out the door. Seeing her mother depart, Gillian starts to fuss and cry. Serena reassuringly notes, "There goes mommy off to work! Bye-bye

Teacher guiding and supporting infant separation and transition

mommy! Yes, you love your mom. It's a little sad to see her go. You'll miss her. She's such a good mommy." Serena soothes Gillian with her voice while acknowledging and affirming her feelings. As Mrs. Jones looks back at Gilly, Serena smiles in encouragement. She pats Gilly's back and slowly heads for the high chair, using soothing touch to help Gillian calm herself and to let Mrs. Jones see that both she and Gillian are alright. As Gillian relaxes and Serena settles her into the high chair for breakfast, Serena hears another parent enter the hallway.

Mr. Smith walks in and puts eleven-month-old Adam's spare clothes and diapers in his basket. As he enters the classroom, Joya greets him: "Good morning, Mr. Smith! Here's Adam, ready for his first full day today! Are you ready for some banana, Adam?" Adam's adventurous temperament makes it easy for him to quickly shift gears from dad to teacher, even though he's just completed two weeks of transition into group care. He grins, says "nana," and reaches out to Joya. As he walks out, Mr. Smith says, "Oh, and I'll put some ointment in Adam's basket for his diaper rash; it says on the tube to put it on four times a day, so will you please do it twice?" Joya responds, "Sure. Please write it down in the communication book along with the approximate times we should apply it. Then the afternoon staff will see it, too, and you'll know he's had it because the teachers will initial the book after they put it on him."

The greetings continue. Babies arrive with their parents, and their parents exchange information with Joya, who is stationed near the door. Joya takes the babies to Serena for breakfast, or she sets them down to play. The children who are finished eating return to the floor or to the mattress to play. Mrs. Kim brings in eight-month-old Jenny, who gives Serena a big smile. Although Jenny was away on a vacation the past week, she seems happy to see her teacher and moves easily into her arms.

By the time the entire group is finished eating, a third teacher has joined them. Serena takes a small group of infants out to the porch for more-active play. When she sets Jenny down on the porch, Jenny begins to fuss. Mrs. Kim had said Jenny was still on East Coast time, so perhaps she is tired, Serena thinks. "Jenny, it sounds like you want me to hold you some more, but I'm going to let you play on your own for a little

bit while I get everyone settled," says Serena. "Then I'll be ready to help you."

And so the teachers continue through their day, attuned to each child's needs. They respond as infants show signs of readiness for a nap, for more stimulation, or for a quiet place to practice a new physical achievement such as rolling over or pushing up onto their knees.

Each Child at Her Own Pace

Information that parents share during drop-off assists teachers in knowing where each infant is likely to be in her usual cycle of eat, sleep, and play. Teachers protect each child's right to progress at his own pace by allowing him time and space to do what he needs to do developmentally, by ensuring that nonmobile babies are kept safe from mobile ones, and by allowing each child to follow her own agenda for learning—whether learning to grasp a rattle, roll over, or pull off a sock. Because children begin to learn language long before they can speak, it's important that teachers also talk with them, respectfully explaining what they're thinking about, feeling, and doing.

When an infant begins attending child care, he may feel overwhelmed. Other babies moving in unpredictable ways and making noise around him can make the world feel chaotic and unpredictable. Meeting new adults can add to an infant's level of stress. Teachers ensure that a new child in a group is given enough time to get comfortable with one adult before that child gets to know another. In the same way, a child unaccustomed to other children is not forced into so much contact with other children that he is overwhelmed by it. The teacher wants to help the child to relax and be at ease, so she uses her voice, eye contact, touch, and gestures to help the child feel safe and protected when other children come close or when noise levels rise. As she gets to know each child, she tunes in to that child's tolerance level for various stimuli, allowing her to proactively teach the child through his trust in her and through her reassurance that the world is safe and all is well. All these techniques help an infant attach to a new caregiver.

A Community of Preverbal Children

"The body says what words cannot." —MARTHA GRAHAM

The video camera has brought much new information into the research and study of brain development, along with new insights for those who work with babies and young children. Careful study of videotapes reveals movements and unspoken messages that communicate much more to a child than the spoken word does. Analyzing how we use actions and words, along with all the subtexts that impact how we communicate, is vital when working and living with young children. It improves a teacher's effectiveness and her ability to articulate the art of early childhood education.

Preverbal children communicate forcefully and purposefully in nonverbal ways, and teachers and parents learn to tune in and communicate right back, both nonverbally and verbally. Educators have long talked about "the dance" between adult and infant, and now new information from miles of video footage captures a system of intuitive communication that is similar across cultures as caregivers address human needs. Scientists study video footage to better decipher an infant's body language, thinking not only about how the infant communicates, but also about how she self-comforts and regulates her brand-new little body. This study has brought about a new area in the field of mental health—infant and toddler mental health—conjuring a picture of Dr. Freud with a wiggly one-year-old on a couch! Infant and toddler mental health is quite different from talk or cognitive therapy, in which a patient sits and learns to reflect on his behavior in the hope of gaining greater self-awareness and growth. Infant and toddler mental health focuses on the physiology of the baby, linking physical well-being with future development.

The Systems Model of Child Development

Infant and toddler development is evaluated on a *systems* level rather than on the *categorical* model of traditional child development. Part of this evaluation examines how systems organize themselves and what causes

them to become disorganized (a temper tantrum is an extreme example of disorganized behavior). All systems work together to make a whole, healthy infant. While these systems address healthy development in the newborn and infant, they remain present and continue to influence the development of the child as he ages. They even, in fact, influence an adult's sense of well-being.

THE FOUR PHYSICAL SYSTEMS

According to the authors of the booklet *Getting to Know Your Baby,* there are four physical systems that experts look at as they assess infant mental health and development: physiological behavior, motor behavior, states of behavior, and self-regulation (VandenBerg et al. 2003).

Physiological Behavior The desired state is a stable, rosy color (indicating even blood flow throughout the body), breathing that is smooth and regular (not overly fast or slow), and a gastrointestinal system organized by stable digestion and regular elimination.

Motor Behavior The muscle tone of a baby's resting body should be balanced between tension and energy. The infant should lie in a "softly tucked" position (neither limp nor rigid); should maintain a flexed, relaxed posture with arms and legs tucked close to the body and hands near the face; and movements should be fluid, with extensions rare.

States of Behavior This refers to sleeping and waking cycles, which lay the foundation for later learning. Babies come into the world ready to socialize; a healthy balance in sleep/wake cycles allows them to interact. An organized, well-modulated baby transitions smoothly from one state to another: progressing from deep to light sleep, becoming drowsy and then alert, and waking.

Self-regulation This is the child's ability to learn to calm herself and cope with her surroundings. In the womb, she self-comforts by sucking on her hands and bracing her feet. In order to maintain balance in her physiology, her motor, and her state systems, the infant learns to organize and regulate all the systems at once.

SELF-REGULATION

How do human beings calm and soothe themselves ? An infant's self-regulating behaviors include (adapted from Als et al. 1982):

- Bringing hands to mouth and face (touching face, covering eyes)
- Bracing feet and legs (pushing feet against surface and straightening knees)
- Clasping hands together
- Clasping feet together (crossing ankles, touching soles of feet together)
- Tucking the body (relaxed curl into fetal position)
- Sucking
- Grasping and holding on
- Gazing (looking and attending)

Like older children and adults, babies choose their own individual self-regulating behaviors. When an infant is distressed, parents or caregivers often respond instinctively to help him find a preferred self-regulating position or activity. Without thinking, we offer a finger to grasp, swaddle him into a tuck position, rock him and sing lullabies, or place him where he can feel secure and protected. We know, however, that adults can only *support* an infant's self-regulation; they cannot regulate for him.

As the brain grows, the human intellect becomes more complex. Teachers continue to attend to a child's physiological systems as the child grows from an infant to a toddler to a preschooler. Teachers also begin to assess and evaluate new areas of development in the child as she ages. As brain capacity increases with age, many of the areas in the infant's *systems development* coalesce in the preschool child into the area generally known as *physical development*. States of behavior, life rhythms, motor behavior, tone, posture, and energy output all affect a child's ability to learn. Perhaps surprisingly, large-muscle mastery is what promotes a child's ability to sit still and to put her energy into developing a thinking mind! The mind then learns to assess, organize, sequence, and structure thought—elements essential to success in elementary school.

In preschool, new developmental tasks and systems take focus. Language development, social skills, emotional maturity and intelligence, physical development, and cognition are the areas supported by preschool teaching. But the concept of systems working together—for example, language skills progress poorly without social skills—never goes away. Previously achieved competencies in the areas of the four key physical systems described earlier—physiological behavior, motor behavior, states of behavior, and self-regulation—form the foundation for an ensuing set of skills, behaviors, and systems. Weaknesses in any one system can be a predictor of future issues in the child's development, mental health, and/ or overall well-being.

In a world full of change, some things remain much as they have always been. Infants grow into an adults, but adults hold on to part of their infant self. They may sleep in a fetal (tuck) position. They may be most comfortable sitting with their ankles crossed (feet clasping). They may derive comfort from a rocking chair or a glider swing. As we grow and change and find new ways to self-regulate and self-comfort, we still return to the infant foundation that is always part of us. This knowledge, drawn from years of seemingly dry and dispassionate scientific analysis, lends great insight into the roots of our humanness.

The Three Key Phases in an Infant's Day

Responsive caregivers have always done their best to make life manageable and comfortable for babies. Survival of the species depends on it! Brain research demonstrates that young children whose lives are stressful—even as infants—develop a permanent shift in brain chemistry that leads to a heightened fight-or-flight reflex, making regulation of emotions more difficult. At any age, optimal learning occurs when a person feels secure and cared for; stress decreases a person's ability to assimilate new information. To ensure that respectful attunement remains intact and that stress stays at bay, three key phases of the infant's day require particular sensitivity on the teacher's part. These key phases are diapering, feeding, and sleeping. When done well, these interactions resemble a dance: the teacher leads, but her steps depend on the baby's response to her lead.

While a teacher is in charge of diapering decisions, only the child can make herself eat or sleep. It is therefore the teacher's job to *control the externals that are under her control*. Because she knows it is in the child's best interest not to be overtired or hungry, she plans the environment and manages her own presence to optimize the child's ability to eat and sleep.

When all these things are done well and the reciprocity of the "dance" is nicely played, the adult's lead also reduces the child's stress and builds the baby's trust in the world as a wonderful place to live, a place where he is cared for and protected.

DIAPERING

In diapering, a teacher might, for example, kneel in front of the baby, make eye contact, and say, "It smells like you need a clean diaper." If the baby smiles back, she picks him up and carries him to the changing table. If he turns to crawl away as fast as he can, she follows, makes eye contact again, and repeats her statement with the acknowledgment, "I see you don't want me to interrupt you now, but I need to change your diaper so you won't get a rash." While being responsive and aware of the child's feelings, she teaches the child that sometimes the adult makes the decision for the child's good.

FEEDING

Where feeding is concerned, a teacher is prepared to honor a child's decision not to eat, knowing that if the child is hungry, is offered appropriate food, and is provided with a calm and pleasant ambience, he is likely to eat. In group care, the ambience may partly be created by helping a distractible child stay focused on the meal at hand. In many cultures, an emphasis is placed on eating to please the mother; children who eat well are thought of as "good" and accepting of the adult's love. However, the teacher knows it is important in her professional role to remain neutral, so the child's experience of the food is directly related to his hunger.

SLEEPING

Infant caregivers spend much of their day helping children fall asleep. Every experienced teacher has known a baby who, even when desperately tired, would fight sleep. This reflects the disorganized behavior of an immature being who is unable to self-regulate or protect herself from external stimuli very well. The adult therefore takes on the role of filter, screening the child from more than he can manage. It may mean trying to help the baby nap a little earlier, before he becomes overtired. It may mean walking her out in the fresh air, or handing her off to a fresh pair of arms. It may mean swaddling him, wrapping him snugly, so he feels secure in space. The

baby is the only one who can sleep, but the teacher is the only one capable of changing the baby's environment to make it conducive to sleep. The teacher regulates herself as well, breathing deeply and slowly, keeping her body relaxed, keeping any motions rhythmic, and disengaging from playful interaction. All these actions are forms of nonverbal communication with the sleepy child; the relaxed muscle tone in the teacher's arms that are supporting the baby's head communicate relaxation to the baby.

As the morning comes to a close, the earliest nappers are waking and being changed, and the older babies are having lunch before their midday nap. Teacher Magda, who stays until the last baby goes home, arrives. Serena, who must leave soon for an appointment, needs to pass information to Magda. Baby Gillian is busy on the floor while baby Jimmy, who has just been picked up from his crib after a nap, snuggles in his blanket on Magda's lap as she sits on the floor.

"Let's see," says Serena, "Adam has a diaper rash so we've been using a soft cloth and soapy water to wipe instead of the baby wipes, and we're putting on the ointment his dad brought in."

"I noticed a little rash yesterday and mentioned it to his dad when he picked Adam up," responds Magda. As she speaks, Jimmy brushes his fingers across her hand, and she begins to open and close her fingers to create a "toy" for him; he responds by alternately squeezing and letting go of her fingers.

"And Jenny is a little unsettled after her vacation; she's needed some extra TLC."

"Oh, is that what's going on? I was surprised to see her napping already when I came in." Magda notices Jimmy leaning out from her lap toward a ball on the floor; she picks up the ball and puts it in his hand. "Did you want to hold the ball?" she asks. Turning back to the head teacher, she asks, "Were they in a different time zone?" As she speaks, the ball drops out of Jimmy's hand and rolls across the floor. She smiles at Jimmy and says, "O-o-o-h, there the ball goes!" As he lunges out after it, she disentangles the blanket, says, "It looks like you're ready to get

Teachers multitasking, with individual attention to each child

on the floor now," and sets him on his stomach, with the ball and a few toys nearby.

Later in the afternoon, Joya and Magda observe something unusual. Seven-month-old Gillian begins to clap the soles of her feet together! Although many children clap their hands together in delight at this age, clapping feet together is less common. How charming to see this little one, who is not yet sitting up, clap her hands together and smile, then lift her legs and clap the soles of her feet together too. How pleased she is with her newfound ability! What a big grin she has as she begins to alternate her clapping, first with her hands and then with her feet, delighted not only with her new discovery but also with her ability to manage her body the way she wants to.

Teacher helping infant to self-regulate

Jenny, a baby who is quick to be distressed and slow to be comforted, has been having a particularly difficult day. As already mentioned, Jenny is just back from a family vacation. While on vacation, Jenny visited grandparents and met lots of adoring relatives, so she is disoriented today, her first day back in child care. In addition, she's also experiencing jet lag. The slightest trouble has pushed her to tears all afternoon. She woke from her early nap, ate, and has been happy as long as Magda holds her, but as soon as Magda sets her down, Jenny begins expressing her displeasure. Jenny has grown accustomed to being entertained by adults, and it will take a few days for her to remember that she can set her own agenda for learning. Magda sings a song and alternates her eye contact between Jenny, sitting and fussing at her feet, and Adam, whose diaper she is changing. When the song ends, she says to Adam, "Jenny is sitting close to my feet because she's waiting for me to hold her. She doesn't sound very happy, does she, Adam? Something is just not right, is it Jenny?" Then, turning to Jenny, she says, "Jenny, I'm going to get cleaned up and then I'll be ready to give you a hug."

Responsive and Attentive Care

In the previous scene, we saw Magda multitasking, as responsive teachers and parents unconsciously do, making sure that everyone who needs her attention has it. She is attuned to Jimmy, knowing he needs to transition out of sleep into play on his own timetable. She also knows she has only

a few minutes to collect the morning's data from the exiting teacher. By constantly moving her gaze, tuning her ears, and processing the input through a fully engaged brain, an attentive teacher is able to tune in to the sounds of many voices, the nuances of tone, the nonverbal messages of bodies and faces, and the need for her physical presence among all the children and teachers present. She may be carrying on multiple conversations, or singing a song to a bouncing baby at the same time she is making eye contact with and smiling at another baby who is rolling over. When a teacher is as sophisticated in her multitasking as Magda, everyone ends up feeling that they get what they need.

CONSISTENT TEACHER-CHILD INTERACTIONS

Every time a baby makes a new discovery, as Gillian did when she was able to clap her feet together, the teachers share in the child's joy. They know that discovering something on one's own gives so much more pleasure than being taught or assisted to do something, and so they resist the urge to interfere with a child's development in seemingly "helpful" ways, such as by propping up a baby to a sitting position with pillows, putting a baby in a bouncy seat for a long period of time, or shaking a rattle in front of him. All these activities seem benign, but in fact they take away some of the baby's interest in and opportunity to explore his world in a developmentally appropriate way.

Teachers who work with infants need to be aware of their personal parenting-style biases and learn to control their impulses to parent the babies as they were parented or as they parent their own children. So while teachers must stay intuitively tuned-in to the babies, they must also be self-reflective enough to be able to stop and evaluate their own "intuitive" behavior, so they can choose how to respond. Each member of a team of infant teachers may have grown up in a different part of the world, but in the group care setting, they must agree to a standard way to interact with the children, so that the children can experience consistency in the way their caregivers respond to them—much the way parents from different backgrounds learn to work together respectfully to form a happy home. Parents and teachers know that young children feel safe and cared for when the world is predictable and consistent, and when surprises are the exception rather than the rule. Predictability forms the order in a child's life, giving her the courage to explore and try new things. Through order,

babies feel supported to develop their own unique abilities and feel free to experiment, which helps form their emerging minds.

The more a baby is free to move, the more opportunity he has to overcome the limits of his immature body. When infants are awake and comfortable, they're ready to explore their world and to experience that world through their bodies. Little ones are placed on their backs so that they can move and see. Teachers stay nearby and are friendly without interfering, helping the child as needed, but focused on allowing the babies to develop control over their bodies and their ability to communicate.

Many programs include children with special needs. As infants, the extent of their physical ability is often unknown. Particularly for the child with special needs, offering every opportunity to learn to move and to use the body to its full capacity is of paramount importance.

Crying and Soothing

Crying is a challenge for all who work in child care. It's hard on everyone—difficult for the adults who want to help, and difficult for the child whose systems are so overloaded that his behavior disintegrates into tears. The newest published research on crying in the littlest babies also has implications for understanding older children.

In 2000, a Johnson and Johnson Round Table Conference brought to light new evidence about crying in infants under three months old (VandenBerg 2004). Babies in this age range are transitioning from the support of their mother's body to independent functioning. Most body systems continue to grow and develop throughout childhood, but big, whole-body systems like breathing and circulation, digestion and elimination, and the sensory or nervous system come into play first, and are the baseline for overall healthy development. After three months, there is a general drop in infant crying. Research from the 1950s blamed early crying primarily on gastrointestinal (GI) disorders, but research presented at the 2000 conference highlights that less than 10 percent of crying in the first three months is GI related. Researchers say newborn infant's crying does not actually tell us the cause of distress. The research states (as most caregivers know) that infants may cry because of overstimulation, environmental sensitivity, hunger, fatigue, or difficulty in regulating

responsiveness. The basis for this behavior is considered to be immaturity of *all* the developing systems, not only the GI system.

The research presented at the 2000 conference suggests that crying within the first three months should be considered "normal." This is an interesting but also potentially dangerous statement: even if true, it only tells part of the story. True, adults should expect babies to cry; it's a form of communication and it's "normal." But the fact that crying is normal doesn't mean adults don't need to respond to it! The research from 2000 recommends that caregivers think about soothing a crying baby's whole body rather than soothing, for example, a stomachache. Interestingly, many of the methods used to comfort GI troubles work for the whole nervous system—swaddling, warmth, and rhythmic movement are effective both for moving gas and for shutting out overstimulation, calming a baby's system so it can reorganize. The researchers also recommend that caregivers try to keep their body still and calm, modify the amount of light in the room, keep noise levels down, and alternate stimulating activities with restful ones (for example, planning a rest time between feeding the baby and giving her a bath). Also, babies like to hold on to something such as a finger or soft cloth, and they are soothed by environments that re-create life in the womb. To re-create a womblike experience, the caregiver can wrap the baby up warmly, hold her close so she can feel regular heart rhythms, soften the light, place her hands close to her face, or hold her feet together.

HABITS AND PATTERNS

Because brains are prone to establish habits and patterns, it's important when thinking about crying and soothing, to look at the habits and patterns being built, especially in the infant, whose wonderful mind is busy trying to understand the world through random cause-and-effect experimentation. If the same response occurs twice, there will certainly be a third attempt to see if the experiment has a consistent outcome! In these early years, patterns of response quickly become hardwired into the brain. Classic early childhood education literature made special note of something that was called "habit training." It does not serve an infant to become hysterical, so responsible adults respond quickly and sensitively to an infant's needs, building a habit that will serve the child. It's important for a baby to learn that if he needs something, his actions will

result in having that need met. However, meeting that need must always stay in balance with the amount of stress a baby can comfortably manage. A thoughtful caregiver does not let a baby get too tired or too hungry, in order to avoid his forming a habit of screaming for what he wants.

Research on crying looks only at crying, not at crying in the context of human development. Raising children is a complex job, and caregivers must factor in other details that may influence a situation. The caregiver who is carefully monitoring a baby's needs will also remember to step back as the baby matures, giving her opportunities to be challenged and stretched in developing her communication skills, as that is what fuels new discovery and learning. If every need is anticipated and accommodated by the time the infant is a toddler, he won't have learned a key developmental lesson: that others have needs and feelings different from his own—the root of autonomy, the key to social development, and the incentive for language as a social mediator. The caregiver must make an important distinction between "stretched" and "stressed."

EMPATHETIC RESPONSE

Crying creates stress because it is the adult who interprets it. An adult knows what it takes to bring her to tears, and how difficult it is to communicate rationally while crying. Such memories and feelings are in the subconscious and can drive a reaction to a crying baby without consideration for what will come next or for how the actions will be received by the child. In order to begin problem solving, caregivers must be able to reflect on their own feelings, responses, and actions. To paraphrase child psychologist David Winnicott, the human brain develops in relationship with another brain. This refers not to proximity but to the relationship, including the associated subtlety and innuendo. A teacher's ability to suspend what she thinks and believes and how she feels counts more than actions or words to children under five. To help babies, children, and loved ones stop crying, an adult first must be able to hold and assess her own emotion, and then avoid letting it drive her response.

"Calm your body and take a deep breath," the first and most important instruction in any situation where crying is concerned, is easier said than done. But because as adults our brains categorize things, we can slow our emotional reaction by shifting our response from the primitive, emotional part of the brain into the problem-solving upper cortex, where thinking

takes place. Crying reflects frustration and a lack of available language (not only a lack of words, but also the lack of ability to be able to pull up those words while flooded with emotion). Therapists refer to crying and temper tantrums as "disorganized behavior," describing what happens when the child's brain gets more data than it can manage (hungry, angry, lonely, tired, stressed). When the child's internal systems are overwhelmed by the world around him and his coping behavior becomes disorganized, his tears reflect that disorganization. Being able to understand this concept and to reframe the meaning of crying helps build compassion for how it must feel to be so little and at the mercy of others in a world where all the variables change constantly.

"Handing off"—asking another adult to take over if your first approach is unsuccessful—can also help. The goal is to find what works to help soothe crying, but not to get too attached to it. As soon as a system seems foolproof, the child ages, her brain connects a few more synapses, and what worked before doesn't work any longer. Many techniques that work to soothe a baby may or may not work to soothe a toddler or a preschooler, but key concepts remain the same. Everyone needs time to calm and reorganize so they can think, talk, and behave in a reasonable way. That is really what a time-out was intended to be. It became a punishment because people didn't really understand the idea behind the action. (This type of misinterpretation is common in adult minds, as we seek a prescriptive cure rather than an understanding of the slow process of shaping a human being for a satisfying life.)

The name of the game when caring for young children is that the details keep changing, the linear solutions work and then don't, but the big picture stays the same—the joy in sharing a young child's life as the mysteries of the world unfold, the fulfillment and awe of unconditional love, the pride and pleasure that come from being a responsible, caring adult shaping a child's experience of the world.

Thoughtful Teaching Fosters Healthy Attachment

If human beings are lucky and have connected, loving parenting in their early years, they develop the ability to attach. With that attachment comes all the parenting instinct imprinted in babyhood. As adults working with

other people's children and having the ability to intellectualize experiences and objectively reflect on and control their behavior, teachers begin the practice of learning to work in a field in which the professionals move back and forth between the critical work of the mind and the intuition of the heart. New teachers learn to look at their own instinctive parenting—perhaps a feeling that babies should never cry; that a baby will eat what a loved adult offers; that adults must carry babies around all the time, prop them up in a sitting position, or keep them in swings or walkers; or that adults should entertain babies in order to keep them happy. New teachers work to develop awareness of their own ingrained habits and to exercise self-control, as they learn to respond slowly, thoughtfully, and respectfully while working together with other teachers as a consistent, predictable team.

In this way, a baby learns to manage herself and to be confident in her ability to elicit responses that are appropriate to her needs. This is the healthiest form of attachment, in which dependence is acknowledged but is not fostered, and the relationship between teacher and child is focused on the child's needs, not the adult's. When this dynamic is established between teacher and child, the teacher is free to decide how best to help the child without being reactionary, and the child is free to explore and return to the teacher for comfort and help on his own terms. This form of attachment is different from parental attachment; it requires a loving neutrality only appropriate to the role of teacher. The teacher's role is not that of substitute parent, but to help children thrive in every domain of their development so they can function in the life of their families as happy, healthy children, bonded and secure in their parents' love.

As evening starts to fall, tired parents come in to reunite with their babies. They have been busy managing the adult world. As they trickle into the center, many have battled traffic and deadlines and all the pressures of modern life. Magda makes sure to greet each parent by name and to share at least a brief minute with each one, knowing how important it is for parents to feel connected to the events of their baby's day. Mr. Smith

is glad to hear that Adam's rash is looking better and that Adam's first long day at the center went well for him.

Mrs. Graham, Darlyn's mom, comes in looking stressed; she moves quickly, and doesn't make eye contact with Magda as she checks the fridge for remaining bottles of breast milk and looks in the bag where the teachers have placed her empty bottles.

"Where is the cover?" she demands of Magda.

Magda, surprised at the tone of voice, asks, "What cover?"

"Every morning, I bring in bottles with covers over the nipples, and every afternoon they're missing! They don't sell them separately, and I need them so I can keep the bottles clean when I bring them to day care," Mrs. Graham says hotly.

"Gosh!" responds Magda. "Let me see if I can figure out what's going on with those covers! It's frustrating, isn't it, to have something you need turn up missing. I know we have some extra ones in the cupboard, so why don't you take those for tomorrow, and I'll check with the other teachers tomorrow to find out what's happening to your covers."

"Thank you!" smiles Mrs. Graham. "I really appreciate that."

Magda notices that of the four bottles in the bag, only one is missing its cover. She suspects that the covers aren't missing every day, but she is smart enough to recognize that this mom, more than anything else, needs to feel support for the challenges of parenting. Magda knows that any other response—questioning, arguing, correcting—would only make the situation more difficult. While she doesn't like the implication that the teachers are careless with Darlyn's belongings, she can be compassionate toward Mrs. Graham and toward the hard job of a working parent. She remarks to a new teacher who has been observing, "The end of the day for a parent who's already commuted and worked for eight to ten hours and has an evening of infant care and housework ahead can often be stressful. The best thing we can do for Mrs. Graham—and for Darlyn—is to make the world a little easier and let Mrs. Graham take a deep breath so she'll be able to relax and smile when she picks up Darlyn for a hug."

Mrs. Jones beams as she hears about Gillian's unique discovery of clapping her feet together! As she and Gillian walk out the door, Magda does her final tidying. She carries the basket of chewed-on toys into the kitchen and drops them in the tub of disinfectant in the sink for Joya to

Teacher building a relationship with parents through empathetic response

wash in the morning, She brings the toys in from the porch, and puts the comforter in the washer so Joya can put it in the dryer in the morning, in order to keep the babies' play space fresh each day by rotating the blankets outside. She leaves a note for Joya to find in the morning, asking her to help figure out the bottle-cover mystery for Mrs. Graham. As she makes her rounds, she processes the day's events, thinking about what went well and what can be done better tomorrow. She remembers that when three babies were on the porch using the tunnel, it got a little too crowded. Tomorrow, she decides, she'll either add another new crawling apparatus or be sure to bring out children with a wider developmental range, so they won't all be trying to do the same thing at the same time.

Magda smiles and chuckles to herself as she closes the door, thinking again of Gillian grinning with her feet clapping away.

The PHYSICAL YEAR: ONE-YEAR-OLDS

3

DEVELOPMENTAL AGE RANGE

10–26 months

T *eachers Katherine and Kamilah stand in the yard with a group of young toddlers. Twenty-two-month-old Ashraf pulls purses out of a box, looking for the right one to carry; eighteen-month-old Brendan strolls around the climber; fifteen-month-old Courtney scoots down the slide; sixteen-month-old Dania and thirteen-month-old Eduardo sit side by side patting sand in the little sandbox; and nineteen-month-old Blanca tosses a ball up in the air with a squeal of delight followed by the pat-pat-pat of little feet in pursuit. A parent passing through the yard pauses to accept four grains of sand offered to him by Dania, plump little thumb and forefinger pressed tightly together. Brendan stops on his journey around the climber in order to pick a few leaves off the jasmine vine growing along the fence. Soon three other little ones join him, carefully pinching and pulling off one little leaf at a time, then intently searching out knotholes in the fence and spaces between boards to poke the leaves through.*

Teachers honoring the pace of young toddlers

Setting Goals

Teachers of young toddlers intentionally and conscientiously give the children many opportunities to explore their world at their own pace, each child following his own interests. Young toddlers often wander until something catches their attention; the teachers make sure the things that will interest them are appropriate. They carefully select and place toys so that children can find them and choose what they want to use, and they ensure that the natural world is also available for exploration. Honoring a toddler's pace is one of the many abstract, yet vital, ingredients shaping the young child's experience in a quality child-centered setting. As illustrated in the opening vignette, the teachers recognize picking leaves and poking them through holes as a valid activity even though it was not planned by adults; in fact, they recognize that it holds greater value because it gives the children an opportunity to invent on their own an activity that satisfies them.

GOALS FOR YOUNG TODDLERS

As with infants, we can identify four goals to guide teachers working with one- to two-year-olds:

- Connection: continue to form trusting, reciprocal relationships with the children
- Comfort: strengthen the regulation of internal schedules (for napping, eating, elimination)
- Pleasure: help young toddlers find safe ways to exercise newfound muscle control and to experience the sensory world
- Joy: help young toddlers find trust through a responsive environment, and feel that the world is a good place to live

---

While the teachers want the children to have interesting experiences throughout the day, their long-term goal is for the children to see themselves as resourceful and interesting people, not as people who need others to create their entertainment for them. Pushing something through a hole is a classic one-year-old activity, both a means of practicing newly acquired physical dexterity, and an embodiment of the symbolism of things disappearing (such as a parent at drop-off time), a variation on the theme of peekaboo and on Piaget's concept of object permanence.

Teacher Kamilah sighs when she checks her box in the office—the note waiting for her says that Katherine is sick today and the center director has arranged for a substitute teacher to fill in. Her group of young toddlers, twelve- to twenty-four–month-olds, will not like having a stranger comforting them, changing their diapers, or helping them eat and sleep. That means Kamilah will be especially challenged in keeping the children centered and comfortable today. She takes a deep breath, and then hurries into her classroom so she can set up and be as prepared as possible to meet the day's needs.

She meets infant teachers Serena and Joya in the kitchen, and lets them know she will be working with a sub today since Katherine is out. She asks them to please keep their ears open for sounds of distress in the toddler classroom, and to check in with her if they have a free moment during the day, to see if she needs help. Because the babies are self-scheduled, Serena and Joya sometimes find themselves with a full nap room and some unexpected "free" time. Most days, they use that time for writing notes in the observation book and to parents, but on a day like this, they're able to offer a little extra support to a neighboring classroom. Joya offers to set up breakfast for the toddlers so that Kamilah can finish her classroom setup and have a few minutes to orient the substitute when she arrives. Kamilah thanks Joya and gets to work.

Kamilah gets freshly washed soft cloth balls out of the dryer and puts them in a basket in the classroom, readily available as a safe option for children when they decide they want to throw something. She notices that the ponchos have also been washed; made of many different fabrics, these "clothes" are simple enough for nearly all the toddlers to

Teacher adjusting to an unexpected staff change, and setting up for the day

pull on over their heads when they want to dress up. She sets the small ponchos next to the play kitchen area. A plastic jar full of rubber ducks goes into the cubbyhole beneath the classroom climber; it will be a fun discovery to dump and refill for any child who happens across it. Kamilah knows it's easy for a toddler classroom to look chaotic and cluttered, so she's careful to place toys that will be dumped in areas that communicate nonverbal containment, such as on a small throw rug or in a cubbyhole. Toddlers may carry a rubber duck from the cubbyhole as they go off to explore, but the rest of the ducks will be close to their plastic jar, making it easy for a passing teacher to tidy them up.

Outside, Kamilah chooses several toy lawn mowers and shopping carts from the shed and stands them against the side of the building, inviting children to push them around the yard. She sets up buckets and shovels around the sandbox, and wipes the morning dew off the low slide and handrails. She sets out three little wooden dogs on strings, made to be pulled by a child, and several riding toys that children can scoot with their feet. She sets a basket of small towels next to the window so children can pretend to wash it. The water table also reflects a washing theme, with little rubber dolls, bits of bar soap, and washcloths for the children to play "bath time."

Creative Problem Solving

The window-washing activity mentioned in the previous vignette came about as a result of some great teacher problem solving. To provide some physical activity for the toddlers on rainy days, a set of stairs was added to the porch, but the only location where they would fit was below a window. At first this location seemed fine, since the window was made of plastic and the children could look inside when they were outside. However, the children didn't just look in—they stood at the window, licking it, banging on it, and calling to the teachers inside! The teachers thought that banging on and yelling at windows was a bad habit to develop, so through consistent, constant redirection they began trying to change the children's behavior. But since toddlers lack impulse control, the teachers soon became frustrated in their efforts. Knowing that it wasn't right to be frustrated with children for doing something they can't resist, they decided this climber next to the window was going to continue being a problem unless they got creative.

One day while most of the children were napping, Kamilah took Ashraf, who awoke early, and went out to clean the window. When Ashraf climbed the stairs to get a closer look at what Kamilah was doing, Kamilah explained, "I'm wiping the window, Ashraf, so it will be nice and clean when the children want to look inside." Ashraf looked at Kamilah's cloth with interest, and then reached for it. Kamilah gave the cloth to her, and Ashraf began wiping the window. Kamilah smiled: here was the solution they'd been looking for! She opened the classroom door and asked Sonia to bring a small basket with dry cloths to the porch. When the children started to bang on the window, the teachers offered them a cloth and suggested they wash the window. This solution has worked out well. The children love to choose a cloth out of the basket, wipe the window, and drop the cloth back into the basket—and they've lost interest in the banging.

Selecting Developmentally Appropriate Toys and Equipment

Typically, children spend their first year gaining enough muscle development and mastery to achieve the basics of gross- and fine-motor movement. The onset of walking launches a year of celebration, as the child celebrates her mastery of her muscles, a mastery that allows her to grasp, to carry, and to move when and where she wants. Walking and crawling are wonderful activities for children this age, so the toddler room is designed with more open space than the infant room. The toys and activities that are popular with these active crawlers and new walkers are toys that provide reasons to move and to practice using their muscles. "One might almost say that the child of this age thinks with his feet," say the authors of *Your One-Year-Old* (1982).

A good toddler climber might more accurately be called a "walker," because it allows children to practice their walking skills more than their climbing skills. Although toddlers can be good little climbers, their actual need is to become competent walkers and runners. Thus, the teachers provide outdoor and indoor equipment that helps with motor skills and walking competence. Low ramps and stairs with railings on both sides

and a nook off to the side of the action where a child can sit in a hole (climbing in and out is almost as interesting as sitting in the hole) provide variety. A toddler can walk up a ramp, down some stairs, and through a low tunnel, all requiring control and motor planning.

There are climbing structures specifically designed for this age group. Teachers should always be monitoring when toddlers are using such equipment, of course, but once a toddler has been in a group for a while, teachers can generally trust that child's judgment to keep himself safe on climbing equipment, so a teacher does not need to stay always within arm's reach. She knows that toddlers rarely put themselves in a situation they cannot manage; it is older preschoolers, distracted by the excitement, the newfound delight, and the bravado of friendships, who might attempt more than they can physically manage. In this respect, the egocentric toddler, who cares only about his own interests, has an advantage.

Clutter and chaos distract young toddlers and make it more difficult to develop focused moments of play. Outdoor areas, like classrooms, need to have a sense of predictability and order. Sandbox toys, riding toys, pull toys, hats and purses, balls and trucks should be put out a few at a time in the same spot every day so that children can easily find them. Two trucks sitting side by side on the sand stand out, framed by the sand. Ten trucks dumped in a pile look very different: young toddlers see the pile rather than the individual trucks. Teachers rotate toys, putting out just enough to catch children's interest, while maintaining a feeling of order.

Regularly changing toys adds variety and makes the world seem interesting and fun—big trucks today, and smaller ones next week; shopping carts and purses one week, and lawn mowers and hats the next. Such rotating selections of toys meet similar ongoing developmental needs but still offer variety. At the same time that they want to add variety and maintain interest for the children, teachers want the basic structure of the classroom to stay quite stable. One-year-olds are moving so much and growing so quickly that toys and equipment need to remain predictable. In a way, being one year old is in itself so stimulating that very little more is needed to keep life interesting! As children learn more about their world, they approach the same toy with a slightly more sophisticated understanding of it, in effect creating a new experience with the same piece of equipment.

The substitute, Nguyen, enters the yard as Kamilah finishes setting up. Kamilah introduces herself and, since she's only seen Nguyen working with older groups at the center, asks Nguyen if she has worked with young toddlers before. Nguyen says, "Well, I usually work with threes and fours, but I have grandchildren and I just love these babies, so it won't be any problem for me."

Kamilah replies, "I won't need your help for the first fifteen or twenty minutes, so that will give you at least a few minutes to let the children see you in the room before you need to start interacting with them. Remember, they haven't ever seen you before, so they'll wonder who you are and why you're in their classroom. And I'll warn you—Courtney and Brendan both get very worried about new people, so it will be best if you try not to get too close or to make eye contact with them until they're ready to approach you. The others will probably be fine as long as you give them a little time and space. As you observe, you'll see that, just like in the older classes, we want to let children explore the environment and manage as much as they can by themselves, so as teachers we stand back and try to be present but not entertaining. And look!" Kamilah says as she turns toward the gate, "Here comes Courtney! Nice to see you, Courtney! Good morning, Mrs. Gray."

Courtney happily toddles into the yard toward Kamilah, but she stops suddenly in her tracks when she sees Nguyen. She then turns, toddles back to her grandmother, and grips her tightly around the knees. After a moment of reanchoring to her grandmother, she peeks over her shoulder at Nguyen and Kamilah. Kamilah quietly asks Nguyen to move closer to the fence, then steps toward Courtney, saying, "It's a surprise to see Nguyen in our yard this morning, isn't it? Nguyen is going to help us today because Katherine won't be here. You don't know Nguyen yet, but you'll get to know her later. Let's go inside with Grandma and put away your things so you can have some breakfast." Courtney accepts her grandmother's hand, and they walk into the classroom, Courtney keeping her eyes on Nguyen all the while.

An Egocentric Worldview

During the first two years of life, children are totally egocentric—not in a "selfish" way, but because they truly believe the world centers around them and their needs, and they perceive the other people in their world as extensions of themselves. The adults who surround him *are* a child's definition of self. This worldview has many implications for those who care for infants and toddlers. First and foremost, it means that when children don't know the adults they're with, it's as if they don't know who they themselves are. This is why Kamilah cautions Nguyen to give the children as much time as possible to approach her. She knows that someone who "loves babies" can overwhelm the toddlers with her enthusiasm, and that the children will be more comfortable if they are given time to approach a new adult on their own terms. Kamilah knows that even the normally outgoing children may be worried by this "stranger" trying to care for them, especially during intimate experiences like diaper changing; that is why Kamilah sighed when she saw that Katherine was out sick. Whenever possible, the center plans a transition period if the children need to get acquainted with a new adult, but there are days like this when that can't happen and everybody has to make the best of it.

REFLECTING BACK A CHILD'S POSITIVE SELF

There is another major implication of the infant's and toddler's egocentric worldview: in order for a child to learn that she is a magnificent, interesting human being, the caring adults around her must be appropriately responsive. A baby who sees his smiles reflected back at him by a caring adult, who finds somebody cooing over him when he cries, or who hears exclamations of excitement when he rolls over sees a reflection of himself as a worthy and wonderful person. Studies have found that a baby cared for by a depressed adult is at high risk of becoming a depressed baby or a baby with attachment disorders. A baby whose caregivers are neglectful or who treat caregiving as a disagreeable chore sees herself as an unpleasant burden. That is why particular care must be taken in selecting infant and toddler caregivers; they must be people whose own life experiences have given them the capacity to give young children the positive feedback they need during this age of total egocentricity.

Child care centers often will try to hire a teacher who functions as the center sub, so the children can get to know that sub over time and the sub will know the rules, routines, and schedules of the group. It's difficult for a sub to help a baby or young toddler who does not know her. The sub needs to show a child that she's worthy of his trust, and this requires time—something subs often do not have. However, a sub can do this by being extremely sensitive, quiet, and unobtrusive. If she allows the children to come to her, the children will sense that she is thoughtful and kind and that she can accurately "reflect" to them who they are. Then they will be comfortable.

The morning arrivals continue. By the time Courtney has taken a seat at the breakfast table, Ashraf is coming in the door. Ashraf doesn't pay much attention to Nguyen, instead following her usual route of running straight to Kamilah for a hug and a bib—eating is always a priority for Ashraf! Kamilah reminds Ashraf to wave good-bye to her dad, and she then serves her rice cereal and banana. Brendan's mom comes in next, with Brendan in her arms. Kamilah sees his body language when he spots Nguyen standing in the classroom; he tightens his grip on his mom's neck and looks worriedly from mom to Nguyen to Kamilah. Mrs. Bonds responds to the tightened grip by following his gaze, then asks Kamilah, "Where's Katherine this morning?" Kamilah explains Katherine's absence and says that Nguyen is here subbing today. As she did with Courtney, she acknowledges Brendan's surprise at seeing Nguyen in the classroom and adds, "I'll help you say bye to your mom and sit down for breakfast, just like Katherine usually does. Nguyen is going to stand there by the fish tank and watch us for a little while, and then she'll help us later." Brendan's mother walks over to the breakfast table with him and tries to seat him in a chair, but he can't quite let go, continuing to look anxiously at Nguyen. Kamilah offers, "Would you like to sit with me for a minute before you eat, Brendan?" He responds by turning away from Kamilah and clutching his mom with determination.

Greeting children and parents, and helping with separation

Finally, Mrs. Bonds looks at the clock and says, "I'm sorry, baby, but I have to get to work. I'm going to give you to Kamilah and I'll see you later. I love you." Brendan bursts into tears as she tries to disengage him from her body; Kamilah needs to grasp him from the back as Mrs. Bonds gently pulls his arms and legs off her. Brendan is frantically crying "No go! No go!" as Mrs. Bonds hurries out the door. After she closes the door, she stops to take a deep breath, listening to Brendan's cries and nearly in tears herself. She looks back at the door but deliberately turns away and heads out of the center and off to work.

The first times Brendan cried like this, Mrs. Bonds kept trying to comfort him so she could leave him in a happy state. Kamilah realized that Brendan, a child for whom transitions had always been a little difficult, was at just the right age to be experiencing this phase of separation anxiety. She arranged a phone conference with Mr. and Mrs. Bonds, and explained her perception of what was happening, letting the parents know that in her experience, a child going through this stage really needed to have his parent leave with as little hesitation as possible. When a child is worried and a parent responds by hesitating to follow the usual routine, it indirectly tells the child, "I'm worried too!" which worries the child even more. By initiating a good-bye routine, Mrs. Bonds could communicate to Brendan her confidence in his ability to manage the separation, said Kamilah, who further noted that she could call Mrs. Bonds later in the morning on most days, to let her know how long the crying lasted (usually just a few minutes) and how the rest of Brendan's morning went. The separations had been getting a little easier over the past two days, but it's likely that Katherine's absence intensified separation time today.

Nguyen hears Ashraf asking for more banana while Kamilah is helping Brendan and his mom separate, so she washes her hands and steps to the table to assist. As Nguyen leans over the table, Courtney eyes her warily and edges her body a little bit away from her, but she stays in her seat and continues eating. Kamilah thanks Nguyen for helping, and Nguyen steps back again, aware that her close proximity is still a problem for Brendan. Kamilah resumes her seat at the breakfast table, with Brendan now clinging to her and tearfully repeating, "No go, Mommy, no go." For a few minutes, Kamilah just holds him, gently rocking him in her arms, murmuring quietly in his ear, "You love your mommy.

Teacher objectively accepting child's feelings

Mommy loves Brendan. It's hard to say good-bye, but mommy will always come back." As Brendan quiets a bit, Kamilah offers him a piece of toast, saying, "When you're finished with your toast, you can sit in your chair and eat some cereal and banana." For a few minutes, Brendan just holds the toast, occasionally sniffling and whimpering as he gradually recovers from his distress. Finally, he begins to chew on the toast, and as he comes to the end of it, he asks for milk. Kamilah sets a cup of milk in front of the chair beside her, pats the chair, and says, "Here is your chair. I'll put some milk here for you, Brendan. Would you like some cereal and banana too?" He accepts her help to get into his chair and to pull a bib over his head. Kamilah keeps a reassuring hand on his back until he leaves the difficult separation behind him and relaxes into the classroom routine. The young toddler, still a novice at self-regulation, is reassured when he can trust the adults around him to help him regain his equilibrium after such an upset.*

Helping with Separation Anxiety

Occurring around the age of eighteen to twenty months old, the "beginning of the end" of total egocentrism is an intense phase of separation anxiety that often heralds the entrance to the age of autonomy. There is security for the child who believes that adults are in some way a part of him; he knows that though they may not be visible all the time, they will surely reappear. When the child first suspects that other people lead independent lives, he also realizes he may be completely vulnerable and alone in the world. As the old Irish fisherman's prayer states, "The sea is so wide and my boat is so small." Thus, the moment of separation from a trusted adult becomes very scary!

Beginning a new caregiver relationship at such a stage can be particularly difficult. Even in a program such as the one illustrated in our vignettes, where a toddler may have been enrolled for a year already, a sudden onset of separation anxiety can make parents worry that something is wrong. Kamilah uses every opportunity she has to share her knowledge of toddler development with parents, so they are less likely to be surprised or worried when stages like this develop. Of course, parents still feel terrible

leaving a howling child, but at least they know it's a normal stage and not due to a problem with the child care setting.

Teacher's flexibility accommodating an individual child's regulation needs

As the children finish their breakfast and begin to play, Kamilah notices an odor each time Ashraf toddles past, so she suggests to her that it's time to change her diaper. Kamilah tells the other children playing nearby that she's going to change Ashraf's diaper and that Nguyen will help them if they need something while she's busy. Brendan drops the doll he's carrying and grabs Kamilah's leg. Kamilah takes his hand and says, "You can come and stand by me while I'm changing Ashraf if you'd like, Brendan." Ashraf runs to the changing table and begins climbing the stairs as Kamilah and Brendan follow.

Kamilah keeps a small basket of books and small toys near the changing table so that children who want to stay close to the teacher have something to look at. While she changes Ashraf's diaper, she talks with her about her blue shirt with the train on it, periodically turning to check in with Brendan as well. Kamilah hears Nguyen telling Courtney and Dania that they can take turns at the pounding bench—one girl has the hammer and the other has the bench. Kamilah waves her arm to get Nguyen's attention, noting, "There's another pounding bench on the shelf, so each girl can have her own." As Kamilah cleans up the changing table and washes her hands and then Ashraf's hands, Brendan continues to hover within reach of her.

Kamilah is glad that just staying close by is enough to keep Brendan comfortable. Knowing that it's difficult for him to be with strangers, she's happy to do whatever she can to help him stay within his comfort zone. She's glad he trusts her to meet his needs, and that her presence gives him enough support so that he feels able to manage stressful situations. She remembers learning that recent research on cortisol, a hormone the body secretes in response to stress, has shown that a child subjected to too much stress can develop a chronic oversensitivity to difficult situations, which in turn affects the child's social and emotional development. This knowledge confirms what Kamilah has always felt, that it is in a child's best interests to protect her from more than she can handle. It helps Kamilah understand why cautious children who develop strong, attached relationships and are given gentle support to develop personal strategies for interacting with the world tend to be more successful in their social development. Kamilah knows she could have spent a long time trying to convince Brendan that Nguyen is perfectly nice and will take good care of him. She realizes, though, that denying a child his perception of the world does not work; it only makes him feel unsupported for being himself. Thus, she's willing to accommodate his need to stay close to her, knowing that in the long run it's his trust in the adults he knows that will allow him accept people he doesn't know well.

Nguyen helps this happen too. Hired to come and help, it can be challenging for a sub to find that her ability to help is restricted by her lack of relationship with the children. Nguyen has done her part by standing back and helping those children who can tolerate the break in routine caused by a sub; in so doing, she has allowed Kamilah to focus on Brendan's needs. Even though she is an experienced grandmother and mother who knows how to comfort distressed babies, Nguyen has controlled her impulse to do so, knowing that her relationship with Brendan will be stronger if he has a chance to meet her on his own terms rather than when he's feeling vulnerable and upset.

"Nguyen," Kamilah says quietly, "I'm going to take three children outside; will you please help the others put on their jackets and then bring them out in a minute?" Kamilah takes Brendan, Courtney, and Ashraf into the cubby area to put on their jackets before they head outside. On her knees helping fasten zippers, Kamilah says, "It's cold outside, so we'll put on our jackets and stay cozy. Courtney, I see you have a drippy nose. I have a tissue in my pocket to wipe it." Rather than ask Courtney's opinion about having her nose wiped, Kamilah helps Courtney think about how her nose feels when it's dripping and she lets her know a wipe is coming. She sees this as part of her role to help the children build awareness of their bodies, and she believes it's as important as keeping them cleaned up and comfortable.

The children go out the door to the outside play area. Courtney goes straight to the climber, with its toddler-sized stairs, ramps, and slide.

Ashraf grabs a shopping cart and pushes it around the yard. Brendan, however, stays close to Kamilah, with his thumb in his mouth, watching.

Nguyen comes out with the second group, and these children disperse as well. Dania steps into the sandbox, picks up two cups, and begins to pour sand from one to the other. Blanca walks by Dania and is intrigued as she watches her pour the sand back and forth; she steps into the sandbox and, sitting nearly on top of Dania, begins to grab the cups. Kamilah quickly steps close and says, "Blanca, let's give you more room and some cups to pour sand too." She picks Blanca up and scoots her several feet away from Dania, handing her cups and showing her how to pour the sand as Dania is doing.

Teacher regulating children's energy output

Brendan, still trailing Kamilah, looks at the lawn mower by the wall. He looks up and, since he doesn't see Nguyen, decides it's safe to step away from Kamilah to go and push the mower. Kamilah smiles as she sees everyone happily at play. She knows it won't last long and so takes time to appreciate the moment. Sure enough, a minute later Blanca stumbles while chasing a ball. As Kamilah gives Blanca a hug, she notices that several of the children are looking clumsy and tired. She asks Blanca if she would like to sing a song and listen to a story. When Blanca says "bus," Kamilah knows Blanca is suggesting they sing "The Wheels on the Bus." Kamilah quietly invites Dania to join them, and then says to Eduardo, who is already sitting in the middle of the mat holding a book, "I'm just going to scoot you over with your book, so we can sit here too." Kamilah and the others sit, and Kamilah begins singing. Brendan, passing by with the lawn mower, abandons it and comes to join them. Soon most of the children are sitting, relaxed and engaged in stories as they rest their bodies. Courtney and Ashraf, however, are busy climbing and sliding, with Nguyen supervising them.

Teacher helping children interpret another adult's actions

Kamilah is just coming to the last picture in a board book when she sees the center director approaching the yard with a camera. As she enters the yard, the director says, "I just need a couple pictures of toddlers for our newsletter." Some of the children who have been listening to the story jump up and begin to clown at the director's feet, saying "Hi! Hi! Hi!" obviously clear about the role they should play when somebody holds a camera. But Courtney hurries down from the climber and backs up to Kamilah with a panicky look, seeing somebody who doesn't belong in the group and who might try to take her picture. Kamilah steps *between Courtney and the director, turns to Courtney, and says, "Here's Mary, ready to take some pictures. If you don't want her to take your picture, we can say 'no picture.'" Courtney keeps a suspicious eye on the director, but feels comfortable enough to go in the opposite direction to find a ball to hold.*

Teaching Self-regulation

Due to their egocentricity, children at this age have not yet learned that others have needs and feelings the same way they do. Taking something from another child seems no different to a toddler than taking something off a shelf—except that, if another child is playing with it, the animation of the object makes it appear more interesting than when it's sitting on a shelf. As they focus on achieving a particular goal, toddlers may sit on, knock over, or otherwise violate the space of other children, totally unaware of the havoc they're creating. Teachers in a toddler room therefore know it's up to them to keep the children safe from each other's mistakes.

At this stage of development, young toddlers are physically driven, virtually unable to stop themselves from impulsive actions or to take another child's point of view. Being preverbal, they also have a limited ability to communicate. That means teachers must stay close so that they can step in as soon as they're needed. While the ultimate goal for all children is to develop internal self-control, for young toddlers, the teacher must provide external control in most situations. Learning that they can trust their teachers to provide this control is a major factor in establishing a child's trust in her environment. She knows that the teachers will "save her from herself," thus making her world safer.

STORY TIME AS A WAY TO REFOCUS ENERGY

Story time in the toddler classroom does not follow a set schedule; instead, the teachers use story time to slow the pace when children seem ready for a quiet moment. As young toddlers learn to self-regulate, the teacher helps them by noting when they're tired and then arranging a little rest. In a few years, the children will need less adult assistance to balance their activities between busy time and quiet time. Trying to force physically

driven toddlers to sit for a preset story time will surely fail; waiting for the right moment to suggest a story results in both a relaxed and inviting story time and a nice refocusing of the children's energy. Both these outcomes meet the teacher's goals to help children learn to self-regulate and to give children opportunities for enjoyable preliteracy experiences.

FIVE EFFECTIVE TEACHING TOOLS TO BUILD TRUSTING RELATIONSHIPS

Kamilah's intervention with Courtney when the director came to take pictures is nearly intuitive to a well-trained, sensitive teacher. At the same time she is supervising a group of children, she can notice the anxiety of one particular child. She uses body language and spoken language to communicate to the child, "I know you get worried about people you don't know. I'm here and I'll be sure you're always safe. I'll help you understand who this person is, that I trust her, why she's here, and how you can make your feelings known. And I'll teach you some words that will help you tell Mary what you want: 'No picture.'" Within a thirty-second interaction, she uses all these good teaching tools:

- accepting and acknowledging the child's feelings
- reinforcing the bond of trust between child and teacher
- giving clear information to the child about the world
- modeling verbal speech
- expressing confidence in the child's ability to manage the situation

Adjusting routines to accommodate different energy levels

After Mary and her camera depart, the children who were focused on her resume their wandering exploration of the yard. Nguyen comments to Kamilah, "My, it's hard to keep up with this group, isn't it! They just keep moving. I guess they have to be a little older before they really sit and play, don't they?" Kamilah agrees, remembering the Ames chart "7 Clocked Minutes of Nursery School Behavior at Different Ages," which dramatizes the difference in activity level found in the play of children at eighteen months, two years, two-and-a-half years, three years, and four years, showing how much the brain and body mature during those years, particularly during the year from eighteen to thirty months old. The chart contrasts the randomness and nonstop nature of a young toddler's movements with the far more purposeful play of a four-year-old. Kamilah makes a mental note that if she has a minute during naptime, she will show the chart to Nguyen and try also to give her a brief refresher course on toddler behavior. At the moment, however, she has to quickly outline for Nguyen the plans for lunchtime, diapers, and nap.

When the time comes to move inside for lunch, Kamilah again oversees the most stranger-anxious children in the group. She's pleased to see that most of the children have been managing all right with the substitute teacher, but she knows that a challenging time of day is just ahead. As children finish lunch and get their diapers changed for nap, they'll be tired and easily upset by changes in routine—and a new teacher is a major change in routine. There's a difficult moment when Courtney, the first one finished with lunch, refuses to let Nguyen change her diaper, and then Brendan begins to cry when Nguyen tries to take Kamilah's place at the table so Kamilah can change Courtney's diaper. However, Courtney is able to sit nearby the lunch table and look at books while she waits for Kamilah to finish up with Brendan. As soon as Brendan is finished eating, Kamilah helps Brendan and Courtney get ready for a nap.

Later, as the first nappers begin to wake, Joya steps into the classroom and says she's available to help for a few minutes. Kamilah says, "Thanks, that's great! I'll just step out to call Mrs. Bonds; I felt bad about not being able to leave the group to call and check in with her this morning. You know how Brendan and Courtney are; they really couldn't have handled being left alone with Nguyen this morning. But Mrs. Bonds looked like she was ready to cry when she left Brendan sobbing today, so I'd really like to talk with her." Minutes after Kamilah leaves the room, Joya hears Brendan waking. She moves close to his cot and smiles at him, saying softly, "Here you are, all done with your nap, Brendan! Are you ready to get your diaper changed?" Brendan rubs his eyes, which open wide as he realizes that it's Joya next to his cot. He immediately bursts into tears and calls out, "'Milah! 'Milah!" Joya quickly bundles him up in his blanket to carry him out of the nap room before he awakens the other children, then soothingly says, "Kamilah is just

Teachers managing challenging transitions

making a phone call and then she'll be back; I'll help you get changed and ready to play while she's gone." Brendan continues crying and calling for Kamilah.

As the other children who are awake sit at the table eating a snack with Nguyen, Joya takes a few minutes to sit and rock Brendan, trying to soothe him with words and motion. "I know you were surprised to see me. You'd like to see Kamilah when you wake up. She'll be back in a few minutes." After another minute's rocking she adds, "It's hard when you wake up and something is different, isn't it?" She rocks some more, periodically murmuring acknowledgment of Brendan's distress, but rather than calming down, Brendan's voice is sounding louder and angrier when Kamilah returns to the classroom.

Joya explains to Kamilah, "Brendan was so surprised to see me when he woke up from his nap! He was wishing that you were here to help him get up." Kamilah takes her cue from Joya and responds, "Brendan, I'm sorry you were surprised to see Joya by your bed. It's been a long time since she was the one who got you up from nap, hasn't it? You were calling Kamilah, too, and I was busy and couldn't come fast enough—that might make a boy feel mad! I'm here now and I can help you get changed." Joya passes Brendan to Kamilah, who continues with many of the same soothing activities that Joya had begun. Slowly, Brendan begins to calm and relax his body, but he is still sniffling as Kamilah puts him on the changing table and begins to change his diaper. Fortunately, by the time Joya needs to return to the infant room, Nguyen's shift has ended and Sonia, one of the usual afternoon teachers, has arrived. Sonia helps the other children while Kamilah focuses on Brendan.

Establishing Trust

The equilibrium of a toddler is easily disturbed, particularly when there's an unexpected change in routine. A toddler's somewhat random and chaotic experience of the world becomes more predictable as she achieves an early understanding of sequence and order. Knowing that washing hands is followed by lunch and then by nap, or knowing that he'll see Katherine in the morning and Sonia in the afternoon, gives a child some ability to

Teacher putting language to child's feelings

predict the future instead of always being surprised by it. Teachers therefore put a priority on keeping life as predictable as possible for young children; they know that a foundation for healthy emotional development is built when children learn they can trust the world to meet their needs and expectations. Teachers also know, however, that one way a child learns to trust the world is by experiencing minor distress and then discovering that caring adults will help him learn to manage such situations. The adult first serves as an extension of self, to help the child learn to self-regulate. After autonomy is established, a child needs less and less adult support to self-regulate.

Early in the day, when Brendan came to school and saw Nguyen, nobody was surprised that Katherine's absence, aggravated by his separation and stranger anxieties, had caused him to fall apart. But after nap, Brendan was upset even when interacting with someone he knows: Joya. Joya was his caregiver from the time he enrolled at the center at three months old until a few months ago when he transitioned into the toddler group. He often sees her during the course of his day and gives her a fond greeting or even a hug, so this situation cannot be explained as separation or stranger anxiety. However, Brendan expects to see Kamilah or Katherine when he wakes, not Joya, and the experience of seeing a person out of the usual context caught him by surprise. His "prediction" that he would open his eyes and see Kamilah or Katherine was incorrect. His fledgling sense of order had been disrupted—and his anxiety was already high because of the stresses of the morning with a substitute. He needed to reconnect with the expected person, the person he trusted to give him the external support he needed to regain his sense of trust in the world; he needed Kamilah to help him.

THE IMPORTANCE OF SEQUENCE AND ORDER

Brendan's budding sense of sequence and order helps him understand and predict what will happen in the world around him, and it forms the foundation for important future learning. He needs a strong sense of sequence, order, and predictability in order to develop skills that will allow him to acquire language and to develop communication skills. Later, these skills will help him sort and categorize, so he can be ready to learn to read, write, and think symbolically (for math and science). The mind of the human baby wants to create order and predictability and the reciprocity

of relationship, but it can't do this without the dynamic, loving support of competent caregivers. When facilitated, supported, and protected from distress, the mind will develop the concepts necessary to function as a whole healthy adult, able to think globally, to understand abstraction and the nuances of emotions and communication, and to manage the details of everyday living. Kamilah's understanding and acceptance of Brendan's stage of development, and her ability to meet his needs objectively and with love and compassion, help establish a foundation for his future learning.

Teacher modeling play extension

While Dania finishes her long nap, the others play in the adjacent play-room. At thirteen months old and new to the group, little Eduardo is working hard to master the stairs on the inside climbing structure. Kamilah asks Sonia to stay close to Eduardo, as she's not quite sure if he has developed enough motor awareness to keep himself safe. Blanca, crawling under the climber, discovers the container of rubber ducks that Kamilah set there this morning, and she happily dumps them out, drops them back in one by one, and then dumps them out again.

Refreshed after her nap, sixteen-month-old Dania picks up a small doll and blanket, which she carries to a corner. She sets the doll on the floor, then works for several minutes to spread the blanket across it. When she's satisfied, she begins to pat, but she's surprised to see that the hand that's patting is not the hand next to the doll—her immature motor planning has activated the wrong hand! She picks up the doll and blanket and walks over to face Kamilah. Dania holds the doll and blanket out to Kamilah, who takes them and says, "Thank you for the doll and the blanket, Dania. Should I pat the baby doll?" She cradles the doll in her arm and pats it gently a few times, then holds it out for Dania to take back. Dania, however, keeps her hands at her sides and keeps watching the teacher. Kamilah cradles the doll again, rocks it, and sings the "night night" song that the teachers sing at naptime. When she again holds out the doll to Dania, Dania takes it back and begins to imitate the teacher's rocking and patting. She is so enthusiastic that Eduardo, who's been watching Dania, leaves the climber and picks up a doll too. Being too young to understand anything about pretending (which requires the abstract ability to have one object stand for another in a child's brain), however, he ends up chewing on the doll's foot.

Modeling

In the previous vignette, although Dania didn't utter a word, Kamilah could see she was asking for advice. The moment when she looked down and saw her right hand patting the floor rather than her left hand patting the doll, Dania seemed to experience a little crisis of confidence. She let the teacher know she had some idea about the doll symbolizing a baby, but she wasn't quite sure what to do about it. Kamilah began by modeling language: naming the doll, the blanket, and Dania. In the process, she also modeled courteous behavior: thanking Dania for bringing her the doll. She could see that Dania needed a new idea, so she modeled a nice way to use a baby doll by patting it. When her brief demonstration didn't seem to be what Dania wanted, Kamilah took the time to draw a parallel for her between Dania's naptime and the way to "pretend" naptime with the doll. That was just what Dania was asking for, and it opened up a new world of pretending for this toddler!

Teachers for preverbal toddler groups model language constantly, with little expectation that it will be reciprocated. They "sportscast" many events in a toddler's day, providing a rich language environment and helping the children understand their world. As they speak, they add drama and physical emphasis to help the children understand the words. For example, when she spies Dania poking her head up from behind a shelf and then hiding again, Kamilah asks, "Where is Dania?" as if totally mystified, looking high and low. As Dania pops her head up from behind the shelf the teacher grins, says *"Peek*aboo!" and opens her eyes wide, as if Dania has caught her completely off guard.

PUTTING FEELINGS INTO WORDS

Teachers use language to help children know they're understood and that a teacher is going to help them. When Brendan was flooded with emotion and able only to cry, the teacher attempted to put words to those emotions: "You love your mommy. Mommy loves Brendan. It's hard to say good-bye,

but mommy will always come back." When it was time to help him move into his own chair, the teacher set a cup of milk in front of the chair beside her, patted the chair, and said, "Here is your chair. I'll put some milk here for you, Brendan." When Courtney worried about Mary coming into the yard with her camera, Kamilah let her know how language could be used to communicate what she wants: "If you don't want her to take your picture, we can say 'no picture.'" Toddlers understand words and follow sentences before they can say the words or put the sentences together, so it's a comfort for them to have an adult put their experience into words; it affirms their experience and creates order and predictability out of their experience. Adults are easier to understand and far more predictable than other children. A teacher's language is calming; it addresses the feeling of unpredictability and chaos that an active group of toddlers can generate.

It's important to Kamilah that the children feel she respects them and wants to include them in her thinking. It's also important to her that they know her actions are purposeful rather than arbitrary interference. That's why when she moves Eduardo on the book mat or Blanca in the sandbox, she explains to the child what she's doing ("I'm just going to scoot you over with your book, so we can sit here too"; "Blanca, let's give you more room and some cups to pour sand too").

TEACHING PERSPECTIVE

Knowing that toddlers are unable to take another person's point of view, the teacher can use a similar "sportscasting" technique to tell toddlers about another person's perspective. For example, if Courtney wants to climb the stairs on a climber, but Dania is sitting on the stairs, the teacher might say: "Courtney, I see that you want to climb the stairs, but Dania is sitting there. You can say 'move' to Dania. Dania, I see Courtney coming up the stairs. Where can you go so that Courtney can come past you? Should I help you find another place to sit? Courtney, I see Dania is standing up so she can move. Let me help you wait here while she gets herself up and then you can finish climbing the stairs. Thanks for moving, Dania. That looks like a place where you can sit and not be in Courtney's way. Thanks for waiting, Courtney. Now there's room for you to climb all the way up the stairs." The teacher could simply pick up Dania and move her or tell Courtney not to use the stairs. However, her goal is for the children to be able to pursue their own interests while also becoming aware of the needs of other people around them. By objectively narrating what she sees, she feeds information to the children that will ultimately help them move toward understanding another's perspective. As their development allows them to take in more information, the children will hear the teacher's voice in their heads directing them to see the bigger picture of the group, rather than just their own interests.

PREPARING CHILDREN FOR COMING EVENTS

A teacher's language can also help moderate surprises children might experience in the course of the day. By describing what is coming, a teacher helps the children prepare for something they might not otherwise expect. For example, as she changes a diaper, the teacher might say, "I'm getting a wipe now for your bottom. It feels a little cold on my fingers, so it might feel cold on your bottom too. Does it feel cold? Now I'm going to use another wipe to really clean you up, and then I'll be ready to put a fresh diaper on you." Or, in another example, if Blanca's father usually picks her up, but today her aunt is coming to pick her up, a teacher can try to prep her a few minutes before the aunt arrives: "Blanca, I remember that daddy said your Tia Tina is going to pick you up today; I bet she'll be here soon! Will you help me watch for her?" Small steps like these can make all the difference for a child, letting her anticipate an unexpected arrival or an unexpected physical sensation.

There is, however, a fine line between enriching children's experiences with language and bombarding them with language to such an extent that they tune it out. A teacher must be careful to remember that sometimes a child's experience is actually richer with no adult interruption. In the opening scene of this chapter, for example, when the children discovered that the leaves they picked off the vine could be pushed between the boards of the fence, the teachers were silent, attentively watching but seeing that the children needed no help from them to fully experience their joy in discovery.

The day winds down

With Sonia's arrival, the class dynamics settle into the usual comfortable pattern for the afternoon, the children able to fully relax into their play without worrying about a stranger in their midst. Midafternoon some of the children relax with a bottle of milk while others enjoy a snack at the table. This group eats often, as most young toddlers have small stomach capacity but burn calories fast with their perpetual motion. Kamilah begins to think about wrapping up her day, jotting notes to parents about how eating and sleeping have gone for their child. Usually she also adds a brief individual note or an anecdote about the day's activities, but today she just posts a note for all the parents that says, "Katherine was out today. The children may want to tell you about Nguyen, who was here substituting. It's been a busy day! Sorry I don't have time for individual notes today." When teacher Bella enters the classroom, Kamilah gives her a quick synopsis of the day's high and low points, including how well Eduardo is doing on the climber and how difficult the morning was for some children without Katherine. She says good-bye to the children and heads to the office, hoping she can have a quick conversation with the director about a better way to arrange for substitutes.

The children and teachers get ready to move back into the classroom as dark begins to fall. As they approach the door, Bella says, "Tia Tina will be here soon, Blanca! Let's change your diaper so you'll be all ready when she gets here." Mrs. Bonds hurries down the path to the yard, eager to reunite with her son, Brendan. When Brendan sees her coming, he turns and runs in the opposite direction. A look of hurt and disappointment comes over Mrs. Bonds's face, and her pace slows. Bella continues inside with the children, Brendan leading the way.

"Hi, Mrs. Bonds," welcomes Sonia at the gate. "Brendan is sure thinking about separations these days, isn't he?"

"I don't understand what he's thinking about!" she replies. "It sounded like his heart would break when I left this morning, and now he's running away from me! I guess he must be mad at me for leaving him all day."

Teacher building a relationship with a parent through professional expertise

"If it's any comfort to you, it's classic toddler behavior to cling to you for dear life one minute and then run away the next! It's part of how he figures out how you connect to each other. Of course, it's always more

comfortable for the child if he's the one running away, not you! I guess you could say it's a way he tries out how it feels to be the one leaving. And the exciting thing about that behavior is that it tells us his brain is maturing and he's getting ready to be a two-year-old!"

"Well, Kamilah did tell me that I shouldn't take his behavior personally, but it's hard not to! I feel like all the things I've learned about parenting are no use anymore. He's changing so much," frets Mrs. Bonds.

"Parenting is sure a roller-coaster ride, isn't it?" Sonia says. "Everytime you think things are running smoothly, the bottom drops out on you again! But you know, the other thing to remember is that transitions have never been easy for Brendan. When a child has his temperament and doesn't like change, a developmental stage like this one, moving into autonomy, can be extra hard. Think about it—development is making this child, who doesn't like change, have to change his whole understanding of the world! And he had a lot to process today, with Katherine out. Kamilah's right—don't take his behavior personally. You're a smart mom, so just go on loving him and doing what you know is right for him, and before you know it, you and he will be in another stage!"

Mrs. Bonds and Sonia move into the classroom. Brendan has been watching the door anxiously, but as soon as he sees his mom he turns away and pointedly ignores her. Mrs. Bonds, reassured by her conversation with Sonia, calls out a greeting and then goes about her usual routine of checking his chart and gathering the things out of his basket to take home. When she catches Brendan's eye sneaking another look at her, she smiles and says, "Peekaboo, Brendan, I see you!" He grins, but turns away again. They repeat the game a few times, Brendan clearly delighted by the opportunity to be in charge of his gradual reengagement with his mother. Finally, Mrs. Bonds approaches him and says, "Where's that Brendan? I need a hug from him!" and when he turns, she says, "Peekaboo, I got you!" and catches him up in her arms. Giggling and snuggling, they walk out the door and head home for the night.

Sonia and Bella smile at each other, pleased to see Brendan's difficult day end so successfully. Part of what he is learning is what is under his control and what is not. He is getting a clear message that he does not get to decide if his mom leaves in the morning, so it's nice that he is also finding that there are times when he can be in charge.

Bella gathers the remaining children to look at books with her while Sonia makes the rounds of the room, straightening up and picking up items to be washed. She adds a few lines to Kamilah's notes to the parents—a reminder that Dania needs more diapers, and a request for spare shoes for Ashraf, whose enthusiasm for water play can leave her with wet feet. Sonia sweeps crumbs from under the snack table, and sets up a tray with dishes for breakfast. She leaves a brief note for Kamilah: "Had a good chat with Mrs. Bonds. It seems like she's hearing us and relaxing a bit about Brendan's anxiety. Tell you more tomorrow."

Sonia and Bella say good-bye to the remaining children and their caregivers as the children leave the classroom: "Good night, Tina and Blanca! Have fun with your special Tia Tina tonight!" "Good-bye, Courtney and Mrs. Gray! See you tomorrow!" "Good-bye, Eduardo! Boy, Mr. Lam, you should see how hard Eduardo is working at getting up and down those stairs!"

As they collect their belongings and walk out the door, Sonia and Bella have a quick discussion about plans for tomorrow afternoon. Sonia had arranged for Katherine to stay late while Sonia went to the dentist, but now, with Katherine's absence, they aren't sure what will happen. Sonia says, "I really have to keep this appointment. My tooth has been killing me, but I know how hard it was for Kamilah today without Katherine."

Bella thinks a minute, then offers, "I usually volunteer in my son's class on Thursdays, but tomorrow they're having their school pictures taken and they won't need me. So I'll tell Mary that if Katherine calls in sick again she should call me, and I'll come in early; I could work a whole eight-hour day. You'll be here by the time my usual shift starts, right? Then at least Kamilah won't have to work with a sub for more than a few hours."

"That would be great—thanks a lot, Bella!" says Sonia. "Have a good evening! See you tomorrow afternoon."

The AGE of AUTONOMY: TWO-YEAR-OLDS

4

DEVELOPMENTAL AGE RANGE

20–36 months

I t's a chilly day. Four toddlers come into the classroom from the yard. Three begin to pull off their jackets as they walk through the door; they then stop and work at getting their jackets hung on hooks. Twenty-five-month-old Colin walks over, stands next to teacher Monique, and ineffectually tugs on his jacket while looking up at her. Monique makes eye contact and asks, "Do you need something?" Colin says "Dacket," and Monique expands his single word into a clarifying sentence, "You want your jacket off?" The child nods and the teacher asks, "How do you open your jacket?" The child looks down and fingers the zipper pull, as Monique turns away for a moment to remind Roberto, whose jacket is on the hook, that Lawanda will hang up her own jacket and he can find a place to play now. Colin drops his hands to his side and looks again at the teacher. She turns back to him and says, "You can pull down on your zipper." Colin pulls awkwardly and unsuccessfully, and looks again at the teacher.

Teacher empowering toddler's independence

85

Monique kneels in front of Colin and, placing his fingers under hers on the pull, shows how to get it down. Colin shrugs his shoulders to get the jacket off, while Monique helps Lawanda find the loop in her jacket that will hold it onto its hook.

Colin's jacket stays on his shoulders, and he again looks to the teacher for help. Monique suggests, "Pull your sleeve with your hand." Colin puts his hand on the sleeve near his elbow and yanks outward, with little result, then looks again at Monique, who is telling Lawanda, "Roberto is sitting in that chair. Do you see another chair for you?" Monique guides Colin's fingers to the cuff of his sleeve and helps him pull downward until the sleeve comes loose. Finally, Colin gets the jacket off, and then holds it out to the teacher. Monique makes no move to take the jacket, instead saying, "You got your jacket off! Now it's ready to go on a hook!" She turns to Lawanda and says, "I see you found a chair to sit in where you have plenty of room to draw with your crayons!"

Colin looks at the jacket in his hand, then walks over to the hooks and pushes his jacket against a hook, as if expecting it to stick. When it doesn't, he lets it slide to the floor, and then walks over to the puzzle shelf. Monique says, "Uh-oh! I see your jacket on the floor, Colin. Let's see if we can get it to stay on the hook." She walks with Colin to the pegs, helps him hold the jacket by the hood, and watches him hang the jacket. "That's great!" exclaims Monique. "Your jacket is right where you can find it when it's time to go outside. Now you're ready to get a puzzle!" Colin grins, says "Gwate!" and goes to get a puzzle.

Ask-Say-Do

Monique is practicing a teaching technique known as Ask-Say-Do. Through Ask-Say-Do, the teachers continually send the message that the children are competent human beings who can learn to take care of themselves. The teachers' goal is self-sufficiency, not efficiency, so they resist the short-term efficiency of having teachers unzip, remove, and hang up the toddlers' jackets. Recognizing that every child develops at her own pace, Ask-Say-Do establishes an escalating system of assistance, which begins by assuming the child can do it himself, then uses a question from the teacher to remind the child of what he knows, then progresses to the

teacher telling the child what comes next, and ends with the teacher assisting the child in performing the task. This system makes no assumptions—even though Colin can easily pull off his jacket at times when he objects to wearing it, he may still be learning that the teacher has given him the responsibility for removing and hanging it at school and thus needs to be prompted through the sequence. So the teacher begins by *asking,* "How do you open your jacket?" When nothing happens, she proceeds to *saying,* "You can pull down on your zipper." And finally, when it appears that Colin needs more support for the process, Monique moves to *doing* by helping him pull the zipper.

Although Ask-Say-Do takes a lot of time and may look to the casual observer as though the teacher is either "doing nothing" or that she is "lazy," the process in fact takes a lot of practice and self-control from a teacher, who must learn to watch the children closely to see if they can manage a situation without prompting and, only after seeing that a child really needs assistance, move into Ask-Say-Do. During the five minutes that the teacher in the previous vignette was helping Colin work out how to remove and hang up his jacket, she was also actively engaged with three other toddlers. She was watching the other children in the class, too, to see if they could independently manage their activities, and where necessary she was giving other children Ask-Say-Do assistance.

GOALS FOR TWO-YEAR-OLDS

Ask-Say-Do exemplifies the four goals we have for this stage of development:

- Autonomy: trust in self
- A sense of capability and independence: trust that it is safe to assert one's own will (this builds on trust that the world is safe, with adults who will moderate the child's drives)
- A more extended and deeper engagement in self-directed play
- The understanding that language acquisition will support their developing social interests

---

Brain Development and the Importance of Structure

Play in a classroom of two-year-olds is more purposeful than that of one-year-olds, reflecting new organization within the children's developing brains. The play of younger children is fairly random and opportunistic, with little intention. As children's brains build more structure, life begins to make more sense. Older toddlers revel in structure and order, and the teachers capitalize on that by helping them learn routines for choosing, using, and replacing toys. Nature and nurture work together to grow the child's brain. While there is an innate interest in structure, order, and sorting that emerges at this age, teachers know that support from the environment will encourage the development of these skills. Repeated experiences with materials that encourage toddlers to play with structure, order, and sorting help shape a toddler's brain to look for sequence and pattern in progressively more complex settings. Ultimately, understanding the sequence of a story (beginning, middle, and end) and the pattern of letters on a page (always starting at the left side) will be essential concepts that support reading.

Teachers are careful to allow ample time so children can make relaxed choices in their play and then get deeply invested in those choices. They want to be sure that when a child is engaged in constructive play, he is "protected" from interruption. They will also look for opportunities for toddlers to extend their play. For example, a toddler who day after day puts blankets over a baby doll and then pats the doll may be ripe for a teacher's suggestion that the doll is ready to wake up and eat breakfast in the high chair. To successfully extend play, the teacher must skillfully observe children's play at the same time she is teaching. Her observation allows her to see when a child's play gets stuck and also to think of an appropriate suggestion to gently move the play forward.

Monique hangs up her purse and gets right to work setting up. Most of the activities in this classroom are arranged for solitary or parallel play

(see appendix D), because the egocentricity of toddlers requires that they each have their own play equipment. She takes the Duplos out, and puts two sets of about fifteen matching, assorted pieces on trays to go out in the yard. In the yard, she sets up two matching strollers with dolls, hangs two toddler-sized backpacks with toy dishes on the fence, and puts shovels into two buckets in the sandbox, lining up two sets of dump trucks and backhoes at the other end.

Monique then heads inside, where she checks the paint cups, washing out the yellow cup that got murky yesterday when Tracy painted yellow on top of red and blue. She fills the cup with just an inch of fresh yellow paint, so she won't feel wasteful if that has to be dumped out tomorrow. She replaces broken chunky crayons in the small dishes designed for a single child's use, and sets up two basins with water and assorted scoops, funnels, and plastic bottles, with plastic aprons on hooks nearby. As she is about to leave the room, she remembers how hard it was yesterday for Roberto not to drink the play water. She stirs some dish soap into the basins to make the water less attractive for drinking, because she wants Roberto to learn to stop himself; along with the teacher's reminders, the soap flavor will give him good feedback. The soap bubbles make the water more fun to play in too!

With the majority of the setup complete, Monique is ready for children to arrive. She uses her last few free minutes to make the play activities on the shelves especially inviting—matching play cups and saucers, putting a wallet and keys inside every dramatic-play purse, and emptying the drop boxes so that their contents sit fully displayed in a dish on each tray. She knows that the toddlers in her class, while beginning to play with toys more intentionally than younger toddlers, are still very concrete thinkers. A full display of a toy's attractions will make it easier for the children to engage with it. To support the most constructive and successful use of the equipment and materials provided to the toddlers in her classroom, she keeps everything as simple and clear as she can. She makes sure that there are enough choices to be interesting, but not so many as to be overwhelming. Four crayons in a dish, fifteen Duplos on a tray, six puzzles on the shelf—she has learned just the right quantity of each item to provide. She knows that setting up play activities very clearly will help children organize their play and also will be satisfying to children whose brains are developing a new ability to organize.

Teacher setting up the classroom for solitary and parallel play

The door opens and Roberto runs in ahead of his dad. "Good morning, Roberto and Mr. Mendez!" welcomes Monique. "Nice to see you in your cozy jacket today, Roberto." After Roberto hangs up his coat, she watches him pull out a chair where breakfast is waiting. She says cheerily, rubbing her hands together, "Oops! Did you forget something?" Roberto catches the nonverbal hand-washing cue, pushes his chair back, and goes to the sink. Mr. Mendez, seeing his son ready to start his day, takes the opportunity before Roberto's hands are wet to give him a kiss and say good-bye. Roberto has been in this classroom for several months and he knows the morning routine; he can wash his hands without any help from Monique. As Roberto sits down again, Monique puts a bowl of cereal in front of him and asks if he'd like a slice of orange.

The door opens again, and Colin's mother walks in with Colin in her arms, his head resting on her shoulder. She is deep in conversation with Lawanda's mom, who is being tugged along by Lawanda's hand. Roberto jumps up from his chair to greet Lawanda with a hug, but Lawanda pulls back against her mom. Monique gently slides her arm around Roberto's shoulders and turns him back toward the table, reminding Roberto that Lawanda will be ready to say hello to him after she says good-bye to her mother. Lawanda relaxes, knowing her teacher understands that she needs a minute to adjust to being at school. Soon Lawanda is giving her mom a hug and a kiss, washing up for breakfast, and happily joining Roberto at the table. Colin, meanwhile, remains fully attached to his mother, who is trying to set him down and seems impatient to be on her way.

Monique asks Colin if he'd like her to hold him while he says good-bye to his mom. He silently lets go of his mother's neck and reaches his arms to Monique. Monique says, "Let's say bye to mom, Colin. She's going to go to work now and daddy will pick you up later!" Although Colin still says nothing, Monique has made sure that he knows his mom is leaving and has given him a reminder to say good-bye if he needs to. Going out the door, Colin's mom says, "He didn't sleep too well last night, so I had trouble waking him up this morning."

As the classroom fills up, teacher Josh, who is assisting Monique today, quietly enters. He greets Monique and returns the hugs of a few children who hurry over to say hello, being careful not to let his entrance distract the children focused on breakfast or on play.

Teaching children that their individual needs are accepted and respected

Joe, twenty-five months old, walks to the manipulative shelf, selects a tray containing a box of small cubes, carries it to the table, and sits down to play. He pulls the blocks out and spreads them over the box lid and tray, and then begins to methodically set them back in the box. Tracy, twenty-nine months old, sits in the chair next to Joe and tries to take some blocks. Joe protects them with his hands and says, "No!" Tracy says, "I'm playing with you, Joe" and puts her hands out again to take blocks. Again, Joe covers them with his hands, tensing his body and pushing her hands away. Josh squats down where he can look each child in the eye, and observes casually, "Joe is playing with the blocks." Tracy says, "I'm playing too." Joe looks worried until Josh says, "I see that Joe took the blocks off the shelf and is using them all by himself." Tracy looks perplexed, but Joe relaxes. Josh resumes, "Tracy, I see more toys on the shelf that you can use while you're waiting for the blocks. When Joe puts the blocks back on the shelf, it can be your turn with them." Tracy gets up to choose another toy, brings it to the table, and sits down to play next to Joe.

Teacher's interpretation facilitating toddlers' play

Modeling Language That Clarifies Toddlers' Interactions

Although two-year-olds can be amazingly verbal, the give-and-take of social interaction is still a mystery to them, to be unraveled in the coming years. When children learn to communicate in words, it opens up an exciting new world of interaction with adults. When a child converses with an adult, the adult typically will compensate for the child's social egocentricity. When a child converses with another egocentric child, however, the results are often unsuccessful. In the previous vignette, Tracy, with her immature understanding of language, thought that by telling Joe she was playing with him, she could make it so. Joe, who is less verbal, could only articulate "No" in response to Tracy's attempt to play with him, though his body language clearly said he would *not* share the blocks.

The teacher's role in this interaction is to clarify the situation for each child. Josh acknowledged Joe's need for ownership, allowing him to stay focused on his play, while he reminded Tracy that it's up to the person using a toy to decide whether or not it's going to be shared. Using very few words and some simple statements of fact rather than overtly directing

behavior, the teacher was able to help each child proceed successfully through his or her play. As Tracy has repeated experiences like this, she will learn that language is a two-way business, requiring sensitivity to the other person's needs even as you articulate your own desires. The teacher knows that verbal toddlers typically "talk without listening." When children get to be two-and-a-half or three and their desire for social interaction outweighs their need for ownership, they then begin to see the need to listen as well as talk.

Encouraging Autonomy

Typically, around the time a child turns two a dramatic shift in self-concept takes place: he recognizes for the first time that he is a separate being from those around him, a concept known as *autonomy*. A baby perceives his world as an extension of himself—and, indeed, to a baby in a nurturing environment, it might well seem that way. The baby feels hungry, and an adult feeds him; the baby feels cold, and an adult warms him; the baby feels the need for human touch, and an adult picks him up. All these things happen without any conscious communication on the part of the infant. As the baby grows, she accumulates evidence that makes her suspect that other people are *not* extensions of her, and her quest to understand this realization drives the stage of autonomy. Virtually all the toddler behavior that frustrates adults and leads to labels like "terrible twos" is the result of a child's efforts to test her new theory about the world and to reconcile herself to it.

The foremost task for a toddler during the age of autonomy is to determine whether or not other people are part of him and under the direction of his will. A toddler's tried-and-true method of testing this is to see what happens when she wants something that the other person does not want, or vice versa. If an adult wants a child to wear a jacket and the child wants to wear a jacket, it's possible they share one will. The way the child tests that theory is to refuse to wear a jacket, and see what happens. The "negativity" that toddlers commonly exhibit is therefore simply an example of the scientific method in action, not an attempt to frustrate an adult's will. "What makes the terrible twos so terrible is not that the babies do things

you don't want them to do—one-year-olds are plenty good at that—but that they do things *because* you don't want them to" (Gopnik et al. 1999).

Intertwined with the effort to establish autonomy is the inability of older toddlers to share. As there can be no "mine" and "yours" if you and I are the same person, labeling objects as "MINE!" is a way to learn about the concept of ownership. Monique remembers a master teacher telling her years ago, "If you can't change the child, change the environment." This is why Monique sets up duplicates of some activities for parallel play; she knows that, counterintuitively, children work out the concept of ownership by having the opportunity to fully own everything they use. Once they've successfully mastered the concept of autonomy and move into the next developmental phase, in which social connections grow in importance, children will spontaneously begin to try to share because they want to have other children play with them.

As energy lags, the teachers quietly plan for lunch, diaper changes, and naps. Colin, whose low energy has persisted ever since he arrived resting his head on his mom's shoulder, will be in the first lunch group. One by one, Josh moves close to Colin, Lawanda, Roberto, and Joe, asking, "Would you like to come and hear a story now?" The first three children begin to move toward the door that will take them to the book area. Joe, however, jumps on a scooter and rides the other way. Josh sees that Becky is just taking off her apron after playing at the water table. He signals to be sure Monique notices the change of plans, and then invites Becky to come for stories. Becky happily joins the group at the door, while Monique shifts position to keep an eye on Joe.

Josh helps the children enjoy a group story experience by being sure everyone has enough room, spreading pillows out so each child can own his space, and by starting to sing as they get themselves positioned. By the time a few finger plays have been executed, everyone is relaxed, focused, and ready to hear two short picture books. After story time, Josh stands near the sink as the children wash their hands and find chairs for lunch. Josh joins the children at the lunch table, asking whether

Teachers improvising to navigate a transition

they'd like milk or water in their cups, serving more noodles or peas as requested, reminding children to scoot their cups back from the edge of the table, and keeping the mood relaxed, so the children can enjoy their meal.

Roberto and Colin finish eating, push back their chairs, and carry their plates, cups, and spoons to the tray for washing. They walk over to the book area and begin to take off their shoes and socks. Josh is nearby to help Colin open the stiff snap on his jeans and pull his pants down past his diaper. He can see that Colin's energy is so low right now that Ask-Say-Do would be needless torment for a little boy who just needs a nap. While Josh changes Colin's diaper, Roberto persists with undressing until he has his socks and pants off. Josh washes up and settles Colin with a bottle, then changes Roberto's diaper. Becky finishes up her lunch and moves to the rug, leaving Lawanda at the table. When Josh has Roberto and Colin settled in their cots, he opens the door to tell Monique there is room for her group to come in for lunch now. She'll be able to help Lawanda finish up lunch while Josh focuses on the nappers. Roberto needs some extra help getting relaxed today, as his parents just stopped giving him a bottle last weekend and have asked that he no longer have a bottle at naptime.

Soon, all the children are fed and napping. One at a time, they wake, get changed, and dress. Reenergized, they put on jackets and go out in the fresh air and sunshine. Two boys stand side by side at a table in the yard as they build trains out of the identical sets of Duplos that Monique set out on separate trays for parallel play. In constructing their trains, both boys have moved the Duplos off the trays and onto the table. Roberto rolls his train over to the edge of the table where Colin's train sits and, looking at Colin, says, "Look at tower! Look at tower! Look at tower!" wanting Colin to notice how high he has stacked the blocks on his train. Colin is completely absorbed in his own building, however, and does not respond.

Teacher nurturing budding social connections

Monique comes close and says to Roberto, "You want Colin to look at your tower? He's very busy!" That satisfies Roberto. Although Colin hasn't responded, Roberto's words have been acknowledged by the teacher, and so Roberto feels he can move on. He begins to say "beep beep" as he rolls his train back and forth. Colin also begins to move his train and to say "beep beep." This play continues for a minute until one of Colin's pieces falls off the side of the table. Colin turns to Roberto and says, "NOOO!" and pushes Roberto's train away. He seems to feel that his train car fell because of Roberto, although that really wasn't the case. At this point, Monique steps closer and says, "Do you need more room, Colin? Roberto, let's move your train over here so Colin has more room."

Helping Children Manage Social Situations

Teachers want to help older toddlers glimpse the satisfaction of playing with another child, even though teachers know the toddlers' immature social development won't be able to sustain it for long. In the previous vignette, the teacher purposely set out the toys on trays that defined a space for each child, but she allowed the children to move their trains off the trays so they could have a satisfying interaction as they "beep beeped" together. She knew she needed to stay close so that she could step in as soon as the children reached the limit of their primitive social and language capacity, for she wants early social experiences like this one to be positive.

Such sensitive teaching keeps life positive for the children and encourages them to keep trying to manage new social situations. Probably in fewer than six months, these toddlers will burst into a long phase of social development—but they aren't there yet. First they need to begin using language with each other and to gain the concept of autonomy. Parallel play, with identical toys next to each other, allows children to begin interacting with others while still having their own space and toys. That way they can occasionally venture closer together without facing unrealistic expectations for sharing.

Lawanda finishes pushing trucks in the sandbox and runs over to the swings. Joe is swinging in one swing; Tracy is just leaving the other. Lawanda jumps into the seat as Tracy exits it. Seeing Lawanda so interested in the swing, Tracy suddenly decides she's not done with it yet. She grabs Lawanda, who pushes the swing back with her legs and causes Tracy to

Teacher interpreting a social misunderstanding

lose her balance. As Tracy tumbles over, Josh sees the problem developing and hurries across the yard. Just as he arrives, Tracy sinks her teeth into Lawanda's leg. Josh is not quite fast enough to prevent the bite. Lawanda and Tracy burst into tears, both screaming "I don't like that!"

"Oh no," says Josh, as he kneels and puts an arm around each girl, "Tracy and Lawanda both want the same swing and Tracy and Lawanda both got hurt. Let me take a look at you and see what happened." He checks the bite wound and brushes sand out of Tracy's hair. "Let's go inside and get you both cleaned up," Josh says, taking each girl by the hand and letting Monique know he'll be back soon. Inside, he washes the wound with soap and water, applies antibiotic ointment, and gives each girl a tissue to dry up her tears. As the girls calm down, he turns to Lawanda and says, "That bite hurt you, didn't it?" He turns to Tracy and says, "It hurts when you bite. Next time, you can tell Lawanda 'My swing' and a teacher will come to help you. If you need to bite, you can get a chew toy."

Offering Positive Alternatives

A young child is dependent on love and acceptance in order to form a healthy self-concept, so she is very vulnerable to words that do not carry a message of love and acceptance. By saying "You can do it this way," instead of "Don't do that," the teacher offers a new possibility and avoids the suggestion that the child is doing something foolish, inadequate, or clumsy, implications that can diminish a child's self-esteem. When, for example, the teacher says "Here's a bucket for the sand," instead of "Don't throw the sand," she's giving the child a good idea about what he can do instead of making him feel bad about doing "the wrong thing." Therefore, Josh let Tracy know that biting hurts—although it's obvious to grown-ups, children don't always realize that other people feel pain the same as they do—and he sent a hopeful message to Tracy when he let her know what she could do "next time." Children often listen only to the last words in a sentence. Rather than saying "No biting," Josh offered Tracy an alternative to biting. In this toddler classroom, there is always a clean supply of "chewies"—hard rubber chew toys for children to bite.

Language Development

As illustrated earlier when Tracy tried to tell Joe that he was playing with her, toddlers are functionally preverbal. When a toddler has an extensive vocabulary and talks a lot, it's easy to be fooled into thinking that she believes in language as a means of moderating her experience in the world. But even the toddler who can relate a long story about going to the zoo has yet to embrace language as a useful tool for solving problems, particularly when strong emotions are activated.

Language develops in higher brain structures, which develop slowly as a child matures. Emotion, which is centered in the primitive brain, is more fully developed at birth, thus dominating a young child's behavior because the higher brain has not yet been trained to override it. That is why Tracy, a pretty good talker, ended up biting: she uses language but has not yet learned to trust language to meet her needs.

The new and delicate understanding of autonomy feeds into what a toddler needs to learn about language. Until a child learns that he is separate from others, it makes sense to think that others always know what he is thinking. While older toddlers are beginning to realize they are separate beings, it takes longer for them to realize that they need to say aloud what they want in order for others to know what they're thinking.

The teachers offer "power words" as a way to bridge the children from physical response to verbal response. Monique and Josh actively teach the children in their group these power words:

No!
Mine!
Go away!
My turn!
I don't like that!
I'm using that!

The teachers know that "Go away!" is not a friendly way to say, "I'm busy now. Come and ask me later." But they also know that the immediate goal is to convince the children that words can tell people what they need—courtesy will come later, when language is more developed.

Along with empowering the children, power words can alert teachers that someone needs help. When Monique hears a child say "Mine!" she knows it is a cue for her to be available to help that child be heard. Often she serves as "translator," knowing that the children are not yet tuned in to each other's language but will usually listen to an adult. For example, if Tracy and Lawanda want to play with the same toy and Monique hears Lawanda say "Mine!" Monique might go to the girls, put her hand between Tracy's hand and Lawanda's toy, and say, "I hear Lawanda saying 'Mine!' Lawanda is still using this toy. Tracy, I see another toy on the shelf for you." Monique knows that using language is more game than reality for toddlers. She has heard children say "No biting" just before they sink their teeth into a playmate! The children have learned that those words go with biting, but they haven't yet learned that words can take the place of biting and they haven't developed enough self-control to stop themselves from biting.

Teacher helping child express feelings

Out in the yard, Colin looks up at Monique and asks for water. Monique reaches for a paper cup on the shelf and hands it to Colin to fill from the dispenser. As he begins to fill the cup, other children come and ask for cups. Each receives a cup and waits for a turn at the water dispenser. Marcus takes a swallow, carefully pours the rest of his water on the ground, watches it trickle away, and then crushes his paper cup. Monique says, "Looks like you're all done with your water, Marcus. The trash can is over there." He drops the cup in the trash can, then reaches over and grabs Becky's cup from her. Although her cup was also empty and crumpled, she screams her objection as he grabs her cup, then throws herself down on her stomach and begins to kick and scream.

At this point, the teacher steps in and points out to Marcus that Becky wants her cup back. Marcus pretends to drink from the cup and then hands it back to Becky, who instantly stops her tantrum and sits up, holding her cup. Monique asks, "Are you ready to throw your cup away, Becky?" The little girl happily drops the cup in the trash can and then goes on her way.

Later, Monique fills Josh in on what happened: "It was nice to see Becky learning about autonomy. I think she needs to have her owner-ship respected while she's sorting out what that means for her. I don't believe that Marcus took the cup to upset Becky; he was just thinking about putting cups in the trash, and wanted to repeat the ever popular and satisfying filling and dumping." Josh asks, "So when you pointed out to Marcus that Becky needed her cup back, you were just allow-ing him to look beyond the cup to Becky's feelings so he could see her need?" Monique replies, "Right. Becky didn't actually need the cup; she just needed to know she'd be allowed to decide when she was finished. As soon as that was clear, she was ready to put the cup in the trash and move on. You know, I'm willing to bet that Becky's big appetite at lunch and her long nap also helped some with her resilience in quickly stop-ping her tantrum."

Self-regulation and Tantrums

Monique was relieved to see Becky regain her equilibrium so easily. Just a month ago, Becky would have been unable to stop her tantrum until she was completely exhausted. Back then, Becky's flood of emotions when things failed to go as she wanted could completely overwhelm her, yet she would not accept any adult assistance. All that Monique could do for her then was to sympathize with her and wait for her to calm a bit. Becky was too distressed to even want to be held, so Monique would keep the other children out of the way and give Becky a quiet corner where she could lie on a rug, kicking and screaming. Every few minutes, Monique would come close to her, gently put a hand on her back, and say soothingly, "That made you so upset! I'll be ready to help you when you're ready for me."

Monique delicately balanced the need to remain emotionally available to Becky with Becky's need to attempt self-regulation. Whereas a younger toddler, knowing he can't soothe himself, readily accepts an adult's assis-tance in recovering his emotional balance after a tantrum sets in, an older toddler is often driven to attempt to self-regulate in the same way he's driven to try to put on his own shoes or perform other tasks—"By myself!" Monique knows there's no point in trying to reason with a child having a tantrum. Often the cause appears to be trivial—milk came in the blue

cup instead of the pink one; mom opened the door that the child wanted to open—but once again, the primitive brain stem has taken charge. In *Emotional Intelligence,* Daniel Goleman describes this phenomenon as the logical brain being "hijacked" by the emotional brain (1995). The toddler, trying so hard to make sense of the world, seems often to feel that the rug is yanked out from under him just as he nearly has it sorted out. In the classic *Your Two-Year-Old,* Ames and Ilg describe this age as being "handicapped by an almost total inability to modulate" (1976). While Becky, the child from the vignette, is still likely to fall immediately into a tantrum when life surprises her, she's learning to right herself again. As Becky's language abilities increase, she'll be more likely to voice her distress, and when she trusts people to listen to her, she'll learn to use language to solve problems, and the tantrums will fade away.

Teacher anticipating and respecting a parent's protective feelings

Josh finds a minute to step out of the room and phone Lawanda's mother. "Hi, Mrs. Johnson," Josh begins, "Lawanda is fine, but I wondered if you have a minute to talk."

"I have time. What's going on?" asks Mrs. Johnson.

Josh says, "I wanted to give you a heads-up about Lawanda being bitten on her leg by another child today."

"Again? Who's biting her? Why does he keep doing it?" she asks.

"Of course, we're working with the child who bit her, and believe me, we don't like it either, even though we know it's normal toddler behavior. I know it's upsetting news, so that's why I wanted to talk with you before pickup tonight."

"Well, you did tell me that toddlers bite, but I hope I won't be getting anymore calls like this," says Mrs. Johnson.

"I hope so too," Josh concludes.

Jana, the late-afternoon teacher, receives a thorough briefing from Josh about the bite on Lawanda's leg. In addition to his phone call, Josh wrote an injury report for Lawanda's parents. When Mrs. Johnson arrives at 5:30, she finds the last group of children listening to a CD. Tracy and Colin each hold a chewy in one hand and an instrument in the other as they make music along with the CD. Jana makes sure each child has enough room to shake an instrument safely, then steps close to the door so she can have a quiet conversation with Mrs. Johnson.

"Hi, Mrs. Johnson," she says. "I wanted to let you know that Lawanda seems fine. She has a little mark left on her leg but she seems to have moved on."

"I'm glad to hear that," replies Mrs. Johnson. "And I'm glad Josh called me, because I'm a lot calmer now than I was when I first heard the news. Something about biting just makes me feel so protective of my little girl!"

At this point, Lawanda spots her mom and runs over for a hug. She leads her mom to her cubby to show her the artwork she made this morning, and they then walk out the door hand in hand, Lawanda telling her mom about how she cut paper with scissors today.

Biting and Other Physical Responses

One of the hardest things about working with toddlers is that they can't stop themselves from reacting physically when they're upset. Hitting, stamping, pushing, yelling, and biting are tools easily available to the toddler. Often, biting seems to peak just before a toddler develops higher verbal skills, almost as if he knows *something* should come out of his mouth, but that *something* becomes teeth instead of words! Many toddlers will bite once or twice; a few will bite a lot. For the child on the receiving end of a physical response, the reaction seems fairly similar whether she is hit, bitten, or pushed—the victim is emotionally offended by the interference, and sometimes is physically injured as well. Once the wound and the hurt feelings are soothed, the event is usually over in the child's mind. However, biting strikes a particularly emotional chord for parents, as it feels so primitive. The teacher must try to be more objective and also put herself in the child's mind; she recognizes these children are very young and immature and that their responses to life are primitive.

When parents enroll their children in group care, they often anticipate the benefits their children will enjoy by being with a group of children, but they don't always consider the possible detriments—illness and injury. Children learn by making mistakes, and sometimes that means they

make mistakes that hurt each other. When teachers have an orientation conference with the parents of a new child in the toddler classroom, they make sure to mention the less-desirable facets of toddlerhood, so that the parents can see biting in the context of overall toddler development. Such preparation helps teachers when they need to tell parents their child was bitten. Of course, parents will still be upset that their child was injured, but they may better understand that it's normal for toddlers to bite and that it doesn't necessarily mean the biting child has problems or that the teachers were inattentive.

PREVENTING PHYSICAL BEHAVIOR PROBLEMS

It's the teacher's job to protect children from emotional floods that can lead to personal injury. Arranging the environment to give each child plenty of personal space, arranging toys and routines to make "owner-ship" clear, and stationing teachers close to children and within reach of each other are all tried-and-true prevention techniques. Teachers can avert many problems through preventive vigilance, but no teacher can promise parents she can prevent injury across the board. Group care does not allow undivided individual attention for each child throughout the day, although there is likely some time every day when each child receives the full attention of a teacher. Part of group care is helping children learn about each other and helping each child feel like she's still a wonderful person even when she makes mistakes.

LEARNING NEW BEHAVIORS

Teachers have strategies they call on when children bite or use other physical means to express themselves. Discipline is about helping a child learn new behaviors, rather than making him feel bad about doing something he can't developmentally stop himself from doing. When two-year-olds hurt each other, it's usually because they're so egocentric—intent on their own activities and unable to take another person's point of view. Some toddlers bite not to express anger but when they love someone so much that they seem to need to "eat them up" (the hug that turns into a bite, for example).

Teachers try to help children learn to use words to express their feelings, and to find something else to bite (chew toys) or hit (pillows) or kick (balls) when the urge comes. They teach a child to notice other children:

"I see Joe is using that toy" or "Roberto is crying. He didn't like it when you sat on top of him." They also observe closely to see if there are certain situations or times of day that are stressful for a child, and if possible, they make adjustments (such as moving that child's lunchtime or naptime ahead fifteen minutes) or they help a child understand how the system works—"I see Lawanda is ready for a turn now that you're done with the swing." Teachers are challenged to balance the goal of giving toddlers opportunities to learn how to play together with the reality that toddlers can manage only a limited amount of social interaction. Thus, teachers make sure a teacher is ready to move in quickly when emotions rise and the children cannot manage the situation. Most of all, teachers trust that with guidance and time to mature, children will become more sophisticated social beings.

The last child is gone, and Jana puts away the instruments and CD player. She doesn't want children to be distracted by seeing these late-afternoon activities in the morning. She leaves a note for Monique to let her know that Josh's call to Mrs. Johnson seemed to help Mrs. Johnson deal with the bite, and to say that the late afternoon went well for Tracy. She makes sure to return the tables and chairs to the arrangement Monique will need for breakfast tomorrow. She washes the chewies and sets them in the drain tray, thinking about how to help Tracy so she'll no longer need to bite. And why, she wonders, has Lawanda been bitten twice in the last week?

As she thinks about Josh's description of the incident today, it sounds to her as if Tracy was done with the swing until she saw Lawanda jump onto it, at which point she suddenly needed to test who "owned" the swing. Last week, in the late afternoon, Tracy had been putting pieces into a puzzle when Roberto began to reach over and pick up a piece to "help." Tracy grabbed his hand and bit it.

Jana has a flash of insight: Tracy's biting may be a sudden reaction to having her ownership challenged. Jana's glad there is a staff meeting scheduled for tomorrow; she can bring up this idea and see if it fits

Teacher making notes about the day, and preparing for the next day

the pattern seen by other teachers. If it does, the teachers can look for opportunities to help Tracy work on ownership—by protecting her play and making sure that when she's using something, the other children are given a clear message about it being Tracy's turn now; and by asking her, "Are you done with that now?" when she leaves an activity, so it will be clear to her that she's leaving the toy and that another child may now play with it.

Jana turns her thoughts to Lawanda. As she thinks through the past week's events, Jana realizes that Lawanda seems to be challenging other children's boundaries—today, by rushing onto the swing that Tracy was just leaving, and last week, by sliding quickly onto a scooter Colin was headed for. Another point to bring up at the staff meeting: Lawanda is also testing ownership.

Jana thinks, "It's nice to know that when we identify children's needs and plant seeds for new behaviors, we can trust development to do its work. I hope that before long Tracy and Lawanda will enjoy more satisfying social interactions. In the meantime, I'll continue to be vigilant and try hard to keep the children safe."

Jana closes the door and heads home, feeling pleased to have some new ideas about how to help Lawanda and Tracy.

BEGINNING SOCIAL OVERTURES: THREE-YEAR-OLDS

5

DEVELOPMENTAL AGE RANGE

30–48 months

Teacher Roulette arrives at school as teacher Cheyenne is putting away the breakfast things and pushing the tables back to their proper place in the classroom. "Good morning," Roulette calls as he glances through the parent communication book. "Anything important for me to pay attention to in here?" he asks.

Cheyenne shrugs. "The usual. Erick's mom brought a ton of toilet-training underpants and sent him in a diaper—what's that tell you? Noriko's grandmother wants her to wear a hat when we go outside. Lars was up late—they have visitors from out of town. I'm forgetting something."

"I saw that Lars has pink medicine in the fridge for an ear infection," notes Roulette. "He needs it after lunch and again after the late snack. I guess his mom will do the early morning and bedtime dose."

Teachers building an effective teaching team

105

"I'll be the meds person for him, then. Did his mom write it down on the meds chart?" asks Cheyenne.

"Yep," says Roulette, and he begins setting up the classroom.

The dollhouse, block area, and book area stay more or less the same all year, with a little adjustment as the children's interests grow and change. The art table needs attention this morning. Activities at the art table change every three days, but crayons, markers, paper, and scissors are always available there. Roulette puts two paste cups with brushes stuck into them on either end of a small tray. Beside each cup, he puts another cup holding a handful of colored noodles. Roulette knows the children will have more success if he sets up the paste in a way that clearly shows them what to glue and if he clearly designates what is theirs to choose from. Two children pasting at a time is all he feels staff can supervise at this point in the year, when so much toilet learning is going on. Toilet learning is their primary focus right now, so he's setting out activities that don't require much adult direction. He sorts stacking cups and puts out ones that match the colors of some small plastic counting bears, setting the bears and cups on two trays on the quiet table that is tucked into a corner of the classroom.

Cheyenne suggests, "Hey, Rou, let's set out the small dollhouse bathroom furniture on the tray near the bathroom. You know, the potty, sink, shower, and bathtub. The kids who are working on toileting love to make the dollhouse family go potty!"

"I was thinking I would do that. Erick must be getting pressure at home," responds Roulette. He sighs. "It's hard to watch folks struggle. Erick's parents love him, but his mom seems unable to help guide his development. You know how hard it is for her to tell him what she wants. It feels like she's driving with one foot on the brake and the other on the gas, and little Erick, in the middle of a willful stage, isn't getting much help from her. We have to remember that parents helping their child learn to use the toilet are taking a big step toward letting their child manage his own life and body. Our job is to challenge parents to let go just a little, to trust, help, guide, love unconditionally, support, and let the child do it himself."

Cheyenne adds, "It seems as if parents simultaneously desire and resist the process, saying they want their child to use the toilet, but subconsciously wanting their child to remain a baby. This has got to be confusing to the child. I wonder if it's true that parents who spend long days away from their young child don't want to spend their limited time together working on learning to use the toilet—maybe the few diapers being changed at home aren't such a big deal to the parent."

"I think you're right," agrees Roulette. "As teachers, we're more objective, and sometimes it can seem as if parents are undermining our toileting efforts. But we can lend valuable support to parents as well as children during this developmental stage by interpreting the child's needs to grow and become independent. Remember, toilet learning really is the child's business. We can help parents learn how to be supportive rather than taking over or undermining the child's own process."

Cheyenne says, "I sometimes get tired of Erick's bossiness and rigidity. He's always telling me and the kids in the class what to do. And he doesn't listen when I try to get him to do something."

Roulette shares, "Remember what my hero Arnold Gesell says in Infant and Child in the Culture of Today about three-year-olds: 'Possibly the main developmental task of the child this age is to strengthen his will, and he does this by practicing dominion. When he is a little more sure of himself he will be able to give in and adapt more easily.' Bossy, domineering children look like they're secure and confident, but they aren't. Erick's attempt to control and manage everything—including you—is a sign that he feels way out of control and is unsure of his ability to manage himself. Along with the mixed messages from his mom, that's why he's not willing to risk peeing in the potty."

"Well, what am I supposed to do?" Cheyenne asks. "Every morning his mom brings all those underpants, and every afternoon she takes home a big bag of wet ones. Yolanda says his mom's complaining about all the laundry."

"I'll tell you what's working for me right now. For one thing, I just don't take it personally when he refuses to do what I ask. I try either to give him lots of time to think about it before he has to do something I want, or I don't really discuss it and just let the routine move him along. You know, like at lunchtime I don't ask, 'Are you ready for lunch now?' I just say, 'It's your turn to wash' or 'I see your spot at the table.' It's the same at potty time. Before we go outside, I draw his attention to the activity in the bathroom by talking about other kids going potty. Then,

when he starts to wiggle, I say, 'OK, time to go.' I take his hand and hustle him off, no discussion. Sometimes that works.

"When he's telling me what to do, I usually ask about his play. I figure if he's worrying about what I'm doing, he's not playing, so I just try to get him to focus back on his business, which is choosing and playing. If he won't lay off me and I can't get him busy, I ask if he wants to sit in my lap. I figure he's feeling so anxious he can't focus, and maybe he just needs the security of being close to an adult. So, try not to take his behavior personally, and remember that he's a good kid—life is just challenging for him right now."

"I'll try to keep those things in mind, Roulette. If I get stuck, will you come help me if you can?" asks Cheyenne.

"Sure," says Roulette. "He may be tougher on you because when he's feeling out of control, he senses your uncertainty and has to test it. He knows me well enough to trust me, including that when I say something, I mean it and I'm going to follow through. He really knows where he stands with me, so he doesn't have to push so hard. Let's observe him closely today and think more about good strategies to help him."

Using the environment as a teaching tool

Roulette shares another idea with Cheyenne: "I've been thinking about Patty and Sue. Let's set up a little differently than we talked about yesterday. I think we need to set up some parallel play for those girls. Patty is so loud and bossy and egocentric. I want to help her experience playing with a friend when it's very clear what is hers and what belongs to someone else, so we can help her get clear about what and who she's in charge of. Here's what I'm thinking. Let's set out the tubs of warm water with the little ponies and flowers and some small hairbrushes and a little soap in those hotel shampoo bottles. Then we can scatter some of those pretty polished stones in the tubs, so the ponies can collect the stones. They'll need a small basket in each tub so the ponies will have a place to put the stones. When you have the tubs set up, get two long blocks from the block area and put them between the two tubs so the ponies can walk along the blocks and 'visit' each other. My plan is to be very clear in the setup about what goes in each tub, and to begin to help Patty see she's in charge of her own things but not in charge of the other children or the things other children are using."

"I follow you. Sounds good," Cheyenne responds. *"When I look through the container of ponies, I'll try to find ones that could go together like a family group. After all, 'mom' knows how to go 'visiting.'"*

"Great idea," nods Roulette. *"Will you set it up on the small table where there's only room for two tubs, so it'll be obvious that only two can play there?"*

"I hope Patty finds it before the other children do," says Cheyenne.

"We'll leave it out as long as children are interested in it," replies Roulette.

Daniel and his dad enter the classroom. *"Good morning, Daniel, and Mr. Nesheim,"* says Roulette.

"Where are the kids?" asks Daniel.

"I'm all ready to open the gate and invite them into the yard," says Roulette. *"Would you like to help me? Give your dad a hug and a kiss bye-bye and we'll go get the kids."*

Daniel and Roulette open the gate to the yard. Roulette takes Daniel by the hand, and they walk over to where Patty and Sue are riding tricycles, so that Roulette can quietly tell them that it's time to enter the classroom and that they might like to look at the water table to see if there's something they'd like to play with there. Then Roulette begins sending the other children inside.

Roulette stations himself near the classroom door, ready to help late-arriving children separate from their parents. While standing there, he hears two little boys and their parents approach the door. As the parents chat, the boys begin to growl. Louder and louder the two boys growl—at each other and at the door.

Thinking this loud unfriendly noise might worry the children inside, who have just separated from their parents and are transitioning away from the intimacy of home into the bigness of school, Roulette opens the door and greets the boys, *"Hi, I'm glad to see you! I can hear you all the way inside. You sure sound ready to come and play at school. Remember to say 'Hi, I'm glad to see you' when you see your friends inside; that way, they'll know you're feeling friendly and ready to play."* Looking at the parents, Roulette says, *"Hi, I'm glad to see you. I guess you're about ready for these busy boys to come to class!"*

Teacher establishing positive tone in classroom

Coaching Children in Social Skills, Establishing Ambience

An old saying comes to mind: "Let your head save your heels." Communication with preschoolers can be more like coaching than parenting or teaching. Telling the two growling boys in the previous vignette to say "hi" to express their pleasure at seeing one another is practical and preventive. The teacher shared useful information that will help the children have a successful experience. Young children have a lot to learn about social interaction; they'll be most successful when they receive clear, constructive information from adults.

GOALS FOR THREE-YEAR-OLDS

- Learn to see other children as friends: parallel play moves into associative play
- Solidify autonomy and independence: increase competence in self-regulation of bodily functions, including eating, sleeping, and speaking
- Develop a greater understanding of self-determination, choices, and management of will
- Establish constructive habits for living with others

Roulette was pleased to observe that the growling boys' parents felt part of a caring community at the center and wanted to have a few moments to connect with each other. The children, too, were happy to see each other. However, the excitement of the moment overwhelmed their emerging language, causing them to growl as a greeting. Because Roulette has a nice relationship with the boys' parents, he knew they would welcome his help and feel support from his intervention. The parents recognized that Roulette's "correction" was not judgmental, but supported the children, who behave in surprising ways when they experience new things.

Though the boys were growling, their parents could tell they were just saying hello in an immature way, so they ignored it. However, Roulette knew, in a way the parents did not, how important the first few minutes of the day can be in setting the stage for the rest of the day in child care. Children who are centered and calm as they come into a group are more likely to have positive experiences with their friends, which will lead to more successful and constructive play throughout the day. Children who have just said good-bye to their parents are in a particularly vulnerable state as they make the emotional shift from home to school. During this time, it's especially important for the school to feel safe, calm, and comforting. Hyperattuned ears will hear unsettling noises from across the building or in the yard and wonder what's wrong. They'll then worry about being apart from a parent who has just gone to work, which will interfere with the children's ability to settle into the rhythm of the day.

SAYING THE RIGHT THING AT THE RIGHT TIME

Coaching is nothing more than anticipating an area of immature development and saying a key word or two at the right moment. It's the "ounce of prevention" that beats a "pound of cure." Here are three examples:

- A teacher notices that Noriko, who has been carefully lining up blocks in a building project, looks worried as she sees rambunctious Ana bouncing in her direction. Noriko is worried that Ana will knock the blocks over, and the teacher realizes that worry might make Noriko protectively push Ana away, so the teacher steps between the girls and says, "Ana, I see Noriko building so carefully here! Are you coming to look at what she's building? Let's ask her where we can stand to see her structure."
- A teacher knows that the minute the gate to the outdoor play area is opened, Erick's inclination will be to run, so the teacher blocks the gate opening with her body, putting herself in front. As the teacher and the children begin to move through the gate, the teacher asks Erick, "Can you use your walking feet, or should I hold your hand to help you remember to walk?"
- A teacher observes that as Morgan and Lars start playing in the dramatic play area, they're both talking about being dogs. The teacher reminds them that at school, dogs use words so their friends will know what they need.

TEACHING SOCIALLY USEFUL LANGUAGE

When "Can I play too?" is met with "No! Go away!" a teacher can step in and rephrase language to create more successful communication, suggesting that instead of "Go away," it would be friendlier to say, "I'm playing with Noriko right now. I'll play with you later." When Ana says to Shawn, "I don't like you," she's actually saying, "I don't know you" or "I can't think of how you could join this play." Two- and three-year-olds lack the imagination to know what a child entering the play might add, and some are rightfully concerned about someone taking away their toys or interfering with their play, which makes "Go away" a reasonable response.

Teachers can also help children think of entry strategies that will result in being welcomed into play. For example, say that a child wants to enter the play of two children pretending to be moms. The teacher can advise that child that saying "I'll be the baby" is more likely to get her included in the play than asking "Can I play?"

By watching and listening closely to children's free play, teachers can help children learn to play together and to develop constructive, healthy social skills. They can coach children to respond to others in constructive, appropriate ways, thereby facilitating social success and meaningful communication among the children.

Teacher helping children work out social conflict

Mohamed and Morgan get settled with the trains. Shawn is drawing at the table. Ana and Noriko are in the dollhouse with Lars, pretending that the girls are big sisters with babies, and Lars is the doggie. Roulette reminds Lars that when you're playing doggie with other children, the dog needs to talk as well as bark, because "People won't know what you want if you just bark." Lars woofs in agreement and Roulette pats him, saying, "Good doggie." Dogs and cats are popular roles for children with immature social skills to play, but the teacher wants the children to speak and listen to each other so their social skills can develop.

The class hums with the children's purposeful activity. Roulette steps closer to Patty and Sue, who are playing with the plastic ponies in the tubs of water. Patty's ponies are hurrying; "Come on baby," Patty calls, splashing the water. "Oh, help! Help! My baby, poor Darling, is stuck."

Sue's pony comes across the board bridging the two tubs, calling, "Swim, baby!" Then Sue tells Patty, "Oh, my Honey needs me! I have to go home."

Patty puts her hand into Sue's tub, taking the plastic flower Honey has been floating on and dumping Honey in the water.

"Hey," says Sue. "Honey was using that!"

"But my Darling is drowning," says Patty. "She needs it!"

Sue looks dismayed, and Roulette asks, "Is it okay with you for Patty to take your flower, Sue?"

"No," says Sue. "She has her own flower." Then, sensing conflict, Sue retreats, saying, "I'm done. I don't want to play anymore."

"When Patty doesn't listen to you and takes your things, you don't want to play?" asks Roulette. "Did you know that, Patty? Sue doesn't want to play when you take her toys."

Patty is silent, and Roulette continues, "She's just like you. You want to play with the toys in your tub, and Sue wants to play with the toys in hers."

"Well, I need that flower and I'm not done. She can't go away!" says Patty.

"We can talk with her. What could we tell her?" asks Roulette, realizing this is a hard question and that it's unlikely Patty will come up with an answer. He asks because he wants to encourage Patty to problem solve and to see her role in the dynamic of play, which will help her build the idea of compassion for Sue as a person "just like her," with her own feelings and desires.

After a moment, Roulette uses his loving support and calm language to soften the emotional charge in the situation: "You could just tell her, 'Oops! I got mixed up! You can have your flower back.' Sue might have an idea about how the two mommy ponies could help little Darling. Sue is a girl who has good ideas, isn't she?"

Sue, standing a little behind Roulette, steps up and says, "Maybe Darling could ride in the little basket. Honey likes it in there."

Patty puts the flower back in Sue's tub. Roulette says, "I wonder if the mommy ponies could pull the babies if we tie a string on the baskets." The girls nod, and Roulette goes to the cupboard for string.

Associative Play versus Cooperative Play

Roulette added his idea of the mommy ponies pulling the babies in order to refocus and extend the girls' play. He'll continue to closely monitor their play, and as soon as they finish playing with the baskets and string, he'll suggest a change in activity. The girls have been playing with some intensity for a while now, so a chance to run and climb and use their big muscles will reduce their tension and let them face the next social challenge with fresh energy. He wants to help the girls end their play on a happy, successful note, so the girls will be encouraged to keep trying to work things out and to get along.

Patty and Sue are at the *associative play* stage (see Mildred Parten's "Stages of Social Play" in appendix D). Their play is imaginative and complex, but they are not truly cooperating. In *cooperative play,* the next stage in play development, it's the play itself that matters more than anything. In associative play, however, the ability to stay in charge and make others acquiesce to one's will is more important than the play itself.

Cooperation requires that each child be able to give up some of what he wants so group play can continue. The three-year-old, a young preschooler, is moving into autonomy, but he still retains a high degree of egocentricity, which makes personal will override any desire to cooperate. Young preschoolers are still learning about who they are. They believe that life is all about them: what they need, how they feel, and what they can get people to do. Sue and Patty like each other, but neither one is willing to let go of what she wants in order to keep their play together moving forward. As they mature, making friends and finding reciprocity in a relationship will become more important and interesting.

Cooperative play requires cooperative language and some ability to see the big picture, which are forms of abstract thought. Associative play is much more concrete. While Sue and Patty's play with the ponies was at times friendly and included sharing and some level of reciprocity, each child's ego and will was actively invested in the play. Three-year-olds are social, but they're usually more interested in the toys and equipment than in the other children, which is why redirection works better with three-year-olds and is less successful with four-year-olds, who are more interested in the other children than in the toys. The same holds true with

being separated from friends when play between several children becomes difficult: four-year-olds usually don't like having to play by themselves, because they want to be with friends, whereas three-year-olds often enjoy the separation.

LANGUAGE AS A KEY TO UNDERSTANDING ASSOCIATIVE PLAY

Associative play is often the most difficult stage of play to understand and recognize, but it's the most typical stage for children in their preschool years. Language is one key to understanding the associative play stage. Children learn language from adults (who, of course, understand the meaning of words with greater depth), and they model the syntax, inference, and emotional tone of adults.

Children start learning language with nouns, useful labels for the things around them, such as *mama, daddy, cup, hat, dog*. Next come power words, such as *mine, more, move,* and (the best power word ever) *NO*. Adults talking with children match children's words, then introduce language that helps the adult manage the child, such as *sit down, come here, don't do that*. As much as adults enjoy listening to children talk, there's not much true reciprocity in early communication. Adults tell children what they want or don't want; they tell young children what they're doing and what they want the children to do. Naturally, children begin talking to their peers this way, ordering them around and demanding that other children do what they want. This has limited success, as other children tune in to and obey their peers far less than they do important adults. When children start to want to be a friend and to have a friend, they're more motivated to attentively tune in to their peers' language.

For example: Patty's loud voice and early language acquisition have kept the other children following her directions over the past year. However, now that the other children have had time to acquire more language and more interests and have practiced saying "no," Patty has found herself less successful in getting the other children to follow her directions without question. Patty thus often feels frustrated, confused, and angry. She may even feel that the children are being mean to her.

Timid, obedient Sue used to do whatever Patty said, and their parents said the girls were best friends. Now, at age three and a half, Sue sometimes expresses a different opinion than Patty. Alert to the developmental shift that was occurring, the teachers started checking in with Sue: "Do

you want to do what Patty says? You can tell her 'I'm still playing here' or 'It's my turn to be first.'" The teachers have been steadily feeding Sue the language that will support her social competence and increase her success at getting her needs met. Their goal is for Sue to build a repertoire of assertive language and to learn how to speak up for herself, even when they're not around. As a result, Sue sometimes tells Patty that she doesn't want to play. At times when Patty refuses to accept this decision, Sue has learned to come ask a teacher for help, so she can hold her ground with Patty.

TEACHER SUPPORT BUILDS CONFIDENCE

Each of these girls needs a teacher's individualized coaching. Sue needs to learn she has the right to make her own choices, and Patty needs to learn that each person decides what's right for himself or herself. With the teachers' consistent support, these girls will internalize these important lessons and remember them throughout their lives.

Every time a child chooses, he learns about himself: "I am the child who knows how to make friends," "I am the child who likes to paint," "I am the child my teacher loves and helps," "I am the child who finds bugs." This self-knowledge builds self-esteem, along with the inner strength that helps children hold their own against the negative elements of conformity. While it's desirable that children learn at age four or five to conform for the good of the whole, there's a danger in conformity without self-awareness. If they learn to know themselves in preschool, children are later better able to resist peer pressure, when peers ask them to do things that don't align with who they know themselves to be.

Teacher guiding children to become independent through toilet learning

Roulette bends close to Noriko, saying, "Noriko, soon it will be time to go outside. Let's go see if you have any shi-shi that is ready to come out." (Shi-shi is the word that Noriko's Japanese American family uses for urine.)

Without looking up, Noriko smiles, ducks her head, and says, "No, go away."

"OK," says Roulette. "I'll see if Daniel wants to try."

Roulette walks off toward Daniel. Seeing this, Noriko stands up and heads for the bathroom. Smiling teachers nod to each other. Without a word, Cheyenne, who is monitoring the bathroom, bends down and turns the button on Noriko's pants, so she can pull the button through the buttonhole without help. Noriko wiggles the button through the hole, pulls down her pants, and climbs on the potty. When there's no instant release, she jumps up again. Cheyenne steps near as Noriko announces, "Nothing's coming out!" Cheyenne replies, "Sometimes it takes a moment for your body to remember what to do. Stay a little longer and see if you can feel the shi-shi inside. Do you feel it down low in your tummy?"

Across the room, Lars yelps and jumps up, knocking over his chair, and then dashes to the potty, tugging on his overalls as he runs. Cheyenne helps him with his buckles as he jumps up and down; he reaches the potty just in time. Noriko, sitting next to him on the other toilet, looks at him with some interest. When Lars begins to urinate, Noriko does too.

"Look, I'm making bubbles in the potty!" says Lars. Cheyenne smiles. When Lars is done, she asks, "Did you wipe?" Lars nods, and Cheyenne smiles as she says, "You're getting so big. You know all about peeing in the potty at school these days, don't you? I don't need to say anything about flush and wash to you, do I?" Lars laughs and flushes the toilet. He then goes to the sink, turns on the faucet, gets the soap, and washes his hands. He turns off the water, finds his hand towel, and dries his hands. Cheyenne comments, "I see the door to the yard is open. You know what that means—time to go outside. Get your sweatshirt and your warm hat. I think it's still chilly outside."

By the time Lars is on his way outside, Noriko has wiped herself, flushed the toilet, and is standing at the sink washing her hands as Ana comes hurrying in. Ana is elegantly dressed in her sister's fluffy hand-me-down party dress. Watching her, it becomes clear to Cheyenne she can't figure out how to get to her underpants through all that dress. She tries to unbutton the back and undo the sash. "Just gather the skirt up and hold it around your waist," suggests Cheyenne, bending down and showing her how to hold up the full skirt in front of her. By now, Ana

is jumping up and down, wiggling and crossing her legs. She gets her underpants down and is on the potty just as the urine is released.

Once done, Ana quickly stands up, ready to wash and then go outside and play. However, the hem of her skirt hits the back of her legs with a surprising dampness. "Wet!!" Ana wails, and begins to cry.

"Oh dear," Cheyenne sympathizes. "You got to the potty just in time, and the pee-pee came out just right, but your skirt fell into the potty and got wet in the water." Ana sobs louder. "Well, we know what to do, don't we? We'll get some dry clothes. Do you have extra clothes in your cubby? Let's look," says Cheyenne.

"But I don't have a beautiful dress in my cubby!" wails Ana.

"What a disappointment," Cheyenne says. "No more beautiful dresses in your cubby. Let's see what you have to play in outdoors, and then you can put on a fancy dress when you play house later. And next time when you wear your beautiful dress, you'll do better at keeping it out of the toilet."

Throughout the day, Roulette and Cheyenne continue to monitor the children's toilet learning, suggesting visits to the bathroom at regularly timed intervals. The teachers note when a child wraps up an activity, and step in with a perfectly timed suggestion before the next activity is begun. When Roulette sees Sue put the last block on the shelf and head to the clay cart, he says, "Sue, there's room for you in the bathroom right now, so I'm going to save the clay right here for you to use after you pee and wash your hands." Just as the teachers build the habit of speaking to each other in constructive ways, they're building the children's personal regulatory patterns.

Toilet Learning

Older two-year-olds and young three-year-olds are working on mastery of their own bodies. Very quickly, they develop competence in dressing and undressing themselves, as well as the ability to tune in to their bodies' messages. Developing self-awareness not only allows a child to anticipate his physical needs and get to the potty, but is also a big step on the way to independence and autonomy. Many preschools enroll children once they've completed toilet learning, as child-to-staff ratios can change dramatically with the acquisition of this one skill. In a school that enrolls children from birth to kindergarten, the classroom with older two-year-olds and young three-year-olds has the challenge and excitement of toilet learning as one of its most significant learning goals, along with the major internal developmental shifts that go with it.

For generations, the "developmentally appropriate" expectation of early childhood educators in the United States has been that children should be able to do the following when toilet learning begins—generally around the age of twenty-four to thirty months:

- independently manage the dressing and undressing required for toileting
- show awareness of the feelings of needing to urinate and defecate
- be able to communicate needs
- be autonomous enough to want to achieve independence in toileting

DIFFERENT APPROACHES TO TOILETING

The United States houses a great diversity of cultures, many of which hold very different expectations about toileting. In some cultures—particularly those without easy access to washing machines or to money with which to buy disposable diapers—it's common to teach children to urinate on command at as young as six months of age. This is usually an interdependent process managed by the parent, who trains the infant to release urine in response to a certain sound. To succeed, the adult managing this process must be in close physical contact with the infant and closely tuned in to the child's bodily rhythms. There was a time when educators disparaged such toilet training with the comment "The child is not trained; the mother is trained." It's important for infant and toddler teachers to remember that, while the child care center being described in this book subscribes to the "American" system of toilet learning, there are many possibilities that may be appropriate in different situations. The teachers at a center need to make sure that, before enrollment, all families know the center's philosophy in the area of toileting, so there are no surprises when the time comes for their child to begin the process.

When children begin to indicate readiness to learn to use the toilet, teachers should make a plan with the parents. They can ask what words the family uses to refer to urine and bowel movements, and they usually

suggest that the child have a reasonably successful weekend in underpants at home before underwear is worn at the center, since the center is such a busy place. Teachers often also ask parents to supply multiple complete changes of clothes for their child and to try to make those clothes easy for the child to pull on and off (in the previous vignette, Ana's dress was a good example of the wrong clothes for easy toileting). As in all areas of development, children thrive when their individuality is respected and they are supported in their efforts to grow and learn.

Self-regulation

Older children with established toileting habits require less direction and simply need to hear a suggestion—"Do you think you need to pee before we go outside?"—but children new to toileting don't really know when they need to pee or not, so it's more effective just to announce it as a part of the routine. Helping children tune in to their bodies is an important part of what a preschool teacher teaches, particularly in a full-day program. When Cheyenne sees a child red-faced and sweating from running and climbing, she suggests to that child that he come look at a book or find a puzzle. Young children can easily become overtired and overstimulated; neither state is conducive to self-regulation or learning. The full-day schedule is designed with the intent of helping young children regulate their energy output, and the teachers offer individualized support.

ROUTINES AND ACTIVITIES SUPPORT SELF-REGULATION

Toileting, nap, and lunch are obvious times when a young child needs to attune her body with the schedule of the day. The program schedule should plan for progressively quieter activities before lunch, so the children can step down from vigorous play to quieter table toys, puzzles, and sensory play, and then settle down yet another step with story time. This progression leads to a social and pleasant lunch time, with the body calm and able to receive nourishment, to eliminate waste, and to settle into a nap.

The group is split for stories so that the children can focus in a small group on the rich language experience. The teachers choose the books carefully, to meet different needs they've observed in the group. If a child has recently experienced a medical procedure, the group may be playing with doctor equipment and showing an interest in stories about visiting the doctor or the hospital. The two- and three-year-olds' class always has some books on the shelf about using the toilet, as well as stories about many kinds of families. Along with books that help the children understand their lives, the teachers also choose books that will broaden children's horizons: imaginative stories about "what if," allegorical stories about mothers finding their children, or stories with wonderful language.

Teacher Cheyenne likes to read poems as she dismisses children from story time to wash hands and go to the lunch table. The children are capable of washing and sitting down at the table with very little adult help. Lunch is served family style, with children learning to say the name of the child they are addressing, asking her to "please pass" what is desired.

The teachers tailor their level of support to the progression of each individual child. All these nurturing activities support and build the relationship between teacher and child. When children experience solid attachment to parents and other caregivers during infancy, they are able as toddlers and preschoolers to build emotionally supportive relationships with their teachers. The attachments of infancy form a platform from which all future satisfying relationships are launched.

Sleep is strongly habitual, so teachers make sure there's plenty of consistency in the pre-nap and naptime routines. Naps occur at the same time every day, the same placement is used for the cots, and the same blanket is used for each child—all these routines support the children's ability to let go and sleep. Children who are restless are patted softly and encouraged to stretch out and close their eyes, relax, and rest. The calm, consistent, caring presence of a teacher allows a child the opportunity to learn to manage his own emotions. If a child has upset a teacher so much that it's difficult for that teacher to maintain objectivity, then another teacher can step in and take over. The nap room is a place where such hand-offs are quite effective, because the best way to get children to sleep is to try not to engage them or stimulate them, but rather to remind them not to talk and to keep their bodies still and their hands down.

Teacher encouraging independence

Cheyenne realizes that Lars, who is pretty independent about toileting but who often waits until the last minute to go, has not been to the bathroom for two hours. So when she sends him to the bathroom, instead of just saying "Time to wash your hands," she says, "Use the toilet and then wash your hands." This saves Lars from being surprised and upset to find urine rolling down his legs as soon as his hands go under the faucet!

Roulette, sitting at the table, reminds children now and then to put napkins in their laps, to stop pouring milk when their glass is almost full, or to listen to the request of another child. Cheyenne puts out cots and a basket of soft toys the children can sleep with. By the time she's done, children are coming to use the toilet or to get a naptime diaper on. Children sit on the rug, pull off their shoes and socks, tuck their socks in their shoes, and pull off their pants, leaving Cheyenne free to change a few diapers and supervise the potty and the hand washing after lunch. Some children in this group are done with diapers, some use a diaper just for nap, and some are still in diapers full time. One child asks for a diaper when he needs to have a bowel movement, but urinates in the toilet. As children get settled to sleep, Roulette and Cheyenne take their places to pat backs and help the children quiet themselves.

After nap, the children use the toilet and get dressed. Most have learned to be, and enjoy being, very independent, but some still struggle a bit. Morgan stands in the middle of the bathroom.

Roulette asks, "Which toilet are you going to use, Morgan?"

Morgan replies, "I can't pull my pants down."

"Hmm," says Roulette. "Did you forget how to put your fingers inside the waistband and pull?"

"I ca-a-n't," responds Morgan.

"Let me remind you," says Roulette. "See, your fingers go here, and then you pull them down. You pull on the front and I'll pull on the back, and we'll get them down together. Then you'll be ready to sit on the potty."

Just as toddlers experience a push and pull between clinging and running away, young preschool children can be quite competent yet

still need to occasionally play a "helpless" role when the fast-expanding world seems big and overwhelming.

The afternoon teacher, Barbara, takes a group to the yard to play while Roulette puts away cots and restocks the room for a change of activities. As he finishes putting the cots away, he notices that Peggy, who has been sitting in the book area with her blanket, has begun to whine: "Teacher, my blankie is all wet."

Looking at the blanket, Roulette sees that Peggy has been chewing on the corner of her blanket. "It sure is wet," comments Roulette. "We can put it in a plastic bag in your cubby and it will be all ready to go home."

"No," wails Peggy, "I need it."

Roulette remarks, "We're getting ready to go outside and play now. I wonder what your friend Amanda is doing outside?"

Roulette looks toward the window. Peggy looks, too, while sucking her thumb and rubbing her nose. "Let me help," says Roulette kindly. He scoops Peggy up, carries her to her cubby, gets her jacket on and her shoes tied, and walks with her to the door to the yard.

"I'd better make a note to discuss Peggy at the staff meeting," thinks Roulette. "Peggy has been such a together, able three-year-old, but I think we're seeing some developmental changes now that she's hit three and a half. I'll call her mom at work and see if she's seeing this behavior at home, and I'll tell her not to worry, it's normal. Well, spring must be coming. Every year around this time in the three-year-olds' classroom, there's a group of children who seem to slip backwards—playing baby, whining, and generally falling apart."

Outdoors, the children are busy playing with a cardboard box: climbing inside, closing the flaps and hiding, popping out and surprising each other. Some children try to fill it with sand, while others want to pull a child sitting inside it, as though the box were a sled. Some practice rolling it over and trying to sit on top of it. Everyone has a turn. The box remains popular, though it's becoming a little dilapidated. Erick pulls a large plastic tub over to the box and hides in the tub instead of in the box. What a big surprise it is to pop out from under the tub instead of the box! Erick puts the tub on his back and announces, "I'm a snapping turtle!"

Teacher adjusting to the ebb and flow of typical development

Teacher keeps play experience positive

Children digging nearby watch the turtle for a while, looking a little worried. Lars gets the funnel off the sandbox shelf and puts it on his finger, saying "poke, poke" quietly to himself as he pushes the end of the funnel into another child's arm. Quietly, teacher Barbara steps closer and comments, "Remember about funnels—they're good for pouring, getting the sand into something with a small opening. Let's find a good container to use with that funnel!" Barbara quietly recites a poem as she helps Lars find a plastic bottle in the sand toys: "One baby turtle alone and new. Finds a friend, and then there are two. Two baby turtles crawl down to the sea. They find another, and then there are three. Three baby turtles crawl along the shore. They find another, and then there are four. Four baby turtles go for a dive. Up swims another, and then there are five."

Creating an Atmosphere of Safety and Caring

When Roulette looked at Peggy, he recognized she was using a series of self-soothing techniques: sucking her thumb, chewing on her blanket, rubbing her nose, and whining. He remembered that children attempt to self-soothe to relieve tension. At age three and a half, many young children become quite stressed, and it's common for them to develop eye ticks, compulsions, or sudden clumsiness, or to begin nail biting, rubbing their genitals, or drooling and stuttering—all from an internal recalibration of who they are and where they stand in the world (Ames and Ilg 1976). By age four, these behaviors are usually gone, but at age three and a half, Roulette knows a young child can still need additional support.

Barbara's teaching (intervening with Lars about not poking another child with a funnel) is so subtle that it could easily go unnoticed. Her ability to observe and anticipate a problem before it happens keeps stress and conflict at a minimum, and keeps the harmony flowing in the yard. All sorts of behavior arise as children try to figure out how to form a friendship. These creative and intuitive children have been using all their senses to try to manage the world around them and the people in it. As they enter this developmental stage, with its strong drive to be a friend, they try every behavior they can think of to learn how to connect with and manage others. Barbara's quiet, thoughtful coaching shows she understands that gentle, calm direction supports the budding social competence of these children.

Being able to recognize and verbalize feelings, which is an extraordinarily important part of stable mental health, is a very important goal in every preschool classroom. Other children often come to observe or ask questions when they hear another child yell or cry. They take great comfort in watching a teacher's loving support and in noting the consistency and fairness with which rules are applied. The teacher often sympathizes: "Too bad," "I'm sorry that happened," "You'll remember next time," or "Oh dear, this is not working. You'd better play somewhere else."

All the children playing in the yard are taking in information. They're focused on what they're doing and they're tuned in to what everyone else is doing. If Lars had not had Barbara's friendly support, he might have responded in an aggressive way to the scary idea of having a "snapping turtle" nearby. He seemed to be thinking about how to protect himself when he poked another child with the funnel and said "poke, poke." The teacher's reminder of how to use the funnel, and her assistance finding an interesting container to use with the funnel, helped Lars and all the children around him know that they were safe, that the teacher would protect and help them be successful at school. Through her response, Barbara actively created an atmosphere of safety and caring, so the children could stay focused on learning and playing. An attuned, attached relationship between a teacher and a child allows the child freedom to explore and grow.

TEACHABLE MOMENTS

Barbara is aware of the changes that take place in a child's brain development and thinking. She recognizes that Lars is beginning to understand that his behavior may affect the way a friend reacts to what he says and does. A teacher's positive attitude toward children's play shows that with her quiet inner strength she can help the children control themselves because *she* is in control. By giving constructive suggestions, her attitude and language can help a child. On a practical level, Barbara speaks to Lars about the use of a funnel. In the bigger picture of human development, she decided to use this teachable moment to guide Lars's experience by ignoring his clear drift toward using the funnel in a socially unconstructive way (poking a friend) and instead constructing a positive experience for

him. Barbara doesn't say a word about poking; instead, she reminds Lars how to constructively use a funnel.

The surprise Lars felt when Erick popped out from under the tub and the use of the term *snapping turtle* upset Lars's equilibrium. Although Lars knows little about turtles, something that snaps can't be safe. At this age, language development is advancing quickly in terms of vocabulary and syntax, but when feelings and emotions are involved, words are still likely to be overcome by actions. Any comment on the use of the funnel as a poking implement would very likely have stimulated rather than deterred Lars's desire to poke.

The goal of a teacher is to help children manage their own behavior and feel successful in their ability to get along with others. Constructive suggestions that positively reflect on a child's actions build that child's self-esteem, helping her see that she can trust adults to assist her, even when she can't quite trust herself. This teaching technique also helps teachers manage the ambience of the group as a whole.

Outdoor Classroom

Outdoor play gives children different experiences than indoor play. The air on their skin can be fresh and cool or warm and muggy, and natural, organic materials surround them—trees that blossom, fruit, change colors, and lose leaves; sand, dirt, flowers, and bugs; the ever-changing sky and clouds. Outdoors there's also space for large-muscle activities that can't be accommodated inside. At the same time, the most important qualities of children's classroom experiences continue outdoors.

In contrast to an elementary school, the ratio of teachers to children at a child care center remains the same outdoors, for the children are learning whether they're indoors or out, and they need the same supportive coaching and guidance from their teachers. The yard is designed to provide opportunities for all sorts of play, not just for tricycling, ball playing, and running, swinging, and climbing. The sandbox holds containers and dishes for "cooking" activities, and has a section reserved for construction vehicles, lakes, and rivers. An inviting basket of books sits next to the bench under a shade tree. A few child-sized picnic tables are placed next to a shelf holding manipulatives, crayons and paper, and puzzles.

A sensory table holds water, boats, and plastic fish. Dolls, strollers, and cradles sit on a blanket that is spread in a quiet corner near the books. Matchbox cars and ramp-building materials sit on another blanket. As in the classroom, similar activities are arranged in the same location each day, making them easy for children to locate. The teacher's clarity and intentionality in setting up the outdoor environment keep the children's outdoor play equally as purposeful and clear as their indoor play.

By providing many outdoor activities, teachers ensure that children will be able to enjoy their time outdoors whether their energy level is high or low and whether their large-motor or fine-motor muscles need exercise. Playing vigorously develops large-muscle groups while supporting the small-muscle dexterity needed for writing skills and reading. Mastering balance and developing core body strength help children maintain focus when they're required to sit. Vigorous play stimulates growth and blood flow to growing organs while releasing tension.

Outdoor activities can also support intellectual development. For example, children often spontaneously sing as they swing or dig, the rhythms connecting and building synapses in their brain. Outdoors, children also can experience soothing, sensory explorations that stimulate and help develop the nervous system, as well as dramatic play time, which helps build social and emotional competence, empathy, and compassion. Manipulating materials, whether blocks, rocks, or Tinker toys, stimulates intellectual processes such as abstract thought, logic, and order.

When Roulette comes out to the yard, he brings snack supplies and puts them on a table where children can help themselves if they feel hungry. Throughout the afternoon, a few children at a time wash their hands, sit at the table, and serve themselves. Barbara and Roulette keep an eye on the table and circulate closer when they see that a child needs a little reminder about how much cottage cheese or how many pieces of fruit to take in one serving, or when a sponge is needed to wipe up a little overflow of milk or water, or to put the milk and cottage cheese back into the insulated cooler when not being used. This arrangement

Teachers accommodating and respecting individual needs

accommodates children's different rhythms; some are hungry as soon as they wake from a nap, while others need to play awhile before they feel like eating. The teachers want to be sure that each child gets the food he needs to keep up his energy until it's time to go home, and this plan keeps snack a relaxed activity for children to choose according to their level of interest.

At the wash basin, Noriko puts her hands in the water to wash up for snack, but suddenly freezes—the water unexpectedly stimulates her bladder, and she wets her pants. She turns to Barbara and cries, "Shi-shi!" Barbara reassures Noriko, "Don't worry, grandma put more dry clothes for you in your cubby. Let's go inside to get changed and you'll make it to the toilet next time. It takes some practice to remember to pee in the toilet." Barbara keeps her voice positive and matter-of-fact. Just like every new task, toilet learning takes time to master, and in the meantime, accidents will happen. Roulette gets the hose to rinse off the deck while Barbara rounds up a few other children who are due for a bathroom break and then goes inside with Noriko and the others.

Lars and Daniel kick a soccer ball back and forth, chasing it here and there, since their aim is a little wobbly. After fifteen minutes, soccer loses its appeal; Lars puts the ball in its basket, and goes to build a volcano in the sandbox. Daniel climbs with Sue for a few minutes and then stretches out on the sand under a tree, watching the sky through the branches. Roulette observes him for several minutes, then strolls over and asks if he's watching something interesting. "No," he says lazily. "But I might see an airplane—or a helicopter—go by." Roulette smiles and walks away, and Daniel resumes scanning.

Roulette thinks how much Daniel must trust his environment to be able to lie down and relax, feeling physically safe, without worrying that a child will jump on him or kick sand. Daniel trusts his teacher to respect his choice of activity, even when that activity might be interpreted by some adults as "doing nothing." He trusts his body to be able to pace and regulate itself, finding that after running around chasing a ball in the sun, he's ready to lie in the shade and do something restful. He trusts his social milieu enough to know that he can choose to play with others or to enjoy his own company.

Roulette reflects, "This is truly a 'place for childhood,' where the blend of school and home succeeds even though the children are in a

Allowing for and respecting individual and group experiences alike

group of twelve from 7:30 AM to 6:00 PM every day, surrounded by dozens of children in other classrooms as well." Daniel's individual experience of childhood is being honored and supported. This small moment shows Roulette all the lessons Daniel has learned and internalized that increase Daniel's sense of competence to manage his world. That sense of competence directly feeds his self-esteem.

A little later, Roulette takes half the class inside to use the toilet or to change diapers. "Hey, Erick, since you're in front today you can choose which potty you want to use!" says Roulette. He then helps the children choose an activity from among the quieter late-afternoon activities that the teachers set up after nap. For most of the day, the children in this young preschool group have been in a large group, choosing among a large variety of activities. Now, in the last few hours of the child care day, the group is divided in half, each group occupying a smaller space with one teacher who transitions into a more nurturing relationship with the children. While story time usually involves a teacher holding a book opposite a group of children, in the late afternoon, story time means sitting on the teacher's lap or leaning on her arm as she reads, while other children draw or otherwise occupy themselves. Sometimes at this time of the day, simple lotto games or puzzles are worked as a group with the teacher. It is a relaxed, nurturing time, with the teacher helping the children modulate their energy as the children begin to think about moving away from the center to their home and their parents.

After Roulette has everyone settled, he points out to the children that Yolanda has arrived to be with them, and he says good-bye. Yolanda is a semiretired teacher who brings the children a mature, comfortable presence at this low-energy time of the day. Although Yolanda is only with the group for a few hours each day, it's an important few hours, and her years of experience teaching preschool allow her to quickly form warm relationships with the children. At this time in the day, the children are running low on energy and are ready for a comfortable, quiet time with a teacher that they trust to be understanding and supportive even when they're not at their best.

Barbara takes her group into the bathroom for diapering and toileting and then into an adjacent room where they'll spend their last few hours. Patty is with Yolanda, and Sue is in Barbara's group. Another reason the teachers divide the children into smaller groups in the late

Using transitions and routines to close out the day

Teachers attending to children's unique social needs

afternoon is so that "best friends" like Patty and Sue can have some time apart after a long day of negotiating the challenges of early friendship. Though Patty and Sue sometimes ask if they can be in the same group, after a little fussing during separation time they generally accept the teacher's decision. Patty's leadership is still sometimes a comfortable habit for Sue, but Barbara also sees Sue at this time of the day relax and go deep into her play, really able to pursue her own interests without interference from Patty.

Ana's father comes into the room and scoops her up for a hug. "Let's get your jacket from your cubby and go make some dinner," he says.

"I made you a picture with all the colors on it!" replies Ana, finding her drawing on the drying rack.

Dad reads a note from Cheyenne that explains that Ana stayed dry all day, except for the accident of the dress dipping into the toilet. He finds the bag holding Ana's wet dress in the cubby and says, "Too bad your dress got wet, but it sounds like you're doing a great job of getting to the potty, sweetheart! Good for you."

Ana asks, "When can I get some Cinderella underpants like Patty has, Daddy?"

This growing social interest—wanting to have what other children have—is another strong motivator for learning to use the toilet at this age!

Teacher helping parent take the child's perspective

Sue's mom is picking up both Sue and Patty today, as Patty's mom has a late class. Mrs. Greenwald sits with Sue for a minute while Sue finishes her puzzle, then says, "Let's go get Patty. Remember, she's coming home with us tonight for dinner."

"No, Mommy. I want to just go home with you!" Sue says unexpectedly.

"But Susie," Mrs. Greenwald replies with consternation, "Patty is your friend! You love to have Patty come and stay with us!"

"Patty takes all my toys. She doesn't listen to me!" objects Sue.

At this point, Barbara steps in to help explain the changing situation and to give Sue some confidence: "You know, Mrs. Greenwald, Sue has been working really hard at school to tell Patty when she has a different idea than Patty does. It's hard work, isn't it, Sue? You were looking forward to going home to your very own house with just your very own mom, and now Patty's going home with you too. But you know what?

Your mom can help you talk to Patty just like the teachers do, can't you, Mrs. Greenwald? And, Sue, you're learning to be a girl who can tell people what she wants."

Mrs. Greenwald smiles gratefully at Barbara and confirms, "Barbara's right, Sue. I can help you with Patty. I can see how you might be tired after playing with her all day. And you know what? We can make a plan right now about what you and Patty can play with in the kitchen while I'm fixing dinner. Then I'll be close by to help you if she has trouble listening. Do you think you'd like to wash dishes in the sink with her, or should we put some dolls or puzzles on the table?" Sue and Mrs. Greenwald find Patty and then head for home.

Barbara likes the idea that she has helped Mrs. Greenwald carry into the evening the same practice the teachers use throughout the day, with adults reflecting and affirming the children so that each child recognizes herself and feels seen, important, and supported in her world. Barbara knows this practice builds self-esteem, confidence, and the social capacity to empathize. She believes that children learn about their own feelings through an adult's acknowledgment and understanding, and also through the language an adult uses as feelings are identified and an experience is recounted. Barbara enjoyed watching Sue relax as she verbalized Sue's feelings: "You were looking forward to going home to your very own house with just your very own mom" and "I can see how you might be tired after playing with her all day." The verbalization process helped Sue identify what she was feeling, helped her understand herself better, and gave her language to talk about her feelings. Barbara feels confident that her comments to Sue and Mrs. Greenwald have helped both of them move more successfully into their evening.

Yolanda is reading a book with Erick when his mom comes in at six o'clock. "How did the toileting go today? Where did those pants come from?" Mrs. Johnson asks first thing.

"I peed in the potty!" replies Erick happily.

"Oh, you're such a good boy! But why do you have on different pants, then? Why is there wet underwear in your cubby?" asks Mrs. Johnson.

Yolanda intercedes, "Hi, Mrs. Johnson. Erick went potty quite a few times today, but a couple times he didn't make it. He had plenty of underwear but he didn't have enough dry pants, so he's borrowing an

Teacher positively reframing the parent's perception of the child

extra pair we had." She turns back to Erick and says, "You're really doing pretty well with the toilet, aren't you, Erick?"

Mrs. Johnson says, "I don't understand why he can't stay with it! He stays dry, then he doesn't. I just put him back in a diaper last night because I think he must not be ready yet. But I don't know—he stays dry some days, so then I just think he's being uncooperative."

Erick has lost the smile he had when his mom first came in, and he's looking downcast. From his perspective, he had succeeded today in getting to the toilet (thanks in large part to Roulette's thoughtful guidance), and it's disappointing to see his mom's dissatisfaction.

"It can take awhile to develop a new habit," replies Yolanda. "I think about how my grandbaby was so excited to start walking, but she still crawls a lot of the time—it's kind of like that. Every time children learn something new, the novelty makes it interesting, but it takes awhile to get really comfortable and used to doing something different. It seems like each child has a little different process of learning to use the toilet. Over the years, I've realized the best thing we can do for children is to trust that it will happen and to support them through the process. I know Erick wants to grow up and learn lots of new things, don't you, Erick? It won't be long before you're really using the toilet all the time. Here, we usually feel like once children start wearing underpants, it's confusing to put on diapers again, so we don't, except for naptime. I wonder if that's part of what's making things confusing right now." She smiles at Erick. "Peeing in diapers is okay, but when you're in underpants it means 'Quick, run to the potty!' That's remembering two things at once—first, whether you're wearing diapers or underpants, and then to run to the potty. Wow! That's a lot to think about before you go pee."

"Well, I don't know. I just can't think about it right now. Erick, let's go home, baby. It's been a long day," says Mrs. Johnson. "Have a good evening, Yolanda."

Teachers strategizing to address a problem

Yolanda sees them out the door and then straightens up the room for the morning arrivals. Barbara, who's been putting away toys in the closet and overheard the conversation with Mrs. Johnson, comments, "She's sure sounding frustrated, isn't she? It must be hard living with Erick right now."

Yolanda replies, "It seems hard for both of them. I'd sure like to see Erick developing confidence that he can live up to his mom's expectations, and part of that is about helping his mom have reasonable expectations. I hope we can give them both the support they need. Did Roulette say anything about them to you today?"

"Yes," says Barbara, "he was saying he wished you had a little overlap time to talk with him about some strategies. He said he and Cheyenne are trying to be real consistent with Erick in the mornings, and it would be good to be able to get you into the loop as well, since you seem to have a nice relationship with Mrs. Johnson."

"Well, you know I can't get here any earlier than I do. My daughter doesn't get back from work until her older one is out of school at three, so getting here by three-thirty is a push already. But you can tell him to give me a call if he has a minute. Here's the number at my daughter's house."

"OK, I will," says Barbara. "I'll let him know about your conversation this evening too. You did a good job trying to give Mrs. Johnson a little perspective, but she probably needs more than a two-minute chat at pickup time."

JOIE *de* VIVRE: FOUR-YEAR-OLDS

6

DEVELOPMENTAL AGE RANGE

44–66 months

A s Lucy walks into the school, she greets parents and children arriving and going into breakfast. She smiles and nods to parents who have already left their children and are departing for work. She then signs in at the office, looks over the communication book to see if anyone has called in sick, and checks the daily calendar, making a mental note to remember the staff meeting at 1:00 and that the director will be coming through the classrooms with a tour for prospective parents at 2:00.

"Looks like it will be a good day," Lucy comments to Brenda, the office manager, who has been answering phones and answering questions since the school opened. "No one has called in sick."

"Yeah, but the Peabody kids have both been yelling since the moment they got here. Cayenne may need a hand with breakfast," Brenda replies.

Staff setting the stage for a new day

135

Lucy notes, "I heard them as I was coming in. I'll stop by and see if I can help. Who dropped them off?"

"Their mom," says Brenda. "As usual, she was smiling like nothing's wrong. It's weird that those two kids can be killing each other right under her nose and she acts like everything is lovely."

"I'm sure that confuses the children," says Lucy. "I'll call her after lunch, but it sounds like I'd better go see how Cayenne is managing. That yelling will be worrying the children who are trying to separate from their parents and eat breakfast. I want to talk about how to help these children and their mom at the staff meeting, so this is a good opportunity for me to get Cayenne observing and thinking about how to help them too. Mrs. Peabody needs help. I think she just smiles and seems to rise above it all because she just doesn't know what else to do. Once we make a staff plan, we can start giving Mrs. Peabody some clear direction about how to play her part, and then I think she'll start to get it."

Shaking her head, Brenda returns to her desk and the ringing phone.

In the breakfast area, Lucy sees children at various stages of eating. Some are finishing up, putting their dishes away, and going out to play, while others are saying good-bye to their parents and then going to get their food. Now and then a child asks Cayenne for more toast or juice. The age groups are mixed, with some siblings choosing to sit together, and some sitting with friends. The Peabody children, three-and-a-half-year-old Jay and four-and-a-half-year-old Jill, are sitting at separate tables, acting silly; they put toast in their juice, and hold their spoons upside down so that scoops of milk and cereal spill. Watching for a moment, Lucy notes that while howling with laughter, the Peabodys are also keeping an eye on each other and provoking each other.

Lucy makes eye contact with Cayenne and smiles, "Gosh, it's busy in here today, Cayenne! I wonder if children can hear their moms and dads saying good-bye?"

"I know," worries Cayenne. "Jay and Jill are having a hard time settling down to eat. I thought if they sat at separate tables it would help them focus on their eating, but now I'm thinking they might just not be hungry—usually they're good eaters, though."

"Hmm," says Lucy. As she walks toward Jill, she knows that other children and parents in the area are aware of her conversation with Cayenne. Jay and Jill have been listening, too, while continuing to act silly. Bending down next to Jill, she places her body so it blocks Jill's view of Jay, puts her hand on Jill's back, smiles, and makes eye contact: "Good morning, Jill, I'm glad to see you. Here you are at school today. Here you are eating breakfast."

Jill sticks out her tongue, covered with partially chewed cheerios.

"I see, yum. Be careful to keep them in your mouth. Gosh, Jill, something seems not quite right. I was wondering if you need to tell mommy or Jay something so that you can eat your breakfast?"

Jill swallows, looks at Lucy, and says, "Mommy didn't give me a hug. Jay got his high five, but I didn't get my hug."

Jay begins calling to Cayenne, giggling and peeking around Lucy at Jill, "I need more juice! I spilled my juice!"

Lucy makes eye contact with Cayenne, who continues to serve other children and help them separate from their parents. "Oh dear," says Lucy to Jill, ignoring Jay. "That's too bad. Now you're feeling bad and Jay feels bad, too, and then there's a lot of loud laughing, and mistakes like spilling are happening. Why don't you finish up eating, and then you can bring Jay back to our class and we'll write a note to Mommy? We can say 'I love you, Mommy, and I missed my hug.'"

"Yeah," chimes in Jay, "I want to say 'I love you too' and 'how 'bout next time I get a high five and a funny face and Jill gets a hug and four kisses, 'cuz she's four and I'm not.'"

"Well, finish eating and come find me," says Lucy. "I'll tell the yard teacher you're coming. Now I'll quickly help Jay, and then I'll hurry along to get the room ready for the children to come play."

Cayenne hands Lucy a towel, nodding toward the juice she has set on the shelf for Jay. Lucy wipes up Jay's spill, gives him the new glass of juice, and smiles. "Now finish up, and when you're done, come find me with Jill and we'll write to mommy."

Cayenne smiles thanks to Lucy as she goes, and the room settles into its usual relaxed state. Lucy goes to her classroom, puts her purse away, and hangs her jacket on a hook. She checks the parents' communication book for notes from parents—no special instructions today; says hi to Roulette, the teacher in the threes classroom next to hers; and goes

Teacher helping siblings transition from home to school

Teacher setting up the classroom for the morning

to the teacher prep area to get paint for easel painting. She gathers together the supplies she'll need for a fall art project and takes the supplies to the classroom, where she replenishes the paper supply at the drawing table, adds to the children's book area a few new books about fall and puts a few books away, and gets the porch activities ready, setting the messy sensory play away from high-traffic areas and hanging aprons on the chairs for the children. As she washes the snack table and sets up the snack, she looks at the yard setup, making sure it's safe and that activities are ready there: digging in one area, climbing in another, small cars near the blocks, a little wet sand for "cooking" near the playhouse, and, for quiet play, some puzzles and books on a tray at the center of a table.

Jill and Jay call from the gate. Going to open the gate for them, she tries to make eye contact with the yard teacher, who is busy helping a child at the climber. Lucy waves to him, but he doesn't see her. She tells Jill and Jay, "Let's go tell teacher Nick you're coming with me now."

The three walk across the yard, and Lucy tells Nick, "I'm here to take Jill and Jay up to write a note to their mommy."

"I want to come! I want to write to my mom!" says Tasha from the climber.

"I'm helping Jay and Jill right now. If you want to write a note when it's time for you to come in and play, I'll help you then. Just come ask me and we'll do it," says Lucy. "See you later, Nick."

Lucy comments to Jill and Jay, "We'll write to mommy, then Jill can stay with me while I open the gate from the yard and invite the other children up, and, Jay, you can go over to Roulette and get busy in your group."

Together, the three write: "Dear Mommy, I love you. I miss you. Come get me early today. You forgot to give me my hug and I was sad and Jay spilled." Lucy helps the children sign their names and decide whose cubby the note should be kept in for mommy to pick up later.

Jay goes to his classroom and Jill gets busy playing as Lucy invites the other children into the classroom. Standing at the gate, she sees that the three-year-olds are already going into their classroom, and that the fours are still busy at play. The two teachers who will assist her this morning are in the yard. Catching the eye of Nick, she nods, signaling him to begin the transition to the classroom. Nick surveys the group,

looking for children at loose ends or for those finishing up their play. He speaks to each child individually and quietly, letting each know that the classroom is ready and that, if they're ready, they can put their toys away and come in to play. As the children go to the gate, Lucy greets them.

As Lucy speaks with each child, Nick goes into the classroom to help the children settle in to play. Anne, the other teacher in the yard, waits a bit for Nick to get the first group of children settled inside, and then begins to send the rest of the children to Lucy, who continues to greet the children at the gate: "Good morning, Al, I'm glad to see you at school today!" "Here you are, George, all ready to play. Is Whit coming too? You boys did some great digging yesterday—I wonder if you'll dig some more today."

In subtle ways, Lucy helps the children think of what they did the day before, what they like to do, and who they like to play with, while at the same time she lets them know that she notices and cares about them and that she will be there to help them as they play. Lucy wants the children to feel relaxed and to know that everyone will get a chance to play with whatever they want to. When children are lined up to enter a space, they often become competitive with each other, focusing on who is first and pushing each other out of the way, rather than thinking about what they want to do and who they want to play with. This commotion makes it much harder for the children to settle down and get busy in the class.

Lucy connects with the children as she greets them. She'll keep the role of greeter all morning, going to greet the children who arrive late, because she wants each child to know that she's there for them. This activity of greeting serves Lucy in other ways, too: it slows the children's entrance into the classroom, so the children can make choices and settle into play, and it allows her to orchestrate the groups as she subtly separates difficult combinations of children by controlling the order of their entrance into the classroom. Given the opportunity, a few children will start every day at the blocks, bikes, or playhouse. By asking Anne and Nick to send them in at the end of the transition time, she can let other children have a chance to start at these popular areas—and she can direct the children who tend to dominate those areas to something new and different.

Teacher greeting children and helping them transition from the yard into the classroom

Lucy, Nick, and Anne help the children develop friendships by using the morning transition wisely. They've been talking about how Kim seems to be looking for a friend. At a previous staff meeting, the teachers had decided to try matching Kim up with Jeremy, another boy in the group who seems to be looking for a friend. Both boys have good ideas, and both have strong enough personalities that one won't dominate the other. Plus, they both like the small trains, the unit blocks, and drawing. By sending these boys up to the room first and by rotating some fresh train tracks into the block area, the teachers try to set the boys up so they will find each other and perhaps discover that they enjoy playing with each other.

Unique Developmental Challenges

Experienced teachers discover the unique qualities of working with four-year-olds. The typical developmental challenges children face in their fourth year include learning to balance well-developed verbal skills and an increased understanding of the complexities of the world around them with their lack of experience in the world, immature social skills, and unsteady emotional competence.

GOALS FOR FOUR-YEAR-OLDS

- Love of and curiosity for life (*joie de vivre*)
- Acceptance of self and of others' differences (confidence and empathy)
- Articulation of feelings and emotions in social situations
- Development of structure and order in their thinking

Four-year-olds are extremely intuitive and are tuned in to nonverbal communication. They also are aware that the world is a big place full of surprises, and they are thus vulnerable and in need of adult support. They're proud of no longer being "a baby," and their feelings are easily hurt if a teacher treats them like a younger child. Four-year-olds love

to exaggerate, and often fabricate stories to make them appear "better." They may take other people's things, as their distinction between right and wrong seems to pertain to everyone other than themselves, and they usually want things to go their way (and can become quite upset when they do not).

Power and Experimentation

Play at this age is often about power and control. Dramatic play is often focused on games about superheroes, cowboys, ninja turtles, power rangers, and princesses—games that concern who is in charge of whom and who can make the other person do what they want. Four-year-olds are experimenters and are often described in child development texts as "out of control" because they're willing to try outlandish and unappealing activities. For example, they'll happily put discarded candy found in a gutter in their mouths and then argue that they shouldn't be asked to spit it out! They're extremely creative and insightful, and can be delightful companions.

Given all these qualities, it makes perfect sense that four-year-olds scare themselves and that they worry about what is real and what is pretend. Life in general is challenging at this age, and it often feels confusing and chaotic. A teacher's understanding and thoughtful anticipation can keep life clear for four-year-olds, at least while they're at preschool or in child care.

While four-year-olds must work very hard to regulate and moderate their emotional responses, they have pretty well mastered physical routines and systems. Teachers rarely need to remind children this age to use the toilet, and they often observe the children naturally balancing quiet and active play during the course of the day.

The children are all busy playing in the classroom and yard. As the morning progresses, Lucy makes note of the children's level of interest in the various activities set up for them. All morning there have been

Teacher setting up projects for extended play

children waiting for a turn to play at the sand and water table. Lucy's decision to fill it with small garden bark and put in small plastic bugs, strawberry baskets for making "cages," and large leaves from an old silk flower plant has everyone interested. Lucy plans for tomorrow, thinking she will sort the bugs into two or three types and note whether the children make bug families.

The art project is set out with three trays; two empty trays show the children that there is room for two children at a time to work there. The third tray, placed between the two empty ones, holds the supplies: a stack of brown cardboard in assorted sizes, and cups of glue with orange, brown, or yellow paint mixed in. Today, the children can paint on the cardboard with the thick slippery glue. Tomorrow, the same colors of glue will be out for painting, along with small pieces of brown, yellow, and orange paper cut into different shapes. By coordinating the colors in the art area, the resulting art projects always look nice, reflect the season, and please parents while allowing the children to plan their own projects.

Lucy wants to keep expanding the children's interest in the art area. She might later extend the project by adding another color or another item to glue. Modifying the same project over the course of several days helps the children focus on the colors and the pleasure of the art, and cuts down on the mad dash to be the first child at the art area, since the children realize the project will be around for several days. The children have learned to trust that the teachers will always make sure that everyone who wants a turn will have a turn.

As Lucy continues to look around the classroom, she observes a group of children playing with blocks; some are busy building a track for the small trains. Linda has a book open in the book area and is "reading" to Maria. In the "play alone" space, Jim sits on a pillow and strokes his blanket, watching the other children play and thinking about whom he might join when he's ready. Elsewhere, children are settling down to play with the dollhouse. Overall, the children in the classroom are deep in play and the classroom is filled with relaxed conversation— children talking and listening to each other, working out solutions to problems, starting and ending activities.

Suddenly, Michelle comes weeping to Lucy, telling her that Hattie pushed her off the swing. Taking Michelle by the hand, Lucy walks with

her to Hattie, who is now busy digging. Hattie concentrates on her digging as they approach. Lucy says, "Here you are, Hattie, busy playing, and here is Michelle, feeling sad."

"Well, I didn't do anything! I got to the swing first! I can do whatever I want! I don't have to listen to you one bit," says Hattie.

Bending down and putting her arms around both girls, Lucy responds, "Let's let Michelle talk for a moment so we can understand why she's sad. Then you can have a turn to talk. Michelle, is there something you want to talk to Hattie about?"

"Don't push me! I don't like that!" says Michelle through tears.

Hattie, looking away, says, "My mom says I can do what I want! I got to the swing first, so I'm in charge!"

Lucy rephrases Hattie's words, "You'd really like to do just what you want, and sometimes at home you can?"

Hattie has her hands on her hips, and her aggressive stance has timid Michelle moving behind Lucy. Lucy keeps her hand on Michelle's back, physically reminding her of her teacher's support, and continues, "You know, Hattie, if someone is crying and sad, they don't really want to hear what your mom says; they want to hear from you. Michelle would like to hear that you'll remember to use your words so there won't be pushing. Do you think you can remember that next time?"

Hattie sticks to her line, "Well, she's too slow, and my mom said I can do what I want! I don't have to listen to you, you know!"

Lucy asks, "Was Michelle in your way?"

"Yes, Michelle wouldn't get out of my way," Hattie answers.

"Michelle, did you know you were in Hattie's way?" inquires Lucy.

"No, I was getting on the swing." Michelle whimpers.

Indignant and red-faced, Hattie yells, "I just got off the swing to see what Al was doing, and then I saw Michelle getting on my swing!"

"Oh, too bad, too bad that happened," sympathizes Lucy. "I think Michelle really didn't know you were coming back to the swing. She thought you were done swinging. I'll walk inside with you, Hattie, and you can choose something else to do now. Next time you'll remember to use your words and tell Michelle 'I'm not done yet.' You can find something else to do inside now. Later you can try again in the yard. Then you'll remember that pushing never works."

Teacher helping four-year-olds resolve a conflict

Teacher defusing typical four-year-old's attempt at emotional manipulation

Lucy takes Hattie's hand, and Hattie yells, "Let go of me! You're hurting me! I don't have to go inside if I don't want to! I'm telling my mom!"

Lucy still holds Hattie's hand, asking, "Can you walk right in without holding my hand? You know, Hattie, when you're pulling and yelling, I think maybe you're not listening."

Hattie yells, "Go away! Leave me alone! I hate you!"

Lucy responds, "I'm not going away. I'm going to walk inside with you, and later, when you're ready, you can come out and try again. You'll remember about using your words."

"I'm sick, my tummy hurts! Maybe I'm going to throw up! I miss my mommy," yells Hattie.

Lucy, still holding Hattie's hand and moving slowly toward the classroom door, asks, "Would you like to sit on my lap a little bit when we get inside? We could sit a moment, and you could think about your mommy and how much she loves you and how she might let you do just what you want and never, never say no!" Lucy smiles at Hattie, and Hattie has to smile back. Lucy laughs, "That would be funny, wouldn't it, to have a mom who never says no!"

Hattie hangs her head and laughs, so Lucy won't see. Walking inside, Lucy pulls one of the low chairs to a spot where she can see the whole classroom, and then sits down. Hattie climbs on her lap. Despite her recent outburst, Hattie has built a relationship with Lucy over the course of the year and she knows she can count on her teacher to kindly support her. Their attached relationship allows Hattie to accept the boundaries Lucy sets on Hattie's behavior.

Lucy describes what the other children are doing: "I see Wit and Mohamed building with the blocks, and Dee Dee is drawing at the art table. Al is looking at a book."

Hattie looks around, sighs, rests a moment in the safety of her teacher's lap, and then announces, "I think I'll paint a picture for mommy. Every day she says she loves me and she misses me and that she has to go to work but she really wants to stay with me."

Lucy is quiet for a moment, and then comments, "You know, Hattie, moms and dads love their children and they love having time with them, but moms and dads need to work. Just like you love being with your mom and dad and you like being at school too. Once I knew a lit-

tle girl who came to this school who was worried that her mommy was unhappy at work because of missing her, and she thought her mommy wanted her to be sad at school because her mommy wasn't happy at work. That was a mix-up. Grown-ups want their children to learn and be happy at school and at home. That little girl's mom just forgot to tell her about how a mom or dad can miss and love their child and still want their child to have a good time at school. At pickup time, they'll all be together again."

Hattie wiggles a little and says, "I forgot to tell Michelle to get out of the way."

"Yes," says Lucy, "and now you'll remember about that. Words can sure be tricky. It's a good thing we know about how everyone is learning."

"Even when there's a mix-up?" asks Hattie.

"Especially when there's a mix-up!" confirms Lucy.

"Walk Your Talk" (Modeling Behavior)

When conflict arises, teachers are aware and available, helping children help themselves. The children's trusting relationships with their teachers allow them to trust in their own ability to solve problems that may arise. Lucy's respectful teaching supports each child's progress while guiding that child toward the next area of understanding. This process requires a teacher to be as thoughtful, intuitive, and creative as the children she works with. To be effective, a teacher has to "walk her talk," teaching kindness by being kind, teaching tolerance by being tolerant. She must develop her own character and build her own self-control in order to help the children learn to control themselves. By being thoughtful and clear in her language, she helps the children think and speak clearly.

While Lucy teaches, she is thinking about many things: the children and how to facilitate their play; which children need support or space; where the direction of play is taking the children; and how she can guide the play so that all the children can have positive, successful experiences. She may also be thinking ahead to an agenda for a forthcoming staff meeting. At staff meetings, the teachers discuss their work, brainstorm ways to help a struggling child or parent, and discuss curriculum and setup.

Team problem solving at a staff meeting

The teachers meet while the children nap. Cayenne shares observations about breakfast time, and Nick contributes thoughts about early morning yard time. Lucy, Anne, and Nick share their classroom experiences, and Laura adds comments about how the late afternoon is working.

"Can we talk about the Peabody children first?" asks Lucy. "I'd like to call their mom later and see if we can figure out what's going on in the mornings. Cayenne, what are your thoughts? You see them separating from their mom."

Cayenne says thoughtfully, "I'm not sure why it seems worse now, but the more those kids cut up, the more their mom seems to ignore them. I mean, she's standing right there but she's not doing anything; she just stands there smiling. It's frustrating trying to help the kids. They want their mom to help them, and they don't listen as well to me with her there. It's as if she just doesn't know what to do or hasn't the energy to do it."

"She looks so tired to me. When I call, I'll ask her if her mother is sick again," comments Lucy.

Cayenne adds, "I've noticed that when Jill is feeling overwhelmed, she acts so silly! I really think she could hurt herself the way she flops her body around. She's not paying any attention to taking care of herself. Then Jay just starts demanding everything, and if he doesn't get it, he spills or does something that is really hard to ignore."

"Yeah, when he spilled this morning, I could just hear the mess escalate, but I knew I'd better finish with Jill so he'd know she was okay, and then he'd manage better. Cayenne, it was great how you helped me work that. Thanks for being close by and helping," says Lucy.

"I was glad you came in when you did, Lucy. Jay and Jill really needed someone else to help them, and I had a full group of children eating breakfast," replies Cayenne.

"Thank you all for your thoughts. This has helped me. I'll call their mom and ask how her mother is doing. I'll remind her to get down and make eye contact when she says bye-bye to each child, and I'll talk with her about how it's okay to tell the kids when she's feeling tired or overwhelmed and worried. They know it anyway, by the way she withdraws. If she'd just tell them she's worried about her mom being sick,

they'd relax, and that would make life easier for her. I'd like to talk with her about the dynamic between the kids and how to work with it, but that's for another day," concludes Lucy.

"Lucy, I'm glad we're meeting today," begins Laura a moment later. "I want to bring something up too. Yesterday afternoon I noticed Jake and Al playing off by the bush in the far corner of the yard. They were being kind of secretive, so I went closer. Jake had his pants down and Al was, you know, checking him out! They jumped apart when they saw me, and Jake said Al told him to do it. I wanted to bring it up so everyone would pay a little extra attention to those two."

"When did you notice this, Laura?" asks Lucy.

"It was about 4:30, after the afternoon transition. Should we separate those boys?" asks Laura.

"Oh, Laura, I'm glad you mentioned seeing that!" adds Nick. "I almost forgot, I saw Al and Amanda in the book area kissing the other day. They weren't just hugging, they were really kissing. Amanda's face was pink."

"What did you do, Nick?" asks Lucy.

"The usual," replies Nick. "I stayed close and said something like 'I see Al is kissing you Amanda.' She said, 'Yes, he loves me.' I said, 'Well, sometimes people who love each other do like to kiss each other, and sometimes they do other things together too. I see the bikes are free in the yard—you could ride bikes together.' Amanda said, 'Yeah, come on honey,' but Al didn't want to go, so I just stayed and talked about what the other kids were doing. You know, I said, 'I see Jeanie and Michelle at the art table making pictures, and Billy and Jeff and Mei Lee are building a house in the blocks.' After a while they started looking around and thinking of other things to do. Then they decided to do something else. I didn't think too much about it—kids see their parents kissing and sometimes they copy what they see. Al has a teenage brother at home too. I just started talking about all the things there were to do, and soon they were interested in something else. But hearing Laura's concern, I'm wondering if we should say something to Al's grandma. Maybe she needs to talk to Ty, Al's big brother, and ask him if he needs to do a better job of protecting Al from seeing such 'big boy things.'"

"How can you be sure a child's not being molested?" asks Anne. "I mean, I know it's normal for kids to want to explore each others'

Teachers intervening in children's sexual explorations

bodies—playing doctor, we used to call it—but what Laura saw sounds a little over the top to me."

"Yes, we always have to take this seriously and be careful not to overreact," says Lucy. "Teachers get information from lots of places. One is by observing, and another is by talking with the parents. It's tricky, though. We don't want to upset parents over nothing, so we want to be thoughtful. You can get information if you tune in to your own gut response when you see such behavior. If you can separate out all your own judgments and personal feelings about sex play and just notice your feelings, it can give you clear insight. How did it feel when you went over there, Laura?" asks Lucy.

"Well, I guess I kind of felt like I 'caught' them. I wasn't too surprised; they were so quiet and hiding, so I guessed they were doing something they knew they shouldn't do. They didn't seem upset about being caught—they weren't stressed or worried," Laura says. "I remember when we had that little girl, Paula, her whole personality seemed to suddenly change. She was such a together little girl and all of a sudden she was just hyper, running all the time, fighting, melting into tears, and clinging to the teacher, not wanting to go home. That was two or three years ago when I came upon her kissing that boy's penis. I've forgotten the boy's name. Remember how distressed and worried Paula was? I felt so alarmed when I came upon her like that, and she reacted like she was terrified. But with Jake and Al it wasn't like that; it just felt like they were exploring and enjoying being naughty in that four-ish way. I remember how hard we worked with little Paula. She just couldn't get her focus off 'playing doctor.' It was so intense and compulsive; she could hardly do or think about anything else. When her mom found out the kid down the street was molesting her, her behavior made sense. She was way over her head trying to understand something that was beyond her, and she kept it a secret too! No wonder she seemed so anxious and distressed, and what a relief that her parents got her some help. It was great to have that therapist come to school and talk with us about how to understand her behavior and to help her. But I didn't get that feeling with Al. You know how he is; he'll try anything. He likes being a rascal and having fun and exploring, and he's so sensory. He loves how things feel—you know how he loves to rub the silky inside of his jacket on his cheek. Any gooey, slimy activity and he's right there."

Lucy sums up, *"Well, it sounds like I should talk with Al's grandma and give her some suggestions about how to help Al through this stage, and maybe I'll see if Ty can be drawn in to help his little brother too. And I think we'd better be on high alert, knowing that he's exploring right now, so we can keep everyone safe. Nick, will you get that nice big anatomy picture book and put it on the children's bookshelf? And everyone remember to watch Al if he goes into a spot that's hard to supervise. As usual, remind children that they need to keep their clothes on at school and that we wear clothes to protect our bodies and our privacy. Redirect the children's interest to looking at the anatomy book or to playing vet instead of doctor. Will you help me remember, Anne, to get the doctor kits and the stuffed animals out? If they want to talk about penises and vaginas, they can go have a look in the anatomy book. The more we talk about it as though it's all perfectly normal conversation, the sooner they'll get the idea it isn't such a big deal, and then their interest in all this will fade.*

"Well, we're running out of time," Lucy continues. *"The children will be waking up and they'll need more than one teacher to help with shoes and to supervise the potty. Good meeting, everyone. Thanks for paying such close attention to the children and for being so thoughtful. Write things down for next time if you think you might forget, and if anything comes up that needs attention before the next meeting, be sure to just come and tell me."*

As the teachers leave, Lucy stays to add information to the children's observation books and to jot notes to parents, planning to make copies of the notes so Laura and Nick will know what she has said to the parents. Later, she'll call Mrs. Peabody and tell her about the discussion about Jay and Jill, and she'll tell her to watch for a note. Smiling to herself, Lucy thinks about Al with his hand in his jacket pocket, rubbing his cheek on the silky lining inside. Maybe she'll see if his grandma could just make him a little piece of silk to keep in his pocket, so his tummy won't get cold this winter from him lifting up his coat.

Sexuality in the Preschool Years

Human beings are sensual, and while sexual organs grow and change over the course of a human life, sensitivity and pleasure in sexual organs are constants throughout life. For young children growing up in a society that uses diapers, which temporarily block access to this sensitive area, access to the genital area often coincides with toilet training. Thus, sexual exploration tends to emerge at around this same time. Children are really getting to know and manage their bodies. In the child's mind, figuring out how to get a sock on and learning to wipe his bottom are not very different; they are both about taking care of the body.

The fact that rubbing their genitals feels good and that children begin to be in contact with their genitals during toilet learning leads quite naturally and innocently to masturbation and exploration. It is common for children to masturbate and rub their bodies on furniture and toys. Like thumb-sucking, masturbation is self-soothing and a way to alleviate stress. If the behavior is more chronic, a teacher may begin to investigate whether the child has developed a self-regulating habit that needs to be redirected, or whether it is a stress-related response. If it is the latter, she looks for the cause of stress that leads to the behavior, in order to eliminate it.

By age four, children are interested in sexual difference and exploration. Playing "doctor" comes up as children become interested in sexual differences (preschools with open bathrooms can eliminate a lot of curiosity). Modesty and self-conscious behavior begin around age five, and crosses all areas of behavior, as children begin to care about how people see and judge them. Before this stage, sex play and experiments and discussion about elimination are often linked to exploration and the fun of being naughty. All of this is healthy and normal. The fact that adults do not approve of such explorations can make them all the more alluring.

Infrequently, preschool children may be victims of molestation and sexual abuse. Below are some things teachers think about when wondering if a child's sexual behavior is normal or if it is a call for help.

Behavior changes in children that *may* indicate abuse:

- Young children are sensuous beings but don't know about adult

sexuality unless they see it, experience it, or are taught about it. Keep your eyes open if children seem to know too much (for example, if a child makes a statement such as "My babysitter's boyfriend's penis sticks straight out of his pants!" or "He said his penis tastes like candy but it doesn't").

- Molestation and abuse cause stress, secrecy, and fear, all of which preschoolers manage poorly. Stress, secrecy, and fear will cause drastic changes in a child's behavior. Anytime a teacher notices big changes in behavior, she knows to watch and listen carefully to the child. A dramatic increase in anxiety will be acted out in anxiety-reducing behavior such as hyperactivity, lots of running, yelling, and an inability to calm down and become still (naptime, for example, may become particularly difficult).

- Deterioration in a child's ability to cope emotionally, an increase in crying and clingy behavior, or withdrawal from people altogether are all cause for concern.

- Children try to understand things that don't make sense to them by playacting about them, so a sudden increase in sex play and hiding, as well as changes in behavior in toilet use, all should be watched.

- Sometimes marks are present on a child's body, or a teacher sees stretched, swollen genitalia or blood in a child's underwear. In such instances, the teacher should request that the child be seen by a doctor.

Many of these warning signs can indicate emotional distress from causes other than sexual abuse, so teachers must be very careful not to read too much into behavior. Generally, an abused child exhibits a pattern of behavior change, not just one single sign, and the observant teacher recognizes the pattern as indicating an abusive situation. While teachers are mandated to report suspected sexual abuse to appropriate child-protection agencies, they also recognize that overreaction to a benign situation can cause serious damage. Perhaps this is why the only information most teachers receive about sexual abuse is what the stages of sexual development are and how to report abuse. Teachers and directors need to be very thoughtful, open, and wise if they suspect a child is in harm's way.

Of course good communication skills and a strong relationship with the family are also particularly helpful in such a situation.

If a teacher sees signs that alarm her, she should talk to her center director and others in a position to help her evaluate the situation. Teachers are required by law to report abuse, but this needs to be carefully planned out and thought through, as it can be very traumatic for all involved and it can break down the trust that all the families in the center feel. Concern about abuse is also present in parents' minds; the teacher who sees a child slip on the bars and land hard on her crotch is wise to let the parent know about the injury, so there won't be worry at bath time that evening.

In the case of Al, the child discussed in the previous vignette by the teachers at their staff meeting, Lucy suspected Al was being exposed to inappropriate behavior at home, so her first step was to talk to the child's grandmother and to draw in the big brother as part of the problem solving, thus strengthening the family and building the school's role as a resource for the family. Then, as with any inappropriate play in the classroom, the teachers made a plan to eliminate it. They decided to open up areas to increased supervision, to remove toys and props such as blankets and boards that children use to hide behind, and to work as a staff to be on the lookout for and stop inappropriate behavior. Reminders such as "We keep our clothes on at school," and innocent comments such as "When I see children with their pants down, I think they need to use the potty," followed by sending the observed child inside to use the bathroom, can take the "fun" out of the play.

Teacher counterbalancing a child's imagination

The teachers arrive back in the classroom as the children get up from their naps or rest time. The teachers put away cots, get out table toys, and help children get shoes on as the afternoon gets under way. Lucy comes back from making phone calls as Alice, with eyes big as saucers, comes to tell her that sixty-six cats jumped out of the tree next door and ran around the yard and tried to get her!

"My word," says Lucy. "Let's go see."

"Oh, they left," says Alice.

"Hmm," says Lucy. "You're thinking about kitties?"

"Yes, mommy wants one, but I say yes, yes, and no, no, and no and yes," says Alice. "A cat might surprise you."

"I see. Cats do like to climb trees and they like to jump and run. You never know what a cat might do or where it might go," observes Lucy.

Alice nods her head. "But mostly they like people, although sometimes they get scared or they're shy," continues Lucy. "They are real, living things though, just like people, so you have to be loving and kind. Alice, I have an idea—would you like to play with the little kitty set? I'll get it for you and you can use it while you think about cats. Here it is in the cupboard. It has a mommy kitty and two baby kittens and a nice kitty bed, and here is the little child who takes care of the kitties. Oh, and here is the food and the dish for a drink of milk."

Lucy settles Alice out of the hustle and bustle of the busy classroom, allowing her to imagine life with a cat. She'll watch Alice play, and when Alice starts looking around at the other children playing in groups, Lucy will send another child over to join her.

Looking weepy, Jody approaches Lucy. "Oh dear," Lucy says, stooping down and putting her arm around Jody as Jody's eyes well up. Jody sobs, "Katie says I can't play! She said 'Go away!' She said she doesn't like me anymore now, she only likes Julie!"

Jody wails and the tears flow freely. Katie and Julie try to ignore Jody, although they glance over at Jody and Lucy now and then with guilty, worried looks.

"Well, let's go talk with them, Jody. What shall we say?" asks Lucy.

"I don't like that!" sputters Jody.

"What don't you like?" prompts Lucy.

"I don't like it when they say 'Go away!' And I don't like it when I'm playing with Katie and she says 'Go away,' because then Julie comes to play, and that's not nice!" Jody articulates.

"Well, let's tell Katie she has forgotten that we can't make other people do things. We can only decide what we want to do. If she wants to be done and go play somewhere else, that's fine, but it's not up to her to decide when someone else is done," comments Lucy. "Do you want a drink of water to help you stop crying? I know that people don't listen too well when people cry and yell at them."

> **Teacher coaching social competence and caring**

As they walk to get a drink, Lucy watches Julie and Katie out of the corner of her eye. She's thinking about how best to handle the situation, how she can let Jody "teach" her friends how to be a friend. Lucy knows Jody needs help to tell her friends clearly and honestly how she feels and what she wants ("I want to keep playing," "I'm not done yet," "I think you don't like me when you say 'Go away'"). Lucy thinks, "My job will be to help the other children listen to Jody and to help Jody feel that her communication was heard, because the conversation is an important part of all three girls' learning—far more important than the particular solution they work out to solve their problem. I have to remember that everyone has times in their lives when they feel rejected, so helping Jody learn how to take care of herself when that happens will be as useful a lesson for her as one on how to rejoin play and not be bossed."

As Lucy and Jody approach Julie and Katie, Julie sticks out her tongue and covers her ears. Keeping her arm around Jody, Lucy bends down and puts her arm around Julie, too, and smiles at Katie. "Jody is sad. See her tears coming down? I think she wants to talk with you. Jody, can you tell Julie and Katie what you want to say?" asks Lucy.

Jody, hands on hips, says, "I'm playing here! That's my baby and my blanket! I'm not done!"

"Well, you left! You went away!" says Julie.

"You look sad, too, Katie. Are you done playing with Jody?" asks Lucy.

"Well, I like Jody and I like Julie, but I don't get to play with Julie too much and I always play with Jody, so when Julie said 'Can I play,' I said 'Yes.' Then Julie said she didn't want to play with Jody."

"I see," says Lucy. "Well, what shall we do? Here is Jody wanting to play, and Katie wanting to play, and Julie wanting to play. I wonder if three girls can play together?"

"No! Only two. This is a two people place," Julie responds.

"I'm going to be sure everyone gets to say what they want. Let's see what Katie wants," says Lucy. Seeing Katie looking pretty miserable, she adds, "Sometimes children say, 'I'm playing with Julie right now. I'll play with you later.' That way Jody knows you still like her and will play with her again a little later."

"Well," storms Jody, "you're not my friend! You can't come to my party! I'll never play with you again."

Katie begins to cry. Lucy gathers her into her arms. "Oh dear, now Katie's sad." Katie drops her head onto Lucy's shoulder.

Lucy's arms enclose all three girls. While she gives her undivided attention to the girls, she continues to keep her eye on all the children in the classroom. She sees children building with blocks, drawing at the art table, nestling with books, making a puzzle, or floating boats in the sink. Lucy listens and watches, smiling and nodding to children in the class as they look at her. If a child approaches her, she'll say, "I'm helping Jody now. I'll come help you when I'm done here."

"I don't want to play anymore," says Katie. "I'm done. I'm going to look at my book."

"She has to clean up!" insists Julie.

"What about you, Julie? Are you done playing too?" asks Lucy.

"I'm done too. I'll put my baby away," says Jody.

"Now I don't have anyone to play with!" howls Julie.

"Well," says Lucy, "you can start to play and see if someone will come and join you. You have such good ideas, I bet the children will be interested in what you're doing and will come to see."

"But when I'm done, they have to come help clean up!" frets Julie.

"Don't worry, I'll be sure everything works out just fine," says Lucy.

Imagination: Exaggeration versus Reality

Four-year-olds have such big imaginations that they can easily slip into lying, as Alice did. She had a genuine concern, but she embellished it a bit to make the whole thing more interesting. Teachers know this is just another way that four-year-olds learn about the world. After all, in their minds the line between what's real and what's pretend is actually quite blurred. Teachers view such exaggerations in the context of a child's development, and thus respond with a light touch, as Lucy did with Alice. There's no reason to explain to a four-year-old the immorality of lying, because in a child's brain, the concept of lying doesn't really make sense until the child is six or seven. This inability to obtain clarity about real and pretend is one of the reasons that four-year-olds tend to be easily

frightened or confused by television and dreams—it's hard for them to know where reality leaves off and imagination takes over.

Play Is a Medium for Learning

Children learn through play, which is a medium just as paint is an artist's medium. With paint, an artist studies light, shape, composition, and texture. An artist may paint the same thing over and over, reworking how to represent an item of interest. So it is with children's play, which is a necessity in their struggle to understand themselves, the world around them, and how they respond and fit into the world.

Children are consumed with their interests. Alice will play kitties. She'll draw them, even *be* them, meowing to her friends. She'll choose books and puzzles about them, and make them out of clay and playdough. She'll cry to be picked up if she sees one—or she'll run and grab it! Alice is studying the world and where she fits within it.

Each year, there are new play themes centered on power and control. Boys are particularly enamored of such themes. They want to be in action—climbing, running, feeling big and strong, getting away from danger, avoiding hot lava and quicksand and monsters. Groups of boys often hurry about the classroom helping each other with an emergency situation, and then rush elsewhere in the room trying to escape another one.

When a new children's movie comes out, the children who see it will reenact the movie for weeks, assigning each other roles: "You be Bill, and you say this." Soon, even children who haven't seen the movie will be playing 'Bill' and verbalizing the movie's script, as all the children get caught up in the excitement of an adventure, the interchangeability of real and pretend, and the satisfaction of succeeding as a member of a social group. Through their play, children consider important questions such as "Am I safe?" and "Can I be strong?"

TEACHER AS "PARTICIPANT OBSERVER"

A teacher's role in children's play is to set the ground rules that will keep everyone safe and that will help the children make choices and not feel overwhelmed by the drama. Often this means slowing down the play and

getting the children to talk about their ideas. "Tell me who you're pretending to be," the teacher might ask.

If children are running away, the teacher should observe carefully to see if there's a designated "bad guy." If there is, the teacher needs to check to see if the person assigned that role really wants to be a "bad guy," because children almost never want that role—even when they've told other children it's okay. Helping a child speak up and stand up for herself becomes the curriculum inside the play. How often does it happen that someone is placed in a role they don't want? What can be done to help children who take the role of victim feel empowered and deserving? These are thoughts in a teacher's head as she works with children, taking on the role of the "participant observer," objectively studying and assessing the situation at the same time she's actively teaching.

Teaching four-year-olds is subtle and opportunistic. The teacher is always observing. Here are examples of times she might step in to redirect, refocus, or extend children's play:

- To clarify language, as in this exchange: "I wonder what you mean when you say he's stupid." "Oh, stupid means he can't tie his shoes, and I can." "Well, he doesn't understand that you're thinking about shoe tying when you say 'stupid.' Maybe you can show him what you know by offering to help him tie his shoe."
- To keep children actively constructive and positive, ensuring that each child has his say.
- To keep the play contained.
- To help children stay within the bounds of school rules.
- To keep one group at play from interfering with another group at play, all the while careful not to interfere with the children's ownership of their play experience.
- To quietly set an appropriate toy nearby to extend the play and allow the children the successful experience of being kind, thoughtful friends.

Literacy and Abstract Thinking

An interest in books and writing often emerges among older four-year-olds, who have a stronger ability to focus than younger children have. Previous exposure to printed materials and observation of adults writing give children this age a strong sense of what literacy is about, even if they're not yet writing and reading on their own. They understand there is a system of communication embedded in the written word, and they want to begin to understand it and use it. For example, children may want to write messages to each other or to their parents. At first, teachers write messages for the children, discussing, as they write, the letters and their associated sounds. Then, as a child becomes more able, she can begin to write for herself.

Some children write easily and become sought-after scribes: "Hattie, will you write a sign for our fort that says 'No Girls Allowed'?" The power of the written word and an interest in the codes and symbols for the sounds will catch fire in a group as their thinking matures enough to comprehend abstract ideas. This ability to think abstractly is a beginning sign of reading readiness.

Fear of the Unknown

Parents often worry about the fears that arise among four-year-olds: children may suddenly refuse to go to the bathroom by themselves, or need all the lights on in their room at bedtime. Monsters, dreams, and death are prominent fears at this age. Because a child's thinking is not yet fully categorized, she begins to fear things she isn't able to understand: What might be there in the dark bathroom? Can the monsters in that movie find my house? A four-year-old can't always distinguish between fantasy and reality. A teacher knows that these fears are signs that a child's brain is growing. Four-year-olds are able to perceive that their understanding of the world is incomplete.

With this in mind, teachers should choose toys for the classroom that stimulate constructive, positive play experiences, keeping monsters, dinosaurs, guns, and other scary and disruptive toys out of the child care environment. Dinosaurs fight, bite, and growl, behaving in ways teachers are trying to discourage as children move toward greater social competence. At home, reading about dinosaurs, thinking about dinosaurs, and talking to grown-ups about dinosaurs are fine activities. However, teachers can still encourage parents to try to eliminate scary stories, violent TV shows, and scary movies at home, to help diminish a child's fears, along with his need to play out his fears and worries at school.

A teacher knows that dinosaurs, monsters, and guns can stimulate aggression and fear, and can put socially immature children in the difficult position of trying to regulate behavior that is beyond their ability to control. A child may play monster or dinosaur by himself in a play-alone area, but the teacher does not allow a child to use such games to scare and intimidate other children. She wants all the children to feel safe at school and to know that they can trust her to help them and to keep them safe. When a child is focused on fear and worry, she's less open to learning, tends to react emotionally, and may feel out of control. The more she acts out of control, the more likely it is that another child will get hurt or a teacher will become dominating and overcontrolling. The delicate balance of power in the classroom relies on proactive teaching, so that children can practice managing themselves and can experience success in their social learning environment.

Emotional Manipulation

Four-year-olds can be emotionally manipulative as they work to build the empathy necessary for successful social experiences. Hurting other children's feelings and then getting their feelings hurt in return seems to be one way children learn about how to be and not to be a friend. It's a difficult shift in thinking to move from treating your friends like you own them and expect them to do what you say to actually caring whether or not they want you as a playmate. As adults, we know that judging ("That's mean") and manipulating ("If you let me play, I'll let you hug my teddy at naptime") are, in the long run, not how people become true friends.

<table>
<tr><td>

Teachers closing out the day

</td><td>

As evening falls, the teachers begin to quiet the children and help them get ready for the arrival of their families. Vigorous play is limited and quiet activities are set out: books on tape that children can manage on their own, toys that can be played with alone, soft toys, and fewer group activities, so children need not compromise or share during this low-energy time of day. Teachers begin tender grooming activities: they comb hair, wash children's faces and hands, and offer a light snack. The teacher's role at this time of the day becomes more parental; teachers offer more support and don't expect children to manage too much on their own. Many of these children have been at school for eight or nine hours, since early morning, and they're tired.

</td></tr>
</table>

An Objective and Neutral Teacher Maintains Calm

Teachers want children and their parents to reunite pleasantly and enjoy their evening together. Knowing how "emotionally porous" young children are to the feelings of adults, the late-afternoon teachers want to fill children with feelings that will help them be happy and positive when they see their parents, so that their family relationship will be strengthened and supported. Teachers know that when they themselves are happy and relaxed, the children will be also. When adults are tense, stressed, or angry, and are in a hurry to go home, then children behave as though they too are stressed. At the end of the day, teachers thus need to try to hold their own feelings in a neutral place, so the children will have the opportunity to experience their own feelings and find support in managing them, without needing to separate their experience from the teacher's reaction to that experience.

When a teacher holds her emotions in check, she also extends respect to the children she's working with, helping them have successful, happy play experiences, so the children can see themselves as people who are competent and worthy of love and respect. A teacher must support a child's developing self-esteem as she helps the child study emotions through his mistakes and hurt feelings. This is an important key to working with young children and it becomes even more important dur-

ing stressful times of the day, such as during morning separation, during nap and waking from nap, and during the transition to home.

Remaining neutral does not mean that a teacher acts without feeling. It means that the feeling the teacher projects is nonjudgmental, that it includes an open curiosity about how a child will face and solve her challenges, and a loving compassion for the complexities of navigating the world as a four-year-old. All young children need to feel loved and cared for, accepted and respected for their own unique qualities. That can best be accomplished from a baseline neutral position. But there is never neutrality in a teacher's joy, love, support, or connection with the children.

READY *for* KINDERGARTEN: FIVE-YEAR-OLDS

7

DEVELOPMENTAL AGE RANGE

56–78 months

Children engaging in cooperative play

racy, a big boy who just turned five, discovers that if he tips the heavy wooden box up and pulls it across the sand he can create a wide, smooth path in the sand. Soon, he's busy dragging the box around the yard, making a track. Max steps onto the track and begins running behind Tracy on it. Vanna and Will watch from the slide, then slide down and join in running with Max. When the box gets too heavy, Tracy calls to Kate, "Come on and help me make the racetrack! This box is heavy!"

Tracy and Kate pull the box awkwardly around the yard once more, then plop it down. "This box can be the starting line for the joggers!" Kate calls out. "Let's go!" Max, Vanna, Will, Tracy, and Kate all jog carefully around the track—knees up, arms bent, fists clenched. When the track gets too full of footprints, the children stop running and drag the box around the yard some more in order to

form a clean track. Other children playing in the yard look up and comment as the racers go by. When Billy wanders out and tries to go the opposite way along the track as the joggers, the joggers defend the path as their territory and their game. Deciding he's not interested in jogging, Billy wanders off.

Completing one of many laps around the yard, Will grabs the box and says, "Hey, I have an idea—bring this big guy to the tree" (he pats the box affectionately). "Then we can climb up and jump out of the tree!"

"It's my box! We're using it!" objects Tracy, sitting down in the box. "We're jogging, and we need it for our track and that is that!"

The teacher, observing from the other side of the yard, steps a little closer to the children.

"How 'bout our track goes by the tree then," suggests Will.

"OK, let's do it!" agrees Tracy.

Will and Tracy drag the box close to the tree and plop it down. As the children line up to start their next lap, Damani runs over and says, "Give me some room, I have my light-up jogging shoes on."

"No more room, we're squished," replies Max.

Damani looks crushed. Tracy says, "Well, we need a starter person. You be the starter person and say 'Mark, get set, go.'"

"OK," agrees Damani. "Your mark, get set, go!"

The children take off again, pleased to have an official starter. As they run close to the tree, Vanna reaches out and slaps it, saying, "First base." Those behind her follow her lead, smacking the tree as they round the corner. When Vanna reaches the box again, she says, "Starter base," and slaps it. Soon the children are all calling out "First base" and "Starter base" as they pass the various landmarks, with Damani periodically calling out "Stop!" or "1, 2, 3, go!"

Cooperative Play

In the previous vignette, the teacher observing the children noted their newly emerging cooperative play. When the play threatened to disintegrate, the teacher stepped closer to reassure the children that she would be there to help them if they needed her. Her presence alone was enough

to give the children confidence to negotiate past the problem. Their social development has reached the stage where they want to play in a group. They're starting to care more about sustaining a group play theme than about doing things each in their own way. They've learned to be flexible enough and big enough in their thinking to be able to shift plans a bit as needed in pursuit of a play goal. And over and over through the years, their teachers have given them the right balance of helpful support and space to figure things out, so they could develop cooperative-play skills.

GOALS FOR FIVE-YEAR-OLDS

- Become part of the group
- Learn to conform to an adult's wishes by setting aside personal desires
- Work independently
- Take responsibility for their own behavior
- Show heightened interest in print, literacy, and math concepts

---

When Will had a bright idea but realized the group was not interested in following it, he was able to come up with a compromise that was acceptable to the group. Vanna's idea of adding "bases" made the play even more compelling, adding an element from older children's play that this group had not yet quite grasped: playing games with goals, bases, and so forth. As the children take roles as leaders and followers, they learn how to be part of a group and to follow another person's plan. This level of flexibility and confidence in their ability to manage, along with their ability to listen to each other and to the teacher, tells the teacher that after a few more months of practicing this kind of play, they'll be ready for kindergarten.

From age four to five, young children change in so many ways. Their arms and legs grow longer and their baby fat disappears—even their posture matures, their "preschool look" nearly gone. Along with a taller, thinner shape come advances in problem-solving abilities, emotional management, abstract thinking, and the expression of needs and feelings. Prekindergarteners also show an increased capacity for empathy and an

improved ability to listen to others' concerns. Their use of words and their interest in vocabulary and print deepens. Rhymes and nonsense words spring up spontaneously as they sing and chant during work and play. Of course, prekindergarteners still need a teacher's guidance from time to time, but many teachers feel the prekindergarten class can almost run itself, so competent and able are the children.

Children at work through playing

In the cognitive area, teacher Anne places a manipulative she invented, consisting of a grid on a square piece paper. In each square is a circle, randomly colored in with a primary color. Next to the paper, Anne sets a small bowl of primary-colored objects to sort: plastic counting bears, colored disks, and wooden beads.

When Anne later observes the children using this manipulative, she notices that the children first count and sort the objects by color. Soon they begin making up games with the objects, saying things such as "Yellow ones get to hop to yellow dots." All the children become interested in the games; some just watch, while others wait for a turn to invent a game.

After most of the children have taken a turn inventing a new game, two boys, Anthony and Jorge, who have been playing outside, come inside and discover the setup. They begin to sort and play, but their play goes in a different direction. Anne notes that the two boys are referring to the sorting objects by "flavor." Instead of saying "yellow" or "red," they say "lemon" or "cherry"—it makes the game even more interesting for them to organize, sort, and think about flavors! The sorting soon changes focus from flavors to "getting a fair share." Both boys happen to have older siblings at home, and the play becomes a vehicle to explore a real-life experience, taking on a deeper value. The boys' thoughts become organized, fluid, purposeful, and imaginative as they discuss who gets "the most" and as they place differing values on different colors: cherry is more coveted than lemon, for example.

Anne stays nearby, listening and supporting Anthony and Jorge's play and redirecting children who want to join the boys: "They're busy

now. You can play with them later." She wants to protect the learning that is going on. Anne knows the boys will likely soon forget about this game, but she also recognizes that this play is important. She knows the boys are learning about how important it is to feel that you're respected and treated fairly. They're also learning such premath concepts as sorting, sets, equal, larger, and smaller. This kind of play will help them throughout their lives: on the Little League team in a few years, with their high-school girlfriends, and, much later, in their business dealings. Anne feeds the boys new vocabulary, occasionally making a comment such as "Hmm, I know candy is sold by the pound, and sometimes people sell sugar by the peck!" Anthony and Jorge don't bother to respond to Anne, but before long they begin referring to "pounds of candy" and "pecks of sugar."

"Squishy!" announces Jon loudly from the drawing table. He is folding a paper airplane when this lovely word pops into his head. "Squishy!" responds another boy, who is building a train track. Both boys repeat "squishy" a few times, have a good laugh, and then go back to their play. An hour later, as the group settles to listen to stories, the boys greet the teacher happily, "Squishy!" Thinking quickly, Anne pulls out a book of poetry to read before she starts the story she'd chosen earlier. The children are obviously interested in the sounds of words and in fun onomatopoetic sounds. The poetry book is full of interesting words and rhyming sounds, and Anne realizes her story time will proceed more smoothly if she reads a book to the children that follows and builds on their interests.

Developing language and literacy through play

Later, next to a bowl of toys, Anne sets a mat with pockets glued onto it and letters of the alphabet written above each pocket. She imagines the internal conversation a child might have as he plays with this equipment. He might recite the alphabet as he searches for the perfect object to put in each pocket. No matter how the play manifests, Anne feels confident that the child's play will be just right. As he sorts and orders the toys in the bowl, saying their names aloud and listening to the sounds they make, and as he sees the corresponding letter for each sound, the child self-initiates his learning.

Anne later notices Anthony, who isn't yet ready to match sounds and letters, playing with the new material. He just pokes any object into any pocket, which, while not the play Anne originally envisioned,

still promotes the good hand-eye coordination that is part of getting ready to write. As he moves objects, Anthony is thinking, trying, and practicing, building confidence, competence, and attention span—all important skills for kindergarten readiness.

Anne observes that Sophie, who rarely explores the manipulative area, is choosing to play in the dollhouse again today. To ensure that Sophie will gain experience with sorting, counting, and other math concepts, Anne earlier placed a wooden birthday cake with candles in the dollhouse to elicit learning behaviors such as counting and singing.

In another area of the room, Jasmine, Jorge, and Ben start to play restaurant. Anne offers them a clipboard with a pencil and paper to write down orders, and she gives them words they can copy if they choose to make a menu. Mimi and Jon wander over to the sand and water table, where they sort sets of plastic fish into "families," with a big daddy, a middle-sized mommy, and two small baby fish. Mimi decides she wants to divide up the fish and sort them by type, instead of families, at which point Jon loses interest and begins to pour water over a design Mimi had made out of stones on the bottom of the water table.

Play Is the Work of Young Children

Anne wants the children to make their own choices according to their own interests, so they will "own" their learning. This style of teaching aligns with children's development and interests, and supports and personalizes learning. Anne realizes that if she had sorted out the toys for the grid she invented, telling the children, "There is one yellow, or lemon; two red, or cherry; and three green, or lime," she would have been leading the children's thinking, and the children's play experience would have been based on Anne's thinking rather than their own. The children's sense of themselves as competent, successful learners would have been undermined. By simply placing a developmentally appropriate toy out where children can find it, she implicitly tells the children: "Explore, discover, think. Whatever you discover is good."

Through their play, children learn things about the world and about how best to interact with others. This is what teachers mean when they say "play is the work of preschool children." When children play and ma-

nipulate materials in fun ways, concepts such as math are much more easily mastered (Healy 1994). Anthony and Jorge explored math concepts as they played: the concepts of *equal, order,* and *sequence,* as well as addition and subtraction concepts such as *take away, less than, more than, next, equals,* and *same as.* But math is only a small part of what the boys were learning. While playing with objects in a *concrete* way, they were also using the objects in a *symbolic* way. They were thinking on many levels at once: sorting colors, counting, imagining the taste that different colored objects might have, and exploring the social dynamic of fairness. They were also building the ability to visualize a problem in their mind.

KNOWING WHAT CHILDREN NEED

As a teacher teaches, she is always observing, noticing children's interests and how they play. This observation of the "big picture," looking into the distance and seeing trends in the children's growth and needs, is essential to effective teaching. Without it, a teacher is unlikely to set up her classroom in ways that will give the children what they need. For example, if a teacher notices a sudden interest in sorting and ordering, she might think about ways to incorporate more sorting and ordering activities into the classroom in order to help the children build those skills for elementary school. She wants to support their explorations, trusting that if they have good materials, they'll bring their own ideas, experiences, and interests to the toys and thus expand their thinking.

CREATING A WORD-RICH ENVIRONMENT

A teacher understands that it's her job to facilitate children's interest in understanding the people around them and the world they live in. She does this through her ability to create a classroom and an outdoor environment that help the children build on their experiences and expand their thinking and understanding through their play. Naturally, language is an integral part of this learning experience. Songs, rhymes, chants, real and made-up words all add to the warmth and joy of a busy, happy classroom.

Most four- and five-year-olds love playing with words. They naturally rhyme, sing, and chant. Just as a babbling infant delights in changing the sounds she makes, four- and five-year-olds love the complexity of rhythm and rhymes. Wordplay helps the ear hear subtle sounds in

language. Fingerplays, poems, songs, and nursery rhymes all help children build an understanding of the complexity of language and attune their ears to the subtle differences between similar sounds.

In her *American Educator* article "Overcoming the Language Gap," Louisa C. Moats writes about "linguistically rich and linguistically poor children" (2001). Moats studied why some young children who learn early on to decipher words and to "read" begin to fall behind by the fourth grade. The children studied didn't seem to have a strong foundation in "word knowledge" via a word-rich environment that provides a context for learning new words. The lack of such a foundation can lead to rote learning of vocabulary with only partial understanding of a word's meaning. When adults use a broad vocabulary, including words children may not know, children naturally expand their own vocabulary. A teacher should use interesting words when she speaks, checking in as needed to see that the children understand what she's saying. She should do this with caring and warmth, in order to build a human connection that opens the children's hearts and minds to learning.

A teacher uses lively, interesting vocabulary in conversations with the children and also chooses quality children's literature to read to them, because the language in books is much richer than that of everyday speech. Books with limited and repetitious vocabulary are designed to help children have successful early reading experiences, not to expand vocabulary. For example, the words in Dr. Seuss's *Green Eggs and Ham,* "I do not like green eggs and ham! I do not like them Sam I am," were chosen specifically to create success for new readers. Contrast those lines with these lines from Robert Louis Stevenson's poem "Time to Rise": "A birdie with a yellow bill / Hopped upon my window sill." A broad variety of authors who use interesting, novel, and challenging language should be represented in the mix of classroom books.

It is through play, however, that the visceral meaning of words becomes established in a way that helps a child remember and understand what words mean. Playing outdoors making mud pies, roads, and rivers using one's hands, and then associating this imaginary play with the words that play creates in the mind (*squishy, slippery,* and *sloppy,* for example) builds a depth of understanding of the meaning of the words that reaches beyond the intellect.

CHOOSING PLAY MATERIALS

When Anne chooses a book, changes toys on a shelf, or sets out something new in the block area or the dollhouse, she thinks about what the children will learn from the experience of playing with the new material. Her success in guiding the children's thinking rests on her attunement to each child's developmental stage and skill and her understanding of what children need in order to be ready for a successful kindergarten experience.

Anne is confident the activities she's chosen are good uses of a child's time. All create readiness for a more structured kindergarten experience in which the children will be asked to do what the teacher says and to learn what the teacher thinks is important. Anne has learned that the first step on the road to the conformity needed for a successful kindergarten experience is early experimentation through play.

"Anne! Anne! How do I make an R? I want to write 'I love you Rikki,' and I don't know how to make an R," Lupe calls out.

"Let's find one," says Anne, as she heads to the book area. "I wonder where we'll find a word with R in these books? RRRR." Anne makes the sound of the letter R.

"Here is The Runaway Bunny. *RRR is in 'run,'" says Lupe.*

"Right," says Anne, picking up the book. "I hear that RRR sound too, and here is R." Anne begins to describe how to draw an R as they look at the letter in the book. "One long line, a round top, and then a long line down. Now you can write the R in Rikki's name. Do you have paper?"

Anne steps back as Lupe gets busy writing. Anne remembers how chaotic Lupe's home environment was when she first started at this school. She was mostly cared for by her deaf grandmother, so her communication consisted of a piercing screech, and she didn't seem to have any concept of books or stories. Lupe had no idea what to do with a book other than to hit people with it. When a teacher opened a book to show her the pictures inside, Lupe's eyes grew round as she exclaimed,

> *Teacher using storybook as the context for writing a letter*

Teacher individualizing curriculum to support social-emotional development

"How do dat?" Lupe hated story time; she fussed and would not sit still or listen.

Gently and quietly, the teachers made a plan to help Lupe. Whenever they could, they made it their job to make friends with her. They let her explore, offered to hold her on their lap during story time, stationed themselves near her to help her with words in social situations, and made eye contact with her as she played, so she would feel safe and cared for. They listened to her carefully and asked her open-ended questions such as "I wonder why?" or "What do you think?"

Before long, one of the teachers discovered that Lupe liked bugs. The teacher showed Lupe how to look under leaves and turn the compost pile by the garden. Together they studied the sow bugs and tried to count their legs; they looked for the white spots on their underside and waited for them to uncurl. Later, the teacher found a simple picture book that included a sow bug picture. Carefully, they counted the bug's legs in the picture. The teacher took the little storybook and put it on the shelf in the book area. Before long, Lupe let the teacher cuddle her up on her lap with a book, as one might read to a baby.

The teacher began by reading the shortest, simplest books to Lupe. Soon Lupe and the teacher had a private reading moment each day. Lupe loved the attention. When other children came around, the teacher welcomed them. Before long, the teacher began to introduce simple stories about grandmas and about going to school, reading to Lupe about things she was familiar with and interested in, to add to the books' value and meaning.

"Looking at Lupe now," thinks Anne, "no one would guess how far behind she was and how hard the teachers worked to help her when she began coming to school here two years ago. She's all caught up now, she loves stories and poems, her attention span is good, her speech is clear, and she listens to the teacher. She knows how to be a good friend, and she shows all the signs of being ready for kindergarten.

Social and Emotional Readiness for Kindergarten

Kindergarten readiness encompasses far more than reading readiness and math readiness; in fact, most kindergarten teachers feel that social and emotional readiness are more important than reading and math skills. A child who can't be a successful member of a kindergarten group will not be able to succeed in school. In 1990 the president and fifty state governors established National Education Goals, the first of which states: "All children in America will start school ready to learn." They developed a research-based document that addresses the needs of the whole child for success in school. The National Education Goals Panel incorporates the following qualities into its assessment of kindergarten readiness (1997; see appendix E):

1. Physical well-being and motor development: The child should be healthy, alert, and energetic, and able to give full attention to learning experiences and other tasks in the school setting.
2. Social and emotional development: A child who has developed a positive sense of well-being will demonstrate the emotional security necessary for successful interaction with peers and teachers.
3. Approaches to learning: Positive attitudes, habits, learning style, and motivation in early childhood will transfer to the elementary school classroom.
4.. Language development: The ability to interact and communicate effectively with adults and peers is essential for success in the elementary classroom.
5. Cognition and general knowledge: Children who are encouraged to explore, experience, and question the world around them in a play-based program are ready for the new, more structured learning experiences of elementary school.

It's safe to say that most children who are not considered ready for kindergarten and who are placed in a prekindergarten classroom probably have greater need to develop social skills and emotional maturity than to develop cognitive skills.

Academics Are Built on an Emotional Foundation

Academic gaps can generally be filled very quickly and easily in a child who is ready to learn. Preschool children learn in undifferentiated ways.

Some of the important skills children need—to be ready to read, for example—are being learned through surprising areas during play. To be able to read, a child's eyes need to be able to track from left to right, to focus at the proper distance, to distinguish individual letters and words, and to be able to keep track of their place on the page. These eye skills are easily developed through vigorous outdoor play: climbing, running, stopping and starting, judging where the foot should go next or how far it is to the other child on the swing. Large-muscle activities are far more effective at developing these skills than is sitting at a table working on a worksheet. Drawing and painting at an easel, however, can be helpful in developing tracking, hand-eye coordination, and small-muscle control.

Typically, children begin reading between the ages of five and seven. Some children start reading earlier, while others are not ready until they're older than seven. The age at which a child begins reading has less to do with a child's intelligence than with brain maturation. Children who are exposed to reading early obviously have more practice reading than those who start later and can therefore seem more advanced in their learning, but as later-starting children are exposed to reading, the difference between the two groups evens out.

Early readers are often better spellers than later readers, which is not surprising since spelling has more meaning to a reader than it does to a nonreader. Because it's easy to test spelling, adults are sometimes fooled into thinking that early reading gives children a greater advantage than it actually does in the long run.

Reading, like math, requires not just decoding but also abstract and symbolic thinking in order to make the connections that will construct meaning from sentences. How does a preschooler develop the ability to constantly adjust his schema to incorporate new knowledge and become an intelligent reader? This mental dexterity occurs over and over again during a child's self-selected play (particularly in thoughtfully designed learning environments) and during a child's everyday living experiences. A child's thinking develops more naturally through play than through overly structured, adult-directed teaching. It cannot occur at any age, however, if the brain is not physically ready.

Young children have an extraordinary ability to memorize. Much of their early learning is in fact dependent on memory. But there's a big difference between memorizing words and comprehending them, and between memorizing numbers and understanding the concepts of sequence and quantity. A child can always be taught to memorize information, but it will have little meaning without the context provided by life experience and play.

In order to learn to read, a child must inherently understand that letters are symbols that represent a sound, and when those symbols are placed together in a sequence, the sounds from the symbols combine to form a word. Toys are also ultimately symbols: a doll, for example, is not actually a real baby, and on some level, two- and three-year-olds know this. They play symbolically with toys of all kinds, which develops their understanding of how to manipulate symbols.

Ordering, sorting, and sequencing are important precursors for the visual dexterity needed to sort letters, words, and numbers. When given the right materials and environment, children can perform such activities almost unconsciously as their brains mature. By the end of a child's fourth year, it's almost impossible to stop children from sorting and ordering their world. These behaviors are clues to teachers about the level and progress of a child's brain development.

Mimi, Bea, and Jasmine have been playing a long time on the climber. While Anne cleans up the porch, she listens to the girls' play. Turning to take some toys inside, Anne sees Bea's grandmother coming to pick her up and take her to the doctor for her five-year-old checkup.

"Gram, Gram," calls Bea, "guess what we're playing?" Before Gram can guess, Bea blurts out, "We played that we were all white girls!"

Gram looks taken aback. "Oh, dear," says Gram, looking upset.

"Yeah," yells Mimi from the top of the climber, "then we played we were all delicious chocolate brown girls!"

Jasmine, smiling, chimes in, "Then we were all lovely yellow marshmallow girls, like me."

Gram, looking a little confused, smiles at the girls, but says to Anne, "What are they talking about? I want my Bea to be proud of her race. Why are you letting them say those things?"

Teacher interpreting developmentally appropriate understanding of racial identity

Anne says, "I think it's important for all the children to be proud of who they are, and race is certainly an important part of that. But today these children seemed to be interested in sorting and organizing. They were talking about skin color in that context. They weren't thinking about race, just about sorting and classifying. Sometimes I have to remind myself that even though children say grown-up things, they don't think like grown-ups. I'm glad it was you who came in just now. If Mrs. Smith had walked in, she would have heard them deciding she was the fattest mom in the school. With her baby due any minute, I imagine she doesn't need the honor of being called the fattest mom in the school!"

"I imagine not," remarks Gram. "Anne, you know I take race very seriously. I don't want Bea to feel anything but good about her color. This is very important to me. I think you should have said something to those other girls. You should not let these children call people 'fat' either; it's rude."

"I understand," responds Anne. "If I'd felt they were saying anything racist, about any of the races they were talking about, I would have stepped in and clarified any misunderstandings. But because they really were focused on talking about sorting and categorizing everyone, I felt that if I began to make racial interpretations about the things they said, I really would have been teaching racism."

Anne continues, "I did suggest they use the words 'big' and 'small' instead of 'fat' and 'thin' for Mrs. Smith and the other parents, telling them that some people don't like to be called 'fat.' I could tell by their faces that they didn't want to upset Mrs. Smith and I could also tell they weren't buying 'big' and 'small'; those weren't the right words for what they were thinking about. In their minds, 'big' means 'tall' and 'small' means 'little.' I also talked with them about kindness and how some people don't like it when they feel people are thinking only about how they look and not about who they are. They weren't very interested, because they were thinking about sorting and I was talking about something that was abstract, off the topic, and irrelevant to them.

"I'll be on the lookout for any race issues and keep helping the children factor in important qualities like kindness whenever I can. I can assure you that this sorting really wasn't about anything other than observing facts and trying to make some kind of order in this big

wide world. It shows us they're getting ready to think categorically, like they'll need to do in kindergarten."

Anne concludes, "As for what Bea was thinking about race in this situation, I'd just ask her."

Bea's grandmother thanks Anne for her explanation and advice. As Gram and Bea are leaving, Gram asks Bea, "I hear you've been thinking about all the colors people come in. What got you to thinking about that?"

Bea replies, "I was thinking that brown mommies go with brown babies but that J.J. down the street has a brown mommy and a pink dad, and that's a mix-up!"

Gram, thinking about what Anne has just told her, smiles and says, "Well, let's talk about that," as she and Bea climb into the car.

Bill, a high-school boy who does community service in the classroom, rolls into the room in his wheelchair and goes to the book area to read stories to some of the children as they wait for their parents to pick them up. Anne sees Abby run to the bathroom when Bill enters the classroom, and follows Abby to make sure she's okay. Abby avoids eye contact with Anne as she says, "I don't like that new teacher."

"Oh, you're thinking about Bill and his wheelchair, and you don't like him. I wonder what it is you're not liking?" inquires Anne.

"His chair makes a noise," says Abby.

"Hmm, I heard it too. Remember we talked about how he was coming and that he would have a chair with wheels and a motor to help him go? The motor makes a little rumbling noise. That was a surprise."

Abby sighs and looks out into the yard.

"It's kind of different, a chair with wheels and a little rumbling motor," says Anne, putting her arm around Abby.

"I don't want him to come to my school," says Abby, looking into the classroom over the teacher's arm.

"Well, you know about people," smiles Anne. "Everyone is different and everyone is learning."

Teaching about Differences

Asking a child to explain what she's thinking about is a smart way to build a relationship with her as a basis for discussing a difficult topic such as race. This kind of "fact finding" helps a teacher gain closer insight into a child's thinking, giving the teacher an opportunity to more accurately respond to questions and comments. A four-year-old who asks, "Where did I come from?" may not be asking about the facts of life but rather which city he was born in, in which case a long explanation of the facts of life would be off topic. In order to be viewed as a trusted, dependable adult, a teacher wants a child to know he is being listened to and that the teacher is paying attention and thinking about what is being said. This is good modeling behavior that shows the child how people interact with each other and how the teacher would like the child to behave toward her. It also shows that the teacher knows the child is a reasonable, thoughtful human being working to figure out his world. This attitude is especially important when helping children understand people who are different, such as people with disabilities or other special needs.

When children say things about issues of difference that adults think are cute or funny, it's often because the child is working to understand something she hasn't quite figured out. This is, for example, how some children respond to people with special needs. The response usually is *not* funny or cute to the child. Teachers who want to help children build social skills and form relationships and deep attachments need to be sure the children are not looked at as objects with cute, funny, and surprising behaviors. Some children are quite afraid of wheelchairs, unusual sounds, or unusual behavior. Some children think they can "catch" disabilities, which may lead them to behave in unfriendly ways toward people with disabilities. This negative behavior reflects the child's fear and lack of understanding.

Asking a child what he's thinking about is a respectful and sensitive way to find out what's going through the child's head, and his response gives the teacher some idea which direction to take when she responds. A teacher wants the child to know she cares about how he feels, so she's careful to be sure her response is attuned to the child's feelings. She wants to build his confidence, so he'll feel that he'll be taken seriously when talking about his feelings and confusions. Such teacher behaviors build rapport, attachment, and a strong relationship with the child. The teacher also knows that by treating the child with respect and compassion, she's teaching him to respect and care for others.

"Everyone is different and everyone is learning" is a comforting and truthful comment to share with children. It's a variation on the theme that we are all the same and we are all different, a statement that as adults we have all come to know and understand at many different levels. In the depth of such truths and life experiences, the preschool teacher has the opportunity to help five-year-olds as they develop the capacity to think about their own behavior and about the world they live in.

During rest time, Anne reads some poems, followed by a chapter from a storybook, while the children rest on their mats. Those children who have outgrown naps enjoy this restful story time. It was a few years ago that Anne started reading chapter books to the five-year-olds during rest time. The books don't have pictures, so as the children rest they use their imagination to form pictures in their mind to go along with the story. At first the children kept asking to see the pictures, but when Anne showed them the pages of words and the occasional ink drawings they stopped asking for pictures and just listened. The children love special "grown-up" stories, and they remember the stories from chapter to chapter.

Some children doze off and are allowed to sleep even after the others go outside to play. Anne recognizes that five-year-olds are still growing and changing and that they need the child care program to support their growing bodies. Some children rest and others sleep during rest time, but all benefit from the calm and quiet. After rest, they'll digest their lunch better and recoup energy to make it through the rest of the day.

Anne knows how hard it can be for social five-year-olds to settle down and rest. She also knows that an elementary school teacher is likely to expect these children to be able to turn their focus away from

Teacher using story time to regulate the pace of the day

their friends, settle their body down, think their own thoughts, and do their own work.

"Let's see what's happening in chapter seven today," begins Anne, as the children cuddle down on their mats, snug with their blankets and stuffed animals. Reading softly and without a lot of drama in her voice, Anne helps those children who need to sleep relax and drift off, while encouraging the children who don't sleep to listen attentively.

After rest time, the children who are awake get their shoes on, put their mats away, use the toilet, get their sweatshirts or jackets, and go outside to play until the sleeping children get up (or the teachers wake them). Teacher Lucy goes on her lunch break.

Later in the day, Anne puts a big piece of cardboard on the porch and sets up a place for many children to work together on a project. Anne puts out tape, cardboard tubes, string, and paint for the children to use. The children are soon hard at work painting and taping on "parts."

Teacher facilitating cooperative play and learning

"How do you spell 'BEWARE, this is a trap'?" asks Mia. Anne begins to spell, but then says, "I'll write it out on a piece of paper and you can copy it. I need to keep an eye on all the children now."

Each of the children clustered around the cardboard contributes his or her idea about traps. "I'll make the cheese," says Paul, crumpling up a wad of paper and taping it to the cardboard as he begins to paint. "I'm making the hole that catches you," says Andy. "Wait, wait! We need a string to trip up the bad guys," says Jasmine, putting string on the cardboard and taping it so it hangs down off the edge of the cardboard. "I've made a sign that says 'Go away,'" adds Vanna, coming from the classroom with a paper covered with letters she made at the art table. She adds her paper to the trap. And so it goes.

The children work together, having agreed on the project. Anne put out the materials for the project, but the creation of the trap began with one child's idea. As other children expressed interest, the idea expanded. Anne stays involved with the children as they work at cooperation. She watches for tippy paint cups; adds more tubes, string, and paper as needed; and reminds the children that everyone will do their part in their own way.

All the children are talking about the trap. They all know how it feels to be trapped, and this feeling is being expressed through their

work. Anne uses her body and her words to set a calming tone while she supports the children's exploration of the feelings and emotions that go with traps. She wants the children to succeed and to grow in confidence as they learn about themselves, their feelings, and what it means to work together on a project.

Taping the last strips of paper, with holes strategically placed, Paul announces, "That's it—here's the bait." There is satisfaction in the mood of the group. The children seem proud of all they can do. Anne recognizes that her facilitation probably would go unnoticed by an untrained observer, but without her emotional presence, the project could easily have disintegrated. It was her steady presence and the confidence and safety she projected to the children that helped the children complete their project and hold their behavior in check. Anne feels satisfaction that cooperative play occurred; she saw cues in the children's play that signaled they were ready to include more children.

The day draws to a close. Anne smiles as the program director, Mary, comes into the classroom. Mary works the last two hours of the day in this classroom, and as Anne finishes her cleanup, she and Mary chat.

"Just put the trap on the shed roof to dry. I think the children might like to work on it some more tomorrow," says Anne.

"I'm glad to get back to work with the children for a while," says Mary. "Soon I'll be writing kindergarten entrance reports for them. I want to really watch their play so I can write good, accurate first drafts. Then I'll pass the drafts to you for your comments, Anne."

"Sounds good," says Anne. "I think the children are doing so well."

Mary takes the small notepad from her pocket and jots a note about the sign Vanna made. She will add the note to Vanna's report, as it shows just where Vanna is developmentally and it will personalize her report.

The Kindergarten Assessment Report

The evaluations for kindergarten readiness are a rigorous exercise the director and teachers do both for the parents and the children. Parents depend on the reports being objective, so they must be truthful and caring.

Reports, which are written after many days of observation, should take into account the cumulative observations over the child's life at the center. One goal of the report is to help elementary school administrators and teachers who will soon be working with a child understand that child's learning style, academic level of readiness, temperament, and social competence. In some cases, when a family is applying to a private or charter school, the prospective school's staff will use the report to assess whether a child and her family are a good match for the style of their school.

When a parent requests a progress report or a kindergarten assessment, the process might go like this:

1. The teachers begin the process by discussing the child at the regular staff meeting. The director and teachers discuss areas of strength along with areas of concern in the child's growth and development.
2. This meeting is followed by more in-depth observation before a rough draft is written.
3. The rough draft is passed out to the teachers for comments.
4. The draft is finalized and given to the child's parents for their comments and approval.

Teachers need to give an honest, positive, clear picture of the child as she is seen at preschool. The preschool should partner with parents; it's important that the report be shared with parents before it is sent to an elementary school. Doing so acknowledges that the parents, more than anyone else, need to know how their child is doing and in what areas their child might benefit from extra support. It's common for parents and teachers to meet for a conference to discuss the report once the parents have reviewed it. During such a conference, teachers might discuss which schools could be a good fit for the child and her family, if the family is considering something other than their local public school. Even if the child will be attending an assigned public school, parents will be more informed advocates for their child if they have a thorough understanding of the child's learning style and strengths, as well as areas in which the child needs adult support.

Assessments may be done at any time, not just as preparation for kindergarten. For example, parents may request an assessment of their child

when it is needed to support interactions with other professionals, such as doctors or therapists who are working with their child.

WHEN TO RECOMMEND MORE TIME IN PRESCHOOL

Children who have had delays in language development often need more time in preschool before they're sent to kindergarten. The ability to use language clearly and proficiently is usually a reflection of a child's thinking process. Since the bridge between language and thinking is built during constructive free play, children struggling to order words and express abstract ideas such as feelings, worries, and dreams can benefit from extending their preschool experience.

Children with weak social skills also can benefit from more playtime. A preschool teacher must think of the development of the whole child. Teachers recognize how important it is that children receive support for social skills. These skills are embedded in play experience and are an important part of a preschool child's learning. Preschool is perhaps the only time children have the opportunity to get adult support and help with these important life skills.

Other children who might benefit from additional preschool time are children who have experienced trauma or loss. Trauma diverts the typical trajectory of development for children by forcing them to work at understanding the feelings, fears, and confusion that accompany the trauma. Children who've had to face trauma can catch up developmentally through extra playtime, during which they can work out the changes they've experienced.

Readiness Is an Accumulation of Skills

Although teachers working with infants are not exactly thinking about a child's departure from the center to elementary school, they play a role in preparing each child for this eventual transition. As four-year-olds become five-year-olds, the teachers begin to observe all the components that will predict a child's readiness for kindergarten learning. Kindergarten readiness is an accumulation of skills. As a child ages, the information she accumulates becomes more and more complex and interdependent. At each stage, development is carefully observed, supported, and maximized

by thoughtful teachers, so each child can progress wholly and naturally toward the next major shift in the brain's development, the shift that marks a child's ability to succeed academically. At age five, a child is progressing toward this shift.

The five-year-old begins to move toward latency, which will be complete by age seven. Piaget writes of the *concrete operations* that occur at age seven—the ability to hold multiple concepts in the mind at the same time. Erik Erikson views seven-year-olds as entering the age of *industry versus inferiority,* at which point the child moves from *play* to *work.* Kohlberg speaks of the first signs of a conscience appearing at this age.

It is notable how many different theorists, studying many aspects of child development, have incorporated into their stages of development a dramatic shift at age seven. The shift explains why many children do not learn to read until age seven and why many schools do not teach reading until the child turns seven, particularly in other countries. While the American approach to education in recent years has been to try to hurry children's learning—by moving first-grade curriculum into kindergarten or even prekindergarten, for example—the truth is that evolution has not picked up the pace. The human child today needs about the same things a child needed centuries ago. Technology may become obsolete every few years, but the human mind is still growing in the same way it has for thousands of years. The result of that growth is that, somewhere between the ages of four and seven, most children will have built the connections they need in order to learn how to read.

The Multiple Layers of Readiness

School readiness reflects all the complexities and multiple layers that make up a human being, including physical development; social skill and emotional competency; language skill and comprehension; and aesthetic and cognitive ability. As a child grows, each area of development ebbs and flows; different areas dominate at different stages of development. At each stage, accumulated knowledge comes together and forms the foundation from which the next round of information-gathering will grow.

Physical development is very important in an infant. In the fourth year, however, aesthetic development takes precedence over physical de-

velopment, which has, by that time, been mastered to the level of a child's need.

Learning and thinking occur when a person feels calm, relaxed, and loved, so a child's environment and the accompanying ambience need to be kept conducive to learning. It is the responsibility of directors and teachers to create a safe, loving, responsive world at school, one loaded with interesting, achievable activities that have a nice balance of calm, quiet, and busy excitement. Creative ideas occur most often when the body and mind are in a state of homeostasis, at which time random thoughts can unexpectedly percolate into the consciousness. Stress, pressure, physical punishment, competition, and shame interfere with this process or lead to resistance. Humans can be forced to do, memorize, or say things, but they cannot be forced to learn. Learning is a much more delicate process, a little like growth; it must be fed and nurtured so it can develop from within.

A child's freedom to play and to make choices is another important element influencing a child's development. Along with a healthy environment and a teacher's understanding and support, through choice a child learns to self-regulate, manage his energy output, experience the consequences of his behavior, develop self-discipline, and internalize self-control.

Another element is the flow of group play. Teachers control and stabilize the energy of the group. Like a counselor managing group therapy, a teacher knows how to keep emotions from dominating the ambience of a classroom.

Through all these elements and layers, children develop competencies that strengthen their ability to relate to the world and to other people. At each moment in her life, a child takes in new information, integrates it into her existing framework, and then reconfigures it based on her newly expanded understanding of the world.

The Importance of Group Play

When children turn five, a teacher learns to support and anticipate a change in their play. Knowing that five-year-olds will want to play together in larger groups than they did at younger ages, the teacher arranges the classroom with more space for large groups to play, open rug

space, and large tables where six children can sit together and draw. Young children have more successful play experiences when they play in twosomes or occasionally threesomes. Until a child turns five, he rarely has accumulated enough knowledge and experience to be able to manage play with four or more friends, each of whom carries different ideas, abilities to cooperate, and levels of language comprehension and usage. At age five, larger group play can succeed.

As already mentioned, kindergarten readiness reflects an accumulation of skills and abilities, some more obvious than others. One of the most important kindergarten-readiness skills emerges through group play. When the number of children who want to play together increases, the opportunities for children to organize each other and work together increase as well. This play prepares preschoolers for kindergarten, where they will learn to allow the teacher to organize them to work together on a project of the teacher's choice. A child's familiarity with group play will therefore help him understand his role within the kindergarten class.

Another important kindergarten readiness skill learned through cooperative group play is the acceptance of delayed gratification, which, ironically, grows from getting what you need right away when you are young and cannot wait. Having the ability to cooperate implies not only that a child can work in a group and do what someone asks, but also that there is strength and integrity in her sense of self and a maturity in her ego development. These qualities help keep a child from taking things too personally or from always feeling a need to be first or best. Self-control and responsibility for one's actions are also required in cooperative play.

Putting Policy into Practice

The recommendations of the National Education Goals Panel, discussed briefly at the beginning of this chapter and summarized in more detail in appendix E, are based on sound research that acknowledges the unique learning style of preschoolers. The panel recommends that all children "have access to high quality and developmentally appropriate preschool programs that help prepare children for school." Two other objectives address the importance of parenting and health care. To quote the report:

"Taken together, the goal and the objectives represent an important departure from past thinking about 'readiness' in several ways. . . . [They] tacitly acknowledge that narrowly constructed, academically-driven definitions of readiness heretofore widely accepted need to be broadened to incorporate physical, social, and emotional well-being. Finally, the Goal and its objectives affirm the connection between early development and learning, and children's later success in school and in life" (1997).

Such policy, which is based on sound research, can fail in getting legislative approval, sometimes due to political ambitions, and at other times due to a genuine failure to understand that the mind of a preschooler is different from the mind of an elementary school child. Early care and education teachers play an important role in "translating" well-intentioned public policy into appropriate classroom practice. Teachers mandated to meet the goals of national educational legislation such as No Child Left Behind or of publicly funded programs such as Head Start can make opportunities to educate parents and policymakers about how young children learn, and can work together to find creative ways to meet mandated goals.

If a teacher is expected to teach four-year-olds to associate sounds with written words, for example, she can help children develop that skill through their play, recognizing that children's knowledge acquisition through play will be far more meaningful and long-lasting than any that might come from sitting in a circle chanting "buh, buh, buh" while a teacher holds up a book. By sharing with parents her knowledge of children's learning styles and by helping parents know how to prepare their child for school, a teacher can also ensure that *parents* are included in children's literacy education. School readiness activities that parents can do at home with their children include reading with them every day, exhibiting an interest in written materials, and including children in everyday activities such as cooking, fixing things, gardening, shopping, sorting laundry, and setting the table.

The educational goal of preparing children for kindergarten is not so much to teach them specific skills that will be part of kindergarten curriculum, but to mold them into active learners who are confident and ready to take on the many tasks that school will set before them. They will need self-help skills, a sense of independence, and the ability to make new friends, to get along with difficult people, and to follow school routines.

Children who are highly successful in kindergarten typically also enter grade school with a well-developed vocabulary, a love of books, a strong desire to learn to read, logical thinking and problem-solving skills, curiosity, concentration, persistence, and creativity.

ROUTINES, TRANSITIONS, *and* SCHEDULES

8

Routines, transitions, schedules, rules, and procedures are the backbone of any quality preschool or child care center; they establish the flow of the day and give the child and the teacher freedom. While they can be thought of as tedious details, the order they create in a busy school or playroom allows the children and the teachers to move their focus beyond management and safety to the larger goals of learning and teaching. Defining these building blocks, which are essential to a well-functioning playroom and school, draws attention to the value they bring to a learning environment and to the place they hold in creating a culture, vision, and philosophy of a preschool program or child care center.

Programs for young children manifest quality through the wisdom, care, and thoughtfulness with which they create internal structures. In turn, these internal structures promote order and predictability. They are held in place by the teachers' commitment to consistently

implement them, teach them, and reinforce them. Consistently reinforced activities become routines, and routines become habits.

Creating Positive Habitual Responses

Habitual responses often occur before conscious thought does, and they can last a lifetime. Working with young children is a serious commitment, carrying with it responsibilities for the well-being of human life. Teachers must take the weight of their job very seriously, as it has moral and ethical overtones and requires personal discipline. Children learn through the modeling behavior of the people they live with, so teachers and directors must model the behavior they want to see from the children. Knowing that routines quickly turn into habits in the developing brain of a preschooler, it's very important to think carefully about what habits are being created.

Table manners, for instance, are simply a habit. Saying *please* and *thank you* is a habit—and whining, begging, biting, and yelling are also habits. Quality programs structure a child's day so that negative habits are not reinforced but positive ones are. Schedules, rules, procedures, and transitions create and continually reinforce positive lifelong habits. Negative habits such as whining, hitting, and biting often occur accidentally during a child's random experimentation with cause and effect: big reactions encourage repeated experimentation. Biting is a good example of an action that receives a big reaction—both from the child who has been bitten and from the adult who is minding the children.

Guidance and clarity about how to best react in a given situation, proactive behavior management (ensuring that children's needs are being met and that children feel understood and supported), and consistent implementation of schedules, rules, and procedures support the wholeness of a young child's learning. Putting a young child in a quality child care program or preschool is like immersing him in a very controlled world where teachers intentionally support positive learning experiences. This environment builds the child's level of trust as well as his family's level of trust. When a child and his family feel safe and secure, the family will work to support the teachers' work at home, and the natural, crea-

tive energy of the child will come out in the form of play, exploration, and learning.

Providing Security and Predictability

Young children often feel helpless and powerless. They are, in fact, pretty powerless over adults and over the world around them. Routines give a child a sense of control over herself and a feeling of predictability about the world. Routines also teach children constructive habits, such as washing their hands after using the potty. When a child can anticipate what's coming next, her energy is freed up to focus on important learning opportunities.

A child at home with a parent or other caregiver experiences routines that occur unconsciously. In child care centers, routines, schedules, rules, and procedures emulate the sense of order found in a well-run home, while also offering children alternative responses to habits developed at home.

Rules, routines, schedules, and procedures give children a sense of security and predictability, spur the acquisition of self-help skills, and promote independence. When a child is allowed, for example, to wash her own hands and to dress herself, she learns how to take care of herself, gains confidence, and develops trust in her own abilities—behaviors that build healthy self-esteem, resilience, and problem-solving skills, which are important tools for success in elementary school and beyond.

Teaching Social Skills

Sometimes routines expand beyond concrete instruction (how to use a toy or manage one's jacket) to address social skills (how to approach another child and invite play). Teachers create the social culture of the school and classroom by modeling for children how to talk with each other, by making the playroom a safe and comfortable place in which to learn and to make mistakes, and by building a harmonious group dynamic. Here is an example of teacher language used to help establish a routine social approach:

Upon seeing a child standing at the slide yelling out into the yard, the teacher goes to the child, gets down at the child's eye level, and says, "If you want to play with Joe, go right over to him and say his name, so he'll know you're talking to him. You can say, 'Joe, come slide down the slide with me.' Joe doesn't know what you want or that you're talking to him if you stand by the slide yelling, 'Come here!'"

By establishing for children a positive, constructive pattern to help them learn how to ask another person to play, the teacher builds a supportive, friendly, respectful group culture and establishes a framework for a productive learning environment. The teacher is also establishing a habit, summarized by the following formula:

To ask a friend to play:

1. Go close to the friend
2. Say the friend's name
3. Tell the friend what you want

Young children often also need help with making a socially acceptable response to an invitation to play. They need to hear, for example, that yelling "No, go away!" is not socially acceptable, but that saying "I'm playing with Jim right now, but I'll play with you later" is acceptable. It's common even for smart, verbal children to need help when they feel social or emotional pressure. Creating and practicing constructive responses builds social skills and helps children accurately express their feelings and emotions.

Establishing a Consistent but Flexible Schedule

The *schedule* is the order of daily activities laid out in a consistent sequence that usually is tied to a timetable. The midday routine may be:

Time	Activity
11:00 – 11:25	Story
11:20 – 11:30	Washing hands
11:25 – 11:50	Lunch
11:40 – 12:00	Bathroom
11:45 – 2:00	Nap

Once established, the order of the schedule never changes, although times may be adjusted according to the needs of the program. For example: The children are enjoying stories so much that the teacher decides to start story time earlier so she can read longer books; or, the bathroom is getting too crowded after lunch, so one group starts lunch a little earlier so they'll be out of the bathroom before the second group arrives. The flexibility of the schedule takes into account individual needs. Some children eat quickly and then go right to the bathroom and then to bed; others eat slowly and need plenty of time to use the bathroom and prepare for bed. There is therefore overlap in the schedule, during which time some children are involved in completing one activity and others are beginning the next activity.

Although this midday schedule may seem simple and straightforward, it has evolved through the years according to the children and the spaces, and it continues to be adjusted regularly as individual and group needs change. Corresponding to this midday schedule is a teachers' schedule, which indicates who should be where at what time and who is responsible for what. Filling in all the pieces requires a grid. For example:

Time	Activity	Staff Arrangement	Spaces Used
11:00 – 11:25	Story	Ann and Bea, each with half the group	• Inside block area • Outside porch area
11:20 – 11:30	Washing hands	Ann, inside, sends a few children at a time to wash hands, while reading poems to the rest. After all are washed, the group goes to Bea, outside, who sends her group in to wash hands.	• Inside block area and bathroom • Outside porch area
11:25 – 11:50	Lunch	Bea helps the first group settle at the table. Ann supervises hand washing and sends children out as they finish washing. Bea helps children get settled at lunch. Ann comes out with the last children and sits at one table, while Bea sits at the other.	• Bathroom • Outside porch area
11:40 – 12:00	Bathroom	As the first child finishes eating, he clears his dishes and goes into the bathroom, followed by Ann. Bea shifts to supervise both lunch tables. Each child may continue eating until satisfied, then clears dishes and goes to the bathroom. Ann remains inside to supervise children as they come in one by one to use the bathroom.	• Outside porch area • Bathroom
11:45 – 2:00	Nap	After children use the toilet and wash up, they find their nap mat and sit down to take off their shoes and socks and cover themselves with a blanket. Ann stations herself in the doorway between the bathroom and classroom to supervise both areas. When the last children come in from lunch, Bea goes into the classroom and begins to help the children on mats who need attention. Soon, Ann joins her in the nap room.	• Classroom, with napping mats out • Bathroom • Outside porch area

Quality Transitions

A *transition* is the orchestration of the time between the activities. Children transition from home to school, from the play yard to the lunch area, from the lunch area to the bathroom, and from the bathroom to the nap area. The time spent going to sleep is also a transitional time. Between times are part of a child's life experience; they not only set the tone for what follows but also provide opportunities to communicate respect and build self-esteem. If children spend time idly waiting or feel herded along and rushed during transition times, an adult's needs or programmatic requirements are being put above the children's needs, making the children feel disempowered and disrespected.

TREAT CHILDREN AS INDIVIDUALS

Treating young children as individuals is important to the development of good self-esteem. When it's time to transition from one area to another, children who are individually asked to move and who are allowed to complete the activity they're involved in before moving can then move independently while remaining under the teacher's gentle supervision. This allows teachers to avoid moving children in groups or lines, and it demonstrates to the children that the teacher understands their needs.

Developmentally, preschool children see themselves as individuals. They don't think of themselves as part of a group of children until about the time they go to kindergarten. While it's possible to line up preschoolers and move them, for example, from lunch to nap or from yard to classroom, guiding children so that each child is allowed to manage his own transition is developmentally appropriate and reinforces a child's confidence in managing himself. Creating a transition that is a subtle, unobtrusive, gradual change from one environment, play space, or activity to another takes thought and planning.

Teachers work as a team to cover each area as the children move slowly and independently from area to area. One teacher supervises the area the children are leaving, encouraging them to finish up and move along to the next area, while another teacher takes the children who are ready to transition, settles them into play (or lunch or rest), and prepares

to receive and settle more children as they finish their activity in the area with the first teacher.

HELPFUL HINTS AND TECHNIQUES FOR SMOOTH TRANSITIONS

- In choosing which children to ask to clean up and transition, teachers should look for children who appear most ready to change what they're doing.
- The teacher should speak quietly and directly to one child at a time, saying the child's name so the child knows she is being spoken to.
- All team-teaching partners need to be aware of the plan and of their part in the plan before it begins.

Here's an example of a transition from yard to playroom in a group with a ratio of six children to each teacher. This technique can be used almost anytime a teacher needs to move children from one area or activity to another.

What the teacher is doing	What the children are doing
Anna quietly tells four children whose play seems to be wrapping up that it will soon be time to clean up.	Children finish their play.
Anna returns to each child a few minutes later and tells him or her it's time to clean up and go inside. She helps the children clean up, so that they can learn how.	Because of the previous warning, the children are now ready to stop their play and to follow the teacher's model in cleaning up.
When Anna leaves the yard with four children, Blanca repeats what Anna did—warning and then helping four children clean up.	Warned children leave play much easier. When the teachers help them clean up, they're learning that cleanup follows play.
Anna takes the first four children to the hand-washing area, where they use the toilet and wash hands two at a time.	The children go with the teacher, enjoying as much independence as possible. They practice their self-help skills as they use the toilet and wash hands.
When the children with Anna finish washing and toileting, she takes them into the playroom and helps them transition into play.	Children quietly enter the playroom, choose where they would like to play, and settle down at an activity.

What the teacher is doing	What the children are doing
Blanca brings the second group of four children to the toileting area. The children use the toilet and wash, and are then sent to Anna in the playroom, where they will get started playing and learning. There will now be eight children in the playroom with Anna.	Children follow toileting and hand-washing procedures. They then go individually to the playroom, where Anna will receive them.
At the time Blanca left the yard with four children, there were still ten children left with Charlie in the yard. Charlie warns four children, helps them clean up, and gets them ready to go in to use the toilet and play.	These children also are following a procedure for playroom entry that provides predictability and security at school.
Charlie sends four children individually to Blanca, who has remained in the hand-washing and toileting area. Blanca helps the children, and then sends them to the playroom with Anna. Anna now has twelve children in the playroom.	Three teachers are now working together as a team, helping each child transition from activity to activity.
Charlie sends four more children to Blanca. As these children finish with their toileting, Blanca goes with them to the classroom with Anna. Now Anna and Blanca are in the playroom with sixteen children.	Two teachers are now working together to help the children in the playroom. Each child has been able to enter the playroom quietly and find what he wants to do in an unhurried manner.
Charlie engages the two remaining children to help straighten up the yard. He then takes the children to the bathroom.	The final children in this group transition from the yard to the playroom.
Charlie and the two remaining children join the group in the playroom. There are now three teachers and eighteen children in the playroom. The transition is complete.	The children have had the individual attention they need and have been able to focus on themselves as they transition from the yard to the bathroom to the playroom.

Flexible Classroom Rules That Provide Order

Generally, *rules* are standards that have been universally agreed upon throughout the school and that support the safety and harmony of the group. Here are some examples of rules:

Children keep their shoes on at school.
Children who want to play outside on cold days wear a jacket.
Children sit down while they are eating.

Such rules create order and predictability, keep the children healthy and safe, and support the harmony of the group. Because she is always modeling, the teacher follows the rules. Rules such as *Sit on chairs, not on the tables* and *Speak in a friendly way* apply equally to teachers and children. Rules are straightforward, logical, and honest. Jackets are worn when it's cold outside so that children stay warm; shoes stay on feet so that feet don't get injured. Rules that are consistently reinforced soon become routine and no longer need to be mentioned.

Often, new teachers and new children hold tightly to rules as they try to feel at home in a new environment. Two-year-olds, who tend to be developmentally rigid, love rules; four-year-olds, who sometimes act a little out of control, think rules are for everyone but themselves. It's very important that rules have some flexibility during the preschool years. Since preschoolers are individualistic and tend to see themselves not as part of a group or team but rather as an individual in a crowd, a rule can have real effect only if each individual child understands the rule. As children get older, rules begin to involve group agreement, such as when children set the rules for a newly invented game.

Children are usually cooperative if a rule makes sense to them. But even if children agree in principle that, for example, *No hitting* is a good classroom rule since no one likes to get hit, if someone happens to take a toy a child is using, he may still feel perfectly comfortable hitting the child who took his toy. So even when a rule is seen by children as making sense, the teacher still must help the children work toward the goal of following that rule as they learn to manage their impulses and emotions.

Children often respond well to comments that imply they have forgotten a rule. For example, a statement such as "Oops! We forgot your jacket and it's cold outside. I wonder where your jacket is hanging?" will often inspire a child to happily look for the jacket without any need to discuss rules. A word of warning, however—by four-and-a-half, some children are embarrassed about forgetting or making mistakes; if this is the case, a more subtle interaction may be more successful, such as a whispered reminder or a wink and a hand motion with no words spoken. The object is to consistently reinforce the rules while helping the children feel respected, happy, and cared for.

Procedures

Procedures consist of a sequence of behaviors that allow a child to successfully use toys and equipment. For example, the procedure for drawing at the drawing table might be:

1. Check to see if there is a chair for you at the table.
2. Get a paper from the shelf and put it on the table.
3. Choose the material you want to draw with (crayons, markers, or chalk) and take the basket of materials to the table.
4. Sit down and draw.
5. Take your finished picture to your cubbie.
6. Put the basket of crayons away on the shelf.
7. Push in your chair.

Every activity has a procedure, whether it is painting at the easel or washing your hands. Once a procedure has been learned, a child can play freely in the yard and classroom. When procedures for washing hands, eating lunch, going down for nap, or painting at the easel are established for the two-year-olds and stay the same for the three- and four-year-olds, children have a lot of freedom and independence because the procedures then become habit, and they are free to focus on other areas of learning.

Here is an example of meal procedures used at one child care center.

- Each child chooses a spot and sits down at the table.
- Appropriate eating utensils, plate, glass, and napkin are properly arranged and set out at each available eating space.
- The food is in small bowls at the center of the table, to be served family style. Small pitchers of water and milk are also on the table.
- As soon as the children are settled, the teacher sits at the table with the children.

- The teacher demonstrates good eating practices and the proper use of a napkin and silverware. She supervises the passing of the food, and refills the small serving bowls from a larger one as needed. The children serve themselves and pour their own milk.
- The adult sets the tone for a pleasant mealtime. A quiet, calm atmosphere prevails during eating times. Pleasant topical conversation is appropriate for older children, whereas most conversation with the younger children centers on meal activities and food.
- When children finish eating, they get up, push in their chair, take their plate to the dish tub or tray, scrape off excess food into the trash, put the silverware into the proper container, and stack the plates and cups.
- After most meals, preschool children are offered the opportunity to visit the bathroom, wash up, and use the toilet. They then proceed to the next activity.

Many routines and the use of almost all the toys and equipment have procedures to go with them. Knowing the procedures for play allows children freedom in play. Procedures dictate the parameters of the play, not the details. For example, the painting procedure specifies that paint goes on the paper; it does not specify what the child can or should draw. Block procedure specifies how many children may use the block area together and how high a block structure can safely be built; it does not specify what children can or should build. Once children learn how to use the toys and how to put them away when they're finished, they can choose and use whatever they want in the playroom and in the yard, without needing permission or help from the teacher.

PROCEDURES SUPPORT INDEPENDENCE

To create a unified culture in a center, all the teachers in the school must know and use the same procedures under the same circumstances and for the same activities. Once a procedure is instituted, teachers reinforce it as children move from group to group. Children experience mastery,

competence, and freedom. When teachers are consistent and persistent, children learn and automatically follow procedures competently and easily, with pride in their ability to manage their independence. Even the simplest activity or task has a procedure. The point of the procedure is to give children a structure that will allow them the freedom to choose activities that please them as they move freely through the classroom.

The following is an example of an obvious, simple procedure that can be used with children from age two to five for the use of manipulative and table toys:

1. The child selects a toy from the shelf and takes it to table.
2. The child sits at the table and uses the toy.
3. When done with the toy, the child returns it to the shelf.
4 The child pushes in his chair, to ready the space for the next child.

The teacher supervising the manipulative area first observes if a child needs help. She may make suggestions to help the child understand the toy. The teacher wants to support the child's focus on the task he has chosen for himself, so she avoids unnecessary conversation that would draw the child's attention away from the task at hand.

PROCEDURES SUPPORT LEARNING GOALS

While helping a child, the teacher wants not only to support the child's learning experience, but also to help the child meet a certain goal. When a child is putting together a puzzle, for example, the child's goal is to complete the puzzle. The teacher's goal for the child may be something different, however; it may be her goal that the child learns to keep his focus on the task at hand rather than on the children playing nearby. Well-thought-out procedures should free up the teacher, allowing her to meet such goals and to teach on many levels and to several children at once. It allows the teacher to individualize curriculum and to teach to each child's unique skill set, temperament, and abilities, helping each child progress along the typical trajectory of healthy development.

The Teacher's Goals:

- To support the child's self-competence.
- To aid the child with proper use of equipment, if necessary.
- To support the child's freedom to explore the equipment.
- To encourage the child to focus on one toy at a time and to focus on completion of an activity through play.
- To track the child's interest and attention span.
- To draw the child's attention to his behavior in order to build self-awareness and self-control and to encourage problem-solving skills.
- To help the child recognize when he is done with a toy, and to put the toy away when finished.
- To protect equipment from being lost or broken.
- To protect the child from being interfered with by other children (by encouraging other children to choose other toys).

The Child's Experience:

- Learns how to begin an activity.
- Learns to make choices.
- Enjoys free play and exploration.
- Learns through play.
- Enjoys the process of learning about a new activity.
- Learns to complete an activity by returning a toy to the shelf and then moving on to another activity.
- Learns to care for playthings.
- Learns that the teacher has confidence in his ability.

PROCEDURES SUPPORT LITERACY

The book area is a cozy, quiet, pleasant space where children can relax, imagine, and enjoy the joy that books bring, with or without a teacher nearby. Each teacher at the school should follow the same procedure when reading stories to the children. The teacher should draw the children's at-

tention to the book through her calm demeanor and quiet respect. She wants the children to focus on the words and the beautiful pictures rather than on her. Because the children are learning vocabulary as well as developing an imagination, it's important that they hear the same words in the same order each time they hear the same story. The teacher can also help the children by talking about the pictures and asking questions about the story while she reads to the group. However, children over two years old should be encouraged to listen to one short story without interruption. Younger children like to point at and talk about pictures.

Story sessions should be short, in order to ensure successful listening. The teacher needs to be careful to control discussion about the book so that it doesn't distract from the experience of the story. A child who is being disruptive or who would rather talk than listen can be redirected to another activity or held in the teacher's lap.

Here is a sample procedure for story time:

1. The teacher takes a small group of children to a quiet place.
2. The children sit quietly facing the teacher, without other books or toys in their hands or on their laps.
3. The teacher selects a book appropriate for the age group, and holds it so that all the children can see the pictures.
4. The teacher reads the story.

The Teacher's Goal:

- To read books in a quiet voice.
- To set an intimate, cozy tone.
- To model how nice books are, and show pleasure in the pictures and in the story.
- To carefully choose books that communicate appropriate messages through words and pictures.
- To ensure that the story or pictures are about something familiar to the children.
- To show the children that she's looking at the written words, so they are aware of her tracking the sentences.

- To note the beginning and end of the story
- To ensure that the children are comfortable and can see and hear the story.
- To adjust her reading position so there's no glare in the children's eyes and all children can see her.
- To show the children that story time is a pleasant learning experience.

The Child's Experience

- Learns to listen.
- Learns to take delight in books.
- Develops a longer attention span.
- Learns to pay attention to the story and to the words rather than to the other children nearby.
- Memory and imagination are stimulated.
- Becomes aware of the correlation of words on the page to the story.
- Learns to relax.
- Imagines and identifies with the story.
- Listens for rhyming and wordplays.
- Builds vocabulary and literacy skills through labeling of objects and repetition of sounds.

Children enjoy looking at books that have just been read to them, as well as choosing different books from the shelf. Older children need very little supervision in the book area, while younger ones need to be taught how to handle books. It helps to have book rules for children to follow, such as:

- We open the book flat.
- We don't fold books backward, because that damages the spine.
- We turn the pages carefully, because they are delicate.
- We return the books to the bookshelf when we're done.

■ To avoid having books get stepped or sat on, we choose one book at a time, look at it, and put it back before taking another.

PROCEDURES SUPPORT CREATIVE EXPRESSION

Although preschool children are often quite verbal, they continue to experience the world mainly through their senses, through movement, and through big feelings and unspoken intuition. That's why the expressive medium of painting, using color and sensuality, is a tremendously satisfying medium by which to facilitate communication and expression. The following procedure for children painting at an easel was used in nursery schools during the 1940s; it's still being used in schools today.

1. The child chooses an apron, puts it on, and pushes up the sleeves.
2. The child brings a cup of paint from a low table near the easel and puts it in the trough on the easel. The child chooses one color at a time to place in the trough.
3. The teacher (or the child, if able) puts the child's name on the back of the paper.
4. When the child wants to change colors, she replaces the paint cup on the low table and selects another cup of color, which she places in the easel trough.
5. When the child is finished painting, she returns the paint cup to the table.
6. The child gets the clothespins with the hook on top (sometimes called lingerie hooks) from the basket on the low paint table. She attaches the clothespins to the bottom end of the painting paper. Releasing the painting paper from the easel hooks, the child carries the painting by the clothespin hooks to the drying line, and hangs up the painting to dry.
7. The child takes off her apron and hangs it on the easel.
8. The child washes her hands (using the hand-washing procedure) and pulls down her sleeves.

Built into this easel-painting procedure are some interesting controls. By teaching the child to choose one color at a time, the clarity of each color is preserved as much as possible, so other children will also be able to choose and enjoy clear colors. Having just one brush and one cup in use

at a time helps ensure that the paintbrushes are replaced in the cup from which they came, further ensuring that colors stay true. Children can mix colors on their paper if that is their interest. Part of living in a group is ensuring that all children have a clear work space and fresh supplies. Teachers can observe the child's work, admire the painting, and name different colors for the child, but should avoid unnecessary conversation and avoid asking the child what he's painting or suggesting things he could paint. The child's work and the child's experience should take precedence.

Children are primarily interested in the process of using materials. The sensuousness of slippery wet paint, the surprise of drips, and the ways colors mix together are a child's first experience of easel painting. Later, the child enjoys covering the whole paper and creating patterns and designs. For young children, art is often more about process than product—it's the adult mind that wants to inquire, "What will you make?" In order to better support a child's learning and growth, a teacher should rarely share her adult perspective with the child. As a child becomes able to draw representative art, the teacher can join with the child in admiring this newfound ability.

Most classrooms have an art area, apart from the easel painting, where children can color, cut, and sometimes tape things together. Crayons and scissors can be made available to young children throughout the day. While the teacher doesn't participate in children's drawing, she may help with drawing letters or with learning to use scissors. Children can choose paper, crayons, and other materials from a nearby shelf before sitting down at the art table to draw or color. When children are done, they can return to the shelf the materials they used, and then take their drawing to their cubbie or to an area to be displayed, as appropriate.

An art area is often a social spot where children sit and chat and draw variously throughout the day. The teacher therefore needs to put art materials where children can reach them easily, and she should carefully choose art supplies that require little or no adult supervision. The children can work very independently. Art projects that require adult help and attention should be set up at a separate table where the teacher can control the number of children engaged in the project and manage her availability to the group.

Rules, Schedules, and Procedures Support Social Development

Developing sensitive and supportive rules, schedules, and procedures requires specific teaching skills and is the backbone of any play-based program that is developmental. These items create consistency and repetition, build routine and habit, and free up both the teacher and the children from the chaos that can occur when a busy group of young children is exploring and experiencing the child care world. Consistent repetition helps build the social skills and communication competency that will eventually develop into socially acceptable habits. Above all, rules, schedules, and procedures create order and predictability.

Other children most interest a child. A classroom of eighteen or twenty children, however, even when children are focused and busy, can feel chaotic to a child. Adults are generally pretty predictable, but another child might do just about anything. If a child asks an adult if she can play with the blue car, most adults will agreeably hand over the blue car. But if the child asks another child for the blue car, the other child might cry, run away, hand over the car, bite, throw the car, or laugh—the possibilities are endless. When faced with the unknown and the unpredictable, a child may be reluctant to reach out and try new things; she may behave in defensive and resistive ways. Such behavior is not conducive to optimal learning. It's therefore crucial that teachers establish schedules, procedures, and rules to create an orderly environment that is safe, comfortable, and supportive.

Nurturing Communities and Cultures

The world is big and unpredictable for little children. The systems we create in society help make the world feel safe and predictable. We first encounter systems in infancy, through the basic procedures our caregivers follow, such as diaper changing and feeding. As we age, some of the responsibility for maintaining systems shifts from the caregiver to the child; we learn how to implement procedures that help us create order in our individual world.

Just as an infant feels safe and supported resting on a caregiver's chest, hearing the calming heartbeat, so the structures in an older child's day create a beat or pulse of understanding and attunement. In some American Indian tribes, the vibration of the drumbeat is thought to reflect the Earth's heartbeat—the pulse of life. Addressing the wholeness of what it means to be a human being is part of the early childhood teacher's job. It helps children develop into happy, healthy, productive citizens. Thoughtful teachers stop and think about such things, because these things speak to the deep organic part inside us. Observing the correlation between life experiences and a child's response to those experiences gives the teacher an indication of how the child will build his personality, habits, and reactions.

All over the globe, when people come together, they create community. Whether intentional or not, a "culture" of acceptable ways of being comes into play within a company, school, family, church, or temple. Teachers create a culture of living and working together in their school and in their classroom, whether or not they're aware of it. When they *are* aware of it, they can create that culture with thought and intention. This part of the preschool teacher's job is rarely discussed; it's part of the "big picture" awareness that is characteristic of quality care.

Teachers and therapists look for the level of attunement that exists in a child's world—the degree to which the child feels that his true self and his responses to the world around him make sense in the eyes of the adults who love and care for him. Quiet, sensitive parents who happen to have a child who also is quiet and sensitive know just how their child feels when he screams and shakes as the garbage truck makes loud noises; these parents are attuned to their child. The child experiences the attunement as an affirmation that who he is and how he reacts is reasonable and at one with life's flow. This is one way that the adults who care for children communicate to them that they are safe, understood, and "okay." This is the beginning of how children learn to get along with each other and, eventually, become friends with each other. Attunement gives the child a feeling of security and confidence.

SUPPORT FOR THE WHOLE CHILD

There is another kind of attunement that is also very comforting and stabilizing, and that is attunement to nature and the Earth—that "heartbeat"

that brings us to the feeling of "being at one." It is when teachers are aware of this pulse or beat that moves between the big-picture concepts, intentions, and ideals and the practical details and hands-on completion of the work that teachers can create a consistent and predictable internal structure that stabilizes and strengthens the school's culture and heartbeat. Through this process, it is the pulse, the in-breath and the out-breath, the heartbeat of the Earth that creates a school or classroom that addresses the wholeness of the human being. Building a school culture that addresses the body, mind, and soul of the child will in the long run create an adult who is able to be in harmony with the world in which she lives.

The internal structure of the school experience is the detail that brings the big-picture goals into being. Just as the melding flavors in a tasty dish become a unique casserole, so do procedures, routines, schedules, and rules become the culture of the school. It is not uncommon, however, for schools or classrooms to establish a culture quite unconsciously. A teacher who regularly gets frustrated, runs out of patience, and raises her voice can unintentionally create in her classroom a group climate in which children are sneaky and constantly push limits. Likewise, a director who is always too busy, who has no relationship with her teachers, and who ignores the children will create a culture in which families and staff do not feel cared for—and in turn, will not care for their school. Adults who have tumbled through life's experiences realize that the mind works as an important backup for the heart's wisdom. The importance of the heart and mind working together is rarely acknowledged in the study of early childhood education, yet it is this combination that is so essential to the development of the culture of the classroom and the school.

LOVE

It's unconventional to openly discuss *love* in professional child care settings—and yet to leave it out is equally strange. As important as routines, schedules, and rules are, it is love, with all its multidimensional, amorphous qualities, that is the keystone in creating the culture of a child care center. It is most definitely an essential big-picture item. No one would say that a child in a full-day child care setting should go ten hours a day without sharing feelings of warmth, joy, and support with their teachers. Teachers can never replace a parent's love, but no school attempting to create a culture of quality can succeed without the richness

and depth of human connection; in fact, children cannot thrive without this connection.

SELF-ACTUALIZED LEARNING

The culture of a school can establish control over many of the variables that influence a child's growth and development. By establishing a physical environment that is developmentally appropriate, teachers can eliminate many conflicts and confrontations. By building a smart, objective, loving culture in which positive language helps children learn to listen and respond appropriately and in which rules, routines, schedules, and procedures facilitate a child's opportunity to choose and foster a feeling of competence and security, teachers build a school culture of group care that truly supports the individual and the child's enjoyment in self-actualized learning.

Predictability allows children to feel confident and to reach out and explore, so procedures, rules, routines, and schedules must be carefully adhered to. It's the teacher's consistency that creates a child's sense of predictability. The teacher's self-discipline and attention to the child provide predictability, allowing the child to open up to the group experience and discover his own creativity and love of learning. Providing appropriate meals, consistent rest time, and naps helps children stay attuned to their body's needs. The teacher who learns to respond to children in a thoughtful, disciplined way—using her words, tone of voice, timing, and appropriate energy level—establishes in her classroom a habit of positive communication, acceptance, thoughtfulness, and loving kindness toward all, which in turn builds an attitude of friendship and compassion in her classroom, the perfect climate and culture for learning and growth.

This structure is intentionally created, so children can learn to experience success as a member of a larger group. The more positive, constructive, and objective the experience is, the stronger the habit is established to respond to challenges in thoughtful, kind ways while maintaining integrity. The internal structure of the school and classroom give children freedom to go wherever they want, do what they want, and feel safe doing it. The teacher and director model the social behavior they expect from the children. With these practices in place, the children can attune to the pulses and rhythms of life. It is the ability to float within these rhythms that allows us to access inner peace, joy, and harmony.

STAFF RELATIONSHIPS *and* TEACHER TRAINING

9

I t's 8:00 AM—the morning has begun. As teacher Laura signs in, her director, Mary, greets her: "Good morning! I've been meaning to tell you that every time I walk through your yard, I notice how healthy the children's garden is looking. It's such a bright spot!"

Laura smiles. "I'm glad you noticed. You know, I've been so happy to be able to share one of my favorite activities with the children. I really appreciate the effort you made to move that fence so I'd have a garden space in my yard. The children are learning so much about the plants and the seasons from the garden."

Mary responds, "It's been great for the children to see us working together to make the garden possible, and the children enjoyed working together moving the dirt, planning the garden, and planting and watering the vegetables. Soon they'll be eating them too!"

Over the past year, Mary had noticed Laura growing subdued. She began to suspect that since her divorce Laura had been struggling with depression. When Laura asked Mary if there might be a space where she could start a garden project with the children, Mary thought of how often Laura came in on Mondays happily describing what she'd done in her garden over the weekend. Mary knew that a garden would be good not only for the children but also for her teacher, and that the trouble of creating a garden space would be easily offset if it helped Laura regain her equilibrium and if it gave the children pleasure. Although it took a little work to reorganize the yards, once the space was identified and a few parents were recruited on a Saturday to move the fence and haul in bags of soil, the project moved quickly. Even before hearing Laura express her thanks, Mary had felt rewarded by the little sparkle she'd noticed in Laura's eye whenever she'd been working in the garden with the children. Investing in a teacher's well-being was an investment in the center's well-being.

Teachers Are Models for Children

A pitcher needs to be filled before it can pour anything out. In the same way, teachers need to be cared for compassionately so they will be able to offer caring and compassion to children. While many aspects of employment in a child care center are like those in any other business—conforming to state and federal regulations, creating clear job descriptions, training and coaching staff to be their best on the job—there are other factors that make it unique. In the business of relationship-based child care, relationships among the adults are as important as those between the children and the teachers. Caregivers who feel valued, respected, and cared for are better able to wholeheartedly care for and support the children. Young children learning about the world must see healthy, caring relationships modeled every day, so they will have working models for their own relationships. From a business perspective, most of the "product" being sold in a child care center is teaching skill; therefore, teachers are the major asset of the organization.

Caring, respect, and compassion must be more than buzzwords. The director models these traits when she, for example, makes it possible for a teacher to be present at an important family event. The director should know the staff and be available to them for consultation, consolation, or exultation about personal and professional matters. In her book *A Great Place to Work,* Paula Jorde Bloom states, "Because the human factor is the most critical factor in quality child care, programs that are sensitive to the needs of adults are in a far better position to provide optimal learning environments for children" (1997).

At the same time, a director must maintain appropriate business practices and boundaries, being careful to avoid favoritism or uneven enforcement of standards among the staff. Much as the director may want to accommodate a teacher's needs, the director's first obligation is to the children and the overall needs of the center. However, she should recognize that in the long run the center will be stronger with loyal, dedicated staff, so every opportunity possible should be taken to create a supportive relationship that will make a teacher's connection to the center rewarding and sustaining. Finding the balance between the "businessperson" role and "friend" role as an employer in a relationship-based program requires a lot of personal discipline.

Clear Communication Is Critical

Communication is at the heart of all human relationships. Knowing this, teachers carefully choose their words and monitor their nonverbal cues when they work with young children. When they speak to other adults, however, they may be in a hurry or assume the other person knows more about something than she really does, which can easily lead to misunderstandings or hurt feelings. Part of the way that strong relationships are built among adults at a center is through clear, open communication in multiple modes. For example, when a new teacher is hired, she receives written policies and procedures and a job description, augmented by an orientation conference and regular coaching from her supervisor. When this process is successfully executed, the employer's expectations are clear to the new teacher. Regular feedback from her supervisor informs her whether she is meeting those expectations. Such feedback also allows her to *hear* the expectations, rather than just read them, which is

especially helpful for people who don't read carefully or who are aural learners.

PERSONAL AND CULTURAL FILTERS

Everyone carries life experiences through which they filter information they receive from the world. Some of these filters stem from personal history and upbringing. A supervisor who gives the simple feedback, "Remember to make eye contact with the baby before you pick him up," means it as a helpful reminder to improve a new teacher's practice—and it's likely to be taken as such by most teachers. But if the director gives that reminder to someone whose upbringing has made her overly sensitive to criticism, she may be surprised to get a defensive response, such as, "I can't help it. You told me to get that diaper changed and I can't do everything."

Early care and education teachers commonly come from diverse cultural backgrounds, which can add another layer of potential complication to the communication mix. When two teachers who are English-language learners speak to each other, words may be misunderstood. What seems to one teacher to be a minor disagreement may feel like a major conflict to another, and what seems like a trivial issue to one teacher may be very important to the other. In one culture, loud voices mean *trouble;* in another, they mean *fun*. Whereas eye contact in the American culture generally indicates openness and attentiveness, in some cultures a person who makes eye contact with a supervisor would be considered disrespectful.

Also, new teachers bring their own ideas and opinions about child rearing and teaching practices gained from their own families, friends, and communities. To newcomers, it may not initially make sense to see an experienced early childhood teacher standing close by children, not stepping into the children's play until she knows she's needed. Until a teacher learns more about early-care-and-education best practices, she might be more likely to step in quickly to tell a child how to solve a problem, thinking that, since she is called a "teacher," she should be explicitly teaching at every opportunity.

ASSUMPTIONS DERAIL COMMUNICATION

The lesson in all this is that adults need to focus on the clarity of their communication with other adults just as much as they do with their com-

munication with children. While adults are more mature and experienced communicators than children are, that very maturity and experience also add complicating layers not only to the way they hear things, but also to the way they say things.

Adults make a lot of assumptions about what other adults already know and about how other adults see the world—assumptions they wouldn't make with children. For example, if a teacher invites a child to help set up the easel-painting area, she tells the child just what colors to put in which cups, what brushes to use, how much paper to put into the clips on the easels, and so on. If she instead asks a new teacher who has been working in the classroom for just a short time to set up the easel painting, she may think she only needs to say, "Set up the easel paints, please." Later, she may discover there are too many or too few color choices, that the new teacher put watercolor brushes into the paint cups, that paint has been put in the juice cups, and that there's only one piece of paper on the easel! Rather than assume the new teacher was not paying attention or that she was lazy, it's more helpful for a mentor or supervisor to recognize that she herself made a mistake in assuming that the new teacher knew how to set up paints. The mentor or supervisor should then resolve to be more explicit about what she wants the next time she gives directions to the new teacher or asks her for help.

A Framework for Quality Relationships

The framework for quality relationships among teaching staff is built on three key areas of knowledge. First, each member of the staff needs to know what is expected of her as an employee, and must have the skills and resources to be able to perform her job. Second, each member of the staff needs to know what her role is and how she can contribute to her teaching team. Third, each member of the staff needs to know how to appropriately share with other staff information and insights about the children in her care.

CLEAR EXPECTATIONS AND TRAINING
Clear communication begins at the time of hiring, when the teacher receives a job description, information about performance standards, and

her evaluation schedule. Supervisory support should also be established at the start. There are so many layers to the job of working with young children that even a fairly experienced teacher will need time to absorb and sort out all of them, which is why a supervisor serves an important role in filtering information and setting priorities for new employees. This happens in the context of a professional, objective, training relationship, with clear boundaries established by the supervisor in her role as a trainer.

Before a new teacher begins to form relationships with the children, she needs to understand the center philosophy about the role that teachers play in the classroom. In the classrooms described in this book, teachers are expected to guide and support the children while following the children's lead. These teachers do not "play" with the children, but rather help and guide the children in following their own interests. A new teacher coming into this center would need to know this from the beginning. It is part of the supervisor's job to ensure that each new teacher is given the proper tools to do her job and that she understands the program's philosophy and goals for the children.

In Personnel Management 101 we learn that employees should never be surprised. Misunderstandings can be avoided if the employer clearly states:

- job functions and expectations
- feedback received from a supervisor on a performance evaluation
- goals of the program
- expectations for attendance and absence
- pay and benefits

Every center should have a comprehensive and regularly updated employee handbook that each new employee is required to read and to review with her supervisor.

The supervisor prevents additional surprises by anticipating what the new employee needs to know and by providing ongoing feedback and training. A new teacher can't grow unless she hears what she's doing well and what she needs to work on. During orientation, she's told that her supervisor will give her regular and direct feedback. The supervisor makes a point of not just commenting on problems or mistakes, but also commenting on the many things the new teacher does well, with feedback like: "That playdough table looks so inviting" or "You helped Joe say good-bye to his dad so nicely this morning." Such feedback creates the context for a friendly, positive ongoing relationship. It is comparable to the old teaching formula: "Comment on five positive actions for every time you correct a child."

Some teachers in a supervisory role find it difficult to give clear, honest feedback when there are performance issues because they worry that it might hurt the employee's feelings to hear she is doing something wrong. Teachers who easily correct a child's mistakes ("Next time, please put the marker in the box with its cap on tight") may have trouble correcting a coworker ("Next time, please let the child wash her own hands"). The truth is, when a teacher is allowed to keep doing the wrong thing without being told, it can become an undesirable habit that will continually cause problems with coworkers and compromise the quality of care the children receive. The director and managing staff should thus work to establish an atmosphere in which everyone is treated with respect and honesty, so that new teachers learn to see ongoing, direct feedback as a vehicle for growth rather than as criticism.

Giving a new teacher the opportunity to observe experienced teachers working in the classroom is another helpful training tool, as it gives new teachers the chance to see how more experienced teachers interact with the children. While each teacher will develop her own individual style as she works with children, she also must conform to the culture of the school, understand and follow school rules and routines, and speak to and interact with children in a consistent way. When a new teacher is given time to observe the style of the teachers she will work with and to see how those teachers react to the children and communicate with them, she is likely to have more success in adapting and contributing to the culture of the school.

TEAMWORK

Unlike K–12 teachers, who teach alone in their own classrooms most of the time, most early childhood teachers work in teams. The positive side of team teaching is that when team members trust each other and respect each member's role, there is backup and support for each teacher in the group. But a team will struggle if its members are suspicious of each other's motives or don't trust the quality of another team member's

interactions with children. These considerations make the creation and support of teaching teams an important element of staff building.

Candid and respectful communication among team members is essential for building trust and cohesiveness. The best teams consist of teachers with a variety of complementary skills and teaching styles—rational with intuitive, seasoned with new, flexible with firm, structured with creative—who all respect the contributions of the others. If the rational and structured teacher is able to say, "Thanks so much for stepping in to help during that meltdown. I just couldn't seem to get through to him," and the intuitive and creative teacher is able to say, "Thanks so much for helping me learn to explain why a two-year-old needs to have his own space," the team will function smoothly. Diverse cultural and language backgrounds can also add spice and varying perspectives to a team.

It takes effort and thoughtful leadership to create a center culture in which people talk directly to their coworkers rather than complain or gossip behind their backs—or hold on to hurt feelings and sulk in silence. No matter how diverse a staff might be, all people respond well to respectful treatment. When the supervisor is open and honest with feedback to teachers, she provides for the staff a model of how to address concerns openly and how to preserve harmony. Teachers who operate on the assumption that coworkers want to be helpful and cooperative will quickly identify any misunderstandings, which can then be corrected.

To build a cohesive team, each team member must feel included. Full disclosure of information and ensuring that everyone understands new information are critical for creating an atmosphere of inclusion. When a teacher steps out of a group of children or leaves an area, she needs to tell her team members what she's doing. When a parent speaks to a teacher about a child, that teacher needs to inform her team members about what was said—either verbally, by writing it in a staff communication book, or by writing it on the child's daily chart. If part of a team of teachers speaks a language other than English, they need to minimize use of that language while at work. When they do speak their native language, they need to explain to other team members who don't know the language what the conversation is about.

Successful teams plan daily responsibilities for maintaining the classroom and yard. If a team member fails to do her share, it's usually because it was not made clear what is expected of her, or because she didn't under-

stand what is being asked of her. Teams plan who is responsible for daily setup, how the classroom should be left at the end of the day, and how to replace toys in storage so that all the parts are together and equipment can be easily located by others who need it. They agree on standards for maintenance of the classroom, such as wiping up paint spills, sweeping cornmeal or sand off the floor, wiping off toilet seats, and tidying toys on the shelves. In some centers, those matters are left for the end of the session; in others, they are completed as a teacher has time throughout the day. Whatever the culture of the center, a team that discusses and agrees on the small details is a team that will work together in greatest harmony.

SHARING INFORMATION AND INSIGHTS

Besides the ongoing sharing of information among teachers as situations arise, team and staff meetings and observation records are common, effective means of maintaining good communication.

Staff meetings should take place on a regular basis, weekly if possible. At most centers, the time carved out for staff meetings is precious, so the person in charge of the meeting makes sure that the time is well spent. Typical staff-meeting topics include scheduling and organizing staff, menus, the needs of individual children, and reflections on the progress toward goals for a group of children. Whatever the topic, good communication between meetings will result in relevant items of concern being placed on the agenda. Meetings are likely to draw more participation if they include agenda items from many staff members, not just from supervisors or the director. Each teacher's input should be solicited during staff meetings, allowing her to contribute her viewpoint and to brainstorm solutions. Meeting notes should be shared with staff that missed the meeting, and filed for review before the subsequent meeting, to ensure that new plans were implemented rather than forgotten. Seeing concerns noted and discussed, then seeing solutions agreed on, implemented, and followed by a review to be sure the concern was fully addressed, tells each teacher that the time spent in staff meetings is worth the effort to be there.

An observation record is another method a teacher can use to communicate with other staff—and with herself. Regular time to reflect on the development of individual children helps a teacher retain her focus on a

child's growth, and her ability to support that growth. Whenever possible, all teachers who work with a child should have the opportunity to contribute to the child's observation record. Just as multiple viewpoints make for a good staff meeting, multiple viewpoints enrich observations. Each teacher sees the story of the child's development through a different lens. A teacher who is very interested in art might notice something unique in the child's creative play, while a teacher who is more psychologically attuned might notice a shift in the child's behavior during his interactions with other children. Including all teachers' perspectives provides a more complete picture of the child, a picture that is useful to current and subsequent teachers as well as parents.

For example, when a teacher keeps careful track of an infant's dispositions and behaviors, it not only helps her and her teammates tune in to the infant's immediate needs, but also will provide insight for the toddler and preschool teachers when they meet the child a few months or years later. When children enroll in child care as young infants, they may as they grow exhibit signs of special needs that were not obvious during infancy. There again, having a clear record of the child's history can be very helpful during future assessment and planning. In teaching teams in which some of the teachers find it difficult to write in English, teachers might write notes in their native language for another to translate, or the team can share insights about a child and designate one person to write them down in the observation record.

FAMILY-TEACHER RELATIONSHIPS

10

A ll the adult relationships within a school hold a very important place in creating the culture of the school. In order to build a healthy culture and to model healthy behavior for the children, it's essential that adults talk together as partners, solve problems, and make decisions that are acceptable to all concerned. Parents are the most significant adult partners who influence the success of a child's first care and education experience outside the home. Learning to communicate with parents in an open, honest, loving, and compassionate way is critical in order for both child and school to thrive, but that learning takes time, forethought, and personal discipline on the part of the director and teachers.

Working and living with children often triggers parents' and teachers' own memories of and feelings from childhood. Joyful memories of unconditional love and the awe and mystery of the world we felt as

a child can be mixed with memories of feeling powerless, misunderstood, confused, and insecure. As parents, and often new teachers as well, try their very best to do what is right for the child, all these feelings jumble together. It's common and understandable that most adults relive some of their own childhood experiences through the children they care for. Being a parent can be as confounding as it is wonderful, since most parents come to the job with little or no information about the growth and development of children. Parents are usually filled with love for their helpless infant, and most make an inner promise that they will do whatever they can to keep their child safe and healthy as they help her grow. The baby, feeling this love, attaches to the parents and turns to them as primary caregivers (see chapter 2 for more about bonding and attachment).

Fostering Children's Autonomy

The process of bonding and attachment enmeshes parent and child in each other's lives: the baby cries and the mother's breast milk begins to flow; dad is wide awake at 3:00 AM because the house is too quiet. The inner connection between parent and child can be organic and quite deep. Then, as the child ages, he slowly separates and differentiates himself from his parents. He begins to stand on his own, as his own person with his own personality, his own responses to the world, and his own life experiences.

This process of letting go can be emotional and challenging, as it requires the adult to pace his or her parenting expectations with the child's developmental abilities. The child care provider and teacher have a unique opportunity to support the development of this attunement between parent and child. When studying child development and early care and education, teachers learn to help children with this process of separation and independence. It's much easier for a teacher than a parent to help a child in his quest for autonomy and independence, because the teacher is not attached to the child with the same depth as the parent. It's common for the teacher to find that she is coaching both the parent and the child toward maturation in the parent-child relationship.

Work with parents demands a healthy partnership between the teacher, the director, and the parents. Such a partnership does not necessarily mean that parents have to work in the classroom or attend parenting classes, but they must be included and welcomed into the school community and seen as the child's primary attachment and interpreter of her world.

A child must eventually experience life herself, on her own; she can't be protected from all life's challenges any more than she can be protected from all bumps and bruises. She can, however, be taught how to respond and think about her life experiences in constructive ways. That is the role of the parent and the teacher: to understand, to interpret, to care, and to guide, staying closely attuned with the child's ability to take in and assimilate the guidance.

Much of parenting experience is personal, intuitive, and subconscious, and it progresses quite naturally with little input from the child's teacher or other advisors. This is why parents who received thoughtful and compassionate parenting themselves are more likely to become thoughtful, compassionate parents. Child-rearing patterns and cultural styles naturally emerge without conscious thought from adults who care for children, which results in actions taken or words spoken to the child before the adult even realizes it. As adults, many of us have said at one time or another, "I sound just like my mother."

Teachers Sharing Perspective with Parents

Parenting today is changing. Parents have traditionally turned to grandparents and other kin for suggestions and advice about child rearing as they share their love of a new baby. This will continue as long as families have babies. But when people look only to the past for parenting advice, they lose the chance to blend that advice with the growing knowledge in the field of child development, not to mention their own hands-on parenting experiences. Many parents look back on what we now know to be questionable parenting practices and say: "If it was good enough for me, it's good enough for my kid" or "It was the way I was brought up and I turned out okay." Such beliefs provide the child care center's staff with a wonderful role to play in the family culture of today.

Most parents and grandparents have not experienced care in a quality child care setting, so their trust and comfort level are still being formed.

When most adults think of "school," they picture elementary school, not having known preschool or infant care. As they see the wholeness of the early childhood educator's approach, which factors in all domains of human development, they recognize the approach as different from that of the elementary school teacher, whose focus is more on intellect. The child care teacher and director who carefully nurture a family's trust create opportunities to support the family's growth through unique insights and developmentally appropriate strategies.

Professionals with years of experience can guide parents through the challenges of living with the stubbornness of a two-year-old and the exuberance of a four-year-old. They can work with parents to help them understand such behaviors from a developmental perspective, and together they can become a team to help a child learn and grow. Teachers can explain to parents the stages of a child's development and his ability to assimilate guidance and to control his behavior. As an important part of this process, teachers may also model for parents their compassion for the challenges of being a little child and having to learn so much in such a short period of time. Teachers realize that the brain grows very fast during the first five years and that the child's body changes proportion and size very rapidly. It's easy to understand how confusing life can feel to a young child. It's part of the job of teachers and directors to use this understanding to empathize with the child while extending a hand to help the parents do the same.

Teachers can also help parents learn to be proactive and intentional with their words and actions, so parents can set in place a pattern in their developing family structure that is supportive and builds on the loving relationship they established at the child's birth. Because language is often a habit and the meaning of adult speech can be unclear to children, developing constructive communication within the family and in the school community can also be helpful. Center staff establish a welcoming atmosphere to build the kind of trusting relationship necessary for open, constructive communication with parents and children alike.

Good Communication Is Essential

For a parent, enrolling a child at a child care center can be a lot like starting a new job, with anticipation, expectation, and trepidation all intermingled and somewhat overwhelming! Learning to trust the center with the care of a young child, especially a child who is not yet verbal, requires a leap of faith on a parent's part. That's why building in some transition time by setting up an intake and orientation conference some weeks before the child starts can be a big help to new parents, particularly those with infants.

Communication doesn't stop with intake and orientation, of course. It's established as a daily practice, both orally and also in written form (for example, by providing regular progress updates, sharing observation notes and portfolios, and posting notes in children's classrooms or on center bulletin boards). Even with a very good orientation, it takes awhile for parents to learn the routines and rules of a center. Busy parents may not see the postings on a bulletin board, for example, since arrival and departure from school is a distracting time when children's demands must be met and social connections are being made. Learning to look for postings becomes a part of their ongoing education about how to function as part of a school community.

Some programs ask an established parent to be a "room buddy" for new parents, to help the new parents settle in. The buddy serves as an experienced peer representative of the school. This peer support provides the parents with another perspective on the center, and the right buddy can lend perspective to a reassuring parent that teachers and directors cannot.

Be clear with parents about the center's policies; be sure they are in written form, and be sure parents have a copy. The center needs to be particularly clear about policies such as who can pick up the child, what will be done if there is a disaster or other emergency, and what parents can expect if children have to be moved from the premises (where they'll be taken, who they'll be released to, and how parents will find their child if he's picked up prior to their arrival).

All schools thoughtfully develop their own medication policies, sometimes influenced by local licensing regulations. Any medication instructions

need to be written down, including the dosage amount and the times of administration. The teacher giving the medication should sign her name and initial the amount and the times the medicine was given so the parents will know the medicine was given and will be able to give the next dose at the correct time. Some schools only give medicines with a doctor's prescription, though infant programs often may administer Tylenol (with parental permission) to help children who are teething. Requiring a prescription is one way to keep the policy about medicine as objective as possible, as some parents choose to use a lot of over-the-counter medications while others want to let nature take its course.

A child care center must be clear about its philosophy and vision and how it supports the children and the families who are part of its community. Support systems are most successful when they are designed to create functional teams of parents and teachers building a community for the good of the children.

As in every field, inaccurate assumptions or unclear expectations can lead to confusion and misunderstanding, while open communication and trust can build teamwork. One of the teacher's roles is to be as good a communicator with parents as she is with other staff and with the children. When a teacher is clear about her expectations, she can help parents learn their role in the center community.

One parent responsibility is to be the child's primary advocate. A young parent enrolling her baby or young child in group care needs to learn how to uphold that responsibility. The goal of the teacher is to be certain that the parents' relationship with their child will remain strong regardless of the circumstances they may find themselves in. For this reason, teachers respond thoughtfully to parents' questions in ways that build the parent-child relationship. Also, during casual communications, teachers can share interesting tidbits about the day's events, helping parents gain a little insight into their child's day, or teachers can ask how the parent is doing. Most days these conversations are kept light—stories about what the child did during the day, who he played with, how he napped, how much he ate, or how toilet learning is going.

Notes about daily events can be kept on a clipboard for parents to read in case the teacher is busy and can't get away to chat. Notes are usually brief and intended to help parents engage their children in conversation during the trip home. Children live in the moment, so questions such as

"What did you do at school today?" or "Who did you play with?" often elicit a response of "Nothing" or "No one." A leading question such as "I read that you painted a picture with Ellen today. What colors did you girls use?" usually will elicit a response, and helps the parent build a relationship with her child as well as with the teachers and the school.

Sometimes a parent will ask for information the teacher doesn't know the answer to. The teacher can refer her to where she can find the answer. For example, direct her to notes that other teachers may have left, or offer to ask the appropriate teacher and get back to her with an answer. Some schools also use a notebook known as a communication book, in which parents can write notes to the staff or request a call from a teacher. The communication book is helpful for notes such as "I'm picking up Jerrott early for the dentist" or "Please be sure Tamara wears her hat outside today." By writing the note down rather than telling a teacher, the parent can be sure that all of the day's teachers will get the message.

Sometimes parents don't understand the daily schedule and are unclear about which teachers their children are with all day. One parent may drop off his child at school with the teacher who serves breakfast, and another parent may pick up the child at 5:30 from another teacher. If she's asked how the child's breakfast went, the afternoon teacher would have no idea, since she's been with the child only during the end of the day. This example illustrates how important written communication is. The morning teachers can write down information about an infant's routines—diaper changes, bottles, solid foods, naps—both for the enlightenment of the afternoon staff and for the parents at the end of the day.

As children get older, the notes change focus from caregiving information to growth and play interests. These notes serve not only to foster conversation between parent and child, but also to communicate a very important message to parents: the teacher has been tuned in to their child as an individual within a busy group of children.

Parents who drop off a child early in the morning and pick him up late in the afternoon are hungry for an insightful glimpse into the reality of their child's day. For that reason, rather than write a generic paragraph, the teacher pressed for time will write down one line that is specific to the child's experience. When writing a note in a public place, teachers need to be careful to write comments that keep the communication flowing but that are not confidential, as other parents may be looking at the same

notepad. A note that reads "Chris didn't eat lunch, and was very hungry at snack and ate a whole apple, so may not eat much dinner" is objective and helpful, but is not confidential. The teacher should not leave a note about personal or emotionally charged issues; for instance, that "Chris was crabby all morning and bit another child." If the teacher feels the parent needs to know such confidential information, she will call the parent.

It's especially important that teachers write down information about any significant incident that occurred that day—for example, an injury—so that other teachers as well as the parent all know what happened. When a child has been injured, there should be a system to notify parents, such as a note on the child's sign-out sheet explaining objectively, without blaming others, what happened. The note should be written and signed by the teacher who helped the child, so that if the parent has questions, she will know who to ask for more details. A note might say: "Tanya fell down and bumped her arm while she was playing in the yard this morning. She and Karmina were selling sand cakes that they had prepared and lined up on a board on the jungle gym. She bumped her arm hurrying to the shelf to get more containers for the cakes. I washed the scrape and put ice on the bump and gave her a hug. She seems fine now but you'll see the scrape and the bandage near her elbow." If a child has a big bump, or if the teachers know this child's parents tend to react dramatically, a phone call before pickup time is a good proactive step, so the parent can digest the information prior to arriving at the center.

Written notes for other staff members are helpful when a child goes home sick at the end of the day. The admitting teacher the next day needs to know to watch for that parent, to check in specifically to see how the child is doing that morning, and to suggest that the parent have a backup plan in case the child really is not ready to be back at school. Young children rarely "act" sick and want to stay in bed; they usually try to be up and at it, which can fool busy parents into thinking the child is doing better. But the demands of being in a child care group can easily overwhelm a sick child, who will quickly run out of energy and need to go home because he cannot cope with all the activity. Clarity and communication are essential here; the center must be clear about its illness policies. While remaining compassionate about the needs of working parents, the center must still advocate for the needs of the child and of the group.

As a teacher builds relationships with parents through regular and meaningful communication, she strengthens the parents' trust in the integrity of the school. As parents gain confidence in the quality of the care their child is receiving, they will express that confidence to the child in subtle ways that allow the child to thrive in the school's care.

Addressing Children's Behavioral Issues

Generally pickup and drop-off are not the times to express to a parent concerns about a child's behavior. Parents have very little control over their child's behavior while they're away at work, so it's not constructive for a teacher to complain to or admonish a parent about their child's behavior—that would only serve to worry a parent or put her on the defensive, diminishing the quality of the parent-child relationship and the parent-teacher relationship.

While at school, it's the teacher's responsibility to help children manage their behavior and understand its effect on the world around them. The teacher always looks first to adjust the elements under her control when a child's behavior is not working well. If the teacher has been working with the teaching team without success in modifying the child's behavior and feels that the time has come to share her concern with a parent, she requests a conference, so that the parent will feel like a problem-solving partner rather than a person who is expected to "make her child behave."

Sometimes, rather than formally requesting a conference, the teacher will begin to share bits of information that serve to feel out the parents' level of concern for and awareness of the problem. The teacher may call or may mention an ongoing concern over several days. If the concern is one shared by the parent, the parent may proceed to ask for a conference.

In some cases, the parent may not see similar behavior at home—perhaps the behavior is related only to being in a group of children at school, or to being away from the parent—or the parent is simply not tuned in to the child's behavior in the same way the teacher is. Then the teacher would initiate the conference, briefly explaining her concern and asking the parent for an opportunity to have a good discussion about it. Prior to the conference, a staff meeting can allow all the people who work with

the child to coordinate their thoughts and agree how to proceed. One person on the teaching team then can serve as the primary communicator, so parents won't be overwhelmed by hearing the same thing from many people, or confused by hearing multiple messages, each one slightly different from the other.

Sometimes a parent refers to her child as though his behavior means that he is bad or naughty. This gives the teacher an opportunity to remind the parent that all the children are learning and that while children do sometimes make mistakes, the job of adults is to help them learn. If a parent begins discussing his child while the child is present, the teacher should try to steer him away from the child, in order to avoid disrespectfully talking about the child as if he weren't there. If the child will not separate from the parent, the teacher can suggest that she call the parent later, asking what would be a good time to do that.

Children need their parents' love and compassion to help them understand the world around them and to build healthy, positive self-esteem. A teacher can help a parent gain perspective to support that need. It's reassuring for parents to know that when teachers have concerns about a child, they will set up a conference to share those concerns, but that most of the behavior children exhibit is quite typical for their age.

Role Definition

The role of the teacher in child care can easily become blurred. Friendly, caring, responsive, thoughtful, and available, teachers make a point to build relationships with parents that are helpful and nonjudgmental, yet they are not really "friends." Teachers are hired professionals who must be objective and confidential as well as kind. Teachers interacting with parents on school grounds represent the school as well as themselves. To be taken seriously, and to be seen as a professional, means that teachers need to be careful not to act like a kindly neighbor or friend. It's part of a teacher's job to make parents feel trusting and open, able to confide their worries and concerns, even as the teacher maintains professional boundaries. Teachers should talk about a child only with the child's own parents, and they should talk about a child only when she is not present. Gossiping about families or staff or discussing a child as he stands there clearly crosses the professional boundary and will break down all the work a teacher does to build parents' trust.

Like a therapist, a teacher makes confidentiality about personal interactions with children, parents, and staff a high priority. During staff meetings, however, children and parents may be discussed, as all these complicated human relationships are significant in helping young children. The teachers hold these discussions in confidence, as they do parent-conference discussions and any observations and notes about the children and their play.

Occasionally a private family matter becomes public, such as when a child's parent or other family member is ill or dies. The director should be in communication with the family, and notify staff and other families about what has happened and how the child and his family wish to be supported under the circumstances.

The center should stay open and honest with parents about areas that are their concern, such as staff changes, neighborhood issues, or matters of the school community. For example, when a staff member is terminated for incompetent or inappropriate behavior, especially if it involves the children, the school community should be notified. Parents who have built trusting relationships with teachers can be distressed by such an event, wanting to know more than the employer can legally share about the reasons for a teacher's departure. Generally, though, it is sufficient to write a note reminding parents that it is the director's job to be sure that their children receive the best, most thoughtful care, and that, since this employee was not performing to the level expected from staff at the center, she has been relieved of her duties. Of course, if a staff person's behavior was directly harmful to a child—for example, using inappropriate touch or discipline—then a more direct and extreme response is called for, in which case it's best to seek legal counsel for advice. On the whole, such communications build parents' trust in the center. It tells them that the staff is being well supervised, that children are being well cared for, and that they will be told what they need to know.

Parents may be tired, stressed, and struggling with a wide range of feelings, not the least of which is guilt and sadness about being away from their child for a long time. A child care center can be a place where such feelings tumble out. The report of a lost sweater or an injury can sometimes bring an overreaction from a tired parent, so teachers try not to take

things personally by remembering that the whole conversation may turn out to be a misunderstanding.

Occasionally parents use the center (ironically, because it feels like a safe and supportive place) to vent their frustrations from home or work. If a parent starts expressing anger about something, the first priority is to get that parent away from the children. That parent should be taken to the program director or to the director of the center. It is not the teacher's job to make things better. Instead of letting an angry parent upset other teachers or children by prolonging the conversation or by arguing, the teacher can say, "You sound so upset. I'm going to ask the director to join us so we can work this out." If need be, the teacher can repeat this until the parent is in the office. One teacher can stay with the children while another escorts the parent to the office.

Teachers can listen, ask questions to clear up confusion, and remember it is not their job to fix things but to empathize and to provide balanced and useful information. The director can provide additional help or a listening ear for a teacher when the stress and responsibility of handling a difficult situation becomes too much.

Teachers, Parents, Children: A Triad of Support

Each child is treasured for who she is, and an important part of her identity is family. Parents must feel respected and valued, so their child will receive the intertwined support of parents and the school. A child will know if a teacher slights his parent or if his parent feels uncomfortable and does not trust a teacher. It's important to remember that, in order to help a child learn and grow, a teacher must enlist parents as her partner. The teacher functions as a disciplined professional. She welcomes and embraces each parent with compassion for the challenges and joys of parenting, thus establishing and teaching goodwill to all. Once a relationship is established, the teacher will begin to gently support and guide the parents as needed.

It has been said that expectation is the partner of disappointment, but willingness is the dance partner of life. In the child care center, there is a world full of diversity in which every child and family is unique, learning, and progressing. The child care center is careful to guard against making assumptions about children and families, instead allowing each person to make himself known and seen as his authentic self.

In big and small ways, the teacher and classroom offer acceptance and inclusiveness. In the block area, for example, there are diverse enough little people to represent a family, whether it is a grandfather-mother-child household, a mom-dad-child-child-child household, a mom-mom-child household, or a dad-mom-child household. There are books in the book area portraying people with different racial characteristics. The dramatic play area includes adaptive equipment for children to explore. Children see teachers greeting and sharing with all parents, including parents who speak English with an accent and parents who wear head coverings. Teachers are equally interested in hearing about a backyard birthday party and a birthday party at an expensive children's museum. The message children receive over and over again is "You have a great family, and it's just the right family for you."

The child care center accepts and offers support to parents because that helps children learn and grow. Whether or not parents choose to receive support is up to each individual, but when people feel fully accepted, they are more likely to respond to such an offer. There can be no judgment around this kind of family decision, or the help offered to the child will be diminished.

The teachers' primary focus is the children, but parents clearly must be factored in, as part of the triad of child, teacher, and parent. Coping skills and budding personality development are related to a child's experiences away from the child care center. The vulnerable young child, totally dependent on the adults around him, is fortunate indeed when those adults collaborate and support one another to give him the best of themselves. Parents and teachers who respect and care for each other build a strong and resilient foundation for children.

Author Commentaries on the DVD Vignettes, *Snapshots of Age-Appropriate Teaching and Learning at BlueSkies for Children*

The vignettes on the DVD included with this book were filmed on-site at BlueSkies for Children, a private nonprofit child care center founded in 1983 as Association of Children's Services (AOCS).

The first sequence of vignettes, "Hand Washing," demonstrates the developmentally appropriate teaching of this essential skill by age group. The subsequent vignette sequences are listed by age group. These video snapshots will give the reader/viewer an additional experiential perspective on the teaching practices at BlueSkies for Children.

Presented here are some notes about observation in the early childhood setting, followed by author commentaries on the vignettes. We recommend that before you read these commentaries, you first read the age-specific chapter corresponding to the vignette sequence for that age group, and then watch the vignettes, making your own observations and comments as a context for reflecting on our ideas.

Some General Notes about Observation

Through observation, teachers gain insight and understanding into children's behavior, feelings, and language use. Teachers of young children watch not just one child, but all the children. Teachers are multitaskers, simultaneously tuning in to the tone of the playroom while watching to be sure that children can move from one area to another area without bumping into each other or stepping over other children. While attending to the traffic patterns in the play yard and room, teachers notice busy areas where crowding could occur. They also pay attention to voice levels. As they attune to the ambience of the group, they listen to the children's conversations around them, and watch for facial cues or body language that will alert them to impending disharmony. Noticing these clues allows a teacher to step in, clarify, and reorganize conversations so the children can experience greater social success. This sort of proactive intervention requires careful listening and thoughtful, attuned observation to effectively align group needs with a child's agenda. The teacher's careful, objective, accurate observation allows her to develop authentic, empathetic responses to the children's behavior. As the children watch and listen to her, they feel her compassionate support, which creates an atmosphere of trust and safety.

This intentional, creative teaching supports a teacher's ability to objectively observe the children while engaged with them and while holding her own vision and goals for the direction of the children's learning. The teacher's overriding goal is for each child to feel capable and successful. When classroom behavior causes stress or discomfort to an individual child, to a group of children, or to the teacher, the teacher takes a step back, separates herself emotionally, and analyzes and strategizes how to create a more successful experience.

In its ideal manifestation, a teacher or another trained professional objectively observes while not in the teaching role. The observer studies the interplay of the child's behavior and the teacher's behavior, factoring in the effects of the group and the arrangement of the classroom environment on the child's behavior. While this is the best way to learn to observe, once teachers complete their formal education, most do not have the luxury of stepping out of the teaching role very often. They learn to be "participant observers," continuing the teacher role at the same time they're collecting data for later consideration or analyzing and adjusting the environment as a need is identified.

THE TEACHER AS PARTICIPANT-OBSERVER

Teachers learn the most about children by studying them as they play. This is why preschool teachers try not to interfere too much with the natural play process. By watching a child behaving naturally, a teacher can see what the child needs to learn to progress in his development. Knowing that the teacher herself, her use of language, and/or her interactive dynamic with the child might factor into the behavior she's observing, the teacher does her best to step into the child's play only when help is needed, and then step back out of the interaction as soon as the child can work out his own issues. Remaining very attentive and emotionally invested and conveying love and acceptance, the teacher supports the children through her eye contact and presence as the children play around her. The children know she is fully present even though she's not visibly interacting.

A child's first connection to her parent is through gaze and touch. Just as a parent's gaze can calm and affirm a child, the gaze of a teacher across a busy playroom can hold and ground the children. Her mind is active; she is listening, evaluating, and thinking about how the learning experiences of the group are developing. She mentally assesses each child's behavior in terms of age-specific developmental norms and that child's unique characteristics. As children become verbal, she assesses their understanding and comprehension of the language being used. If she senses confusion or misunderstanding, she steps in and clarifies the interaction, then steps back to continue to observe. The more the teacher practices, the more skilled she becomes, and the smoother the classroom runs.

Hand Washing

The video sequence of children washing their hands shows how a teacher's behavior can look very different with different age groups as each age group works toward the common goal of building the habit of washing hands after toileting. Consistent, developmentally appropriate expectations and support are clearly illustrated in this clip, which shows how "consistently" and "differently" can fit together—though the process is different in every group, there is still a way that it is the same. While the long-range goal is for children to wash their hands without a teacher's cue or help, building habit and pleasure in having nice clean hands begins in infancy with the baby's hands being dipped under the faucet after a diaper change.

A teacher meets the children right where they are. If a teacher's four-year-olds' class enrolls a new child who has never been asked to wash his hands independently, she will teach to the two-year-old in that four-year-old, who needs to know how to be competent in the bathroom as well as the classroom. Once this four-year-old has achieved a level of self-competency, the teacher will move on to more sophisticated teaching.

This small task, learning how to wash one's hands by oneself, displays the progression of children's self-sufficiency as they pass through developmental stages.

Infants: The Baby House

While there's often a big temptation to buy fancy toys for infants, "real life" playthings like bowls and cups and cloth napkins with a knot tied in them often make the best toys. Homemade toys are good too: the big jar full of buttons on the infant porch is sealed shut, so the babies can look at it and roll it without having access to the small buttons—a homemade rolling toy! When caring for babies, teachers think about what babies want but can't have, and then try to adapt that object into a safe toy or to create a safe toy that behaves like the forbidden object does (for example, plastic disks on a chain are a safer facsimile of car and house keys on a chain).

"WHAT DO YOU NEED?"

In the opening section of this segment, the teacher is diagnosing what a fussy baby needs. She starts with a hug, which does not satisfy him. Then she offers water (note that the porch is a perfect place to let the babies learn to drink from an open cup), which he happily accepts. But as soon as she begins to disconnect from him, he begins to fuss again. Then she pulls out the cold chew toys that she had stashed ahead of time behind the pillows, knowing that children in the group on the porch are teething. That is finally what soothes him and allows him to return to play. As she goes through all these strategies with Carter, she is also aware of the needs of the three other infants on the porch.

PLAYING ON THE PORCH

The teacher speaks to each child individually, she tells them what she's doing, she keeps them safe from each other's explorations (for example, by helping Mia move away from Tenzin), and she models language (for example, telling Mia to say "Move" to Tenzin). When the climber was inconveniently placed, the teacher pulled it closer so she could easily help all the children. The teacher thinks differently about her use of equipment with young babies than the teachers working with older children think about furniture and equipment. In the infant play area, everything is mobile, and teachers move equipment to keep children safe and happy. They are not concerned with teaching traffic patterns or using equipment to designate different play spaces. If the setup is not working, the teachers in the infant room move equipment or even put it away; they know there's no sense in trying to change a baby's mind and make him do something else. The teacher's whole job is to help the babies do what they want and to see that they get what they need—but while she does that, she makes sure that what they have available to want is safe.

When it's time to go inside, the teacher merely opens the door and allows the children to come in at their own pace. Clearly, these infants have done this before. They have had multiple experiences with this teacher, who is attuned to their rhythm, and they trust her to know when they have had enough time to explore the porch area and are ready to eat. When the door opens, they need no help to move inside for lunch.

NAPTIME

We've all watched and helped babies go to sleep. This everyday activity is worth studying, however, because it's one that is central to a positive experience of life for young babies, who generally nap at least twice a day. When an infant begins to transition into a group care setting, the teachers get as much information as they can about how the baby likes to be held, fed, and put to sleep. These activities will form a large part of the infant's day, and even if the techniques in group care eventually evolve away from those used at home, they give the teachers a starting point for each child's individual preferences and needs.

As we watch the babies in this video going to sleep, we see the dance between teacher and child. No one can force another person to go to sleep. Teachers know this, but they also know that babies need lots of sleep in order to grow and be ready to learn, so the teachers learn as much as they can about how to help the little ones relax. Note the many different strategies the teachers use and how well organized they are in supporting the infant's need for sleep. They have bottles and pacifiers ready (the one who began the process by holding a baby on her shoulder had his individual burp cloth there for him). Sometimes they sit, sometimes they stand, and they hold the infants in many different positions. The last infant we see, lying across a pillow on the teacher's lap, is a child who fights sleep and needs the teacher's help to still herself so she can relax and get the sleep she needs. In this case, we see only the final minutes of a long winding-down process. The teacher is taking responsibility for guiding the baby's regulation so the child can develop a habit of falling asleep before she gets overtired or overstimulated.

One-Year-Olds

The one-year-olds' teachers do a lot of talking! They narrate the children's experiences, giving them language to accompany all their activities. The teachers don't expect a response; they're simply helping the children learn that there are words that go with everything they do and see. Like adults learning a second language, children often understand language before they can come up with their own words. The teacher notices how calming it is for the children when she supplies language for them. We call this type of language usage "sportscasting" because it's similar to the way TV sportscasters observe a sports event and talk about what they see.

"WHERE IS ANNIE?"

Note how the teacher is using her body to teach: her arm becomes a gate, and her lap becomes a waiting spot; she shifts position to send messages to the children that they can or cannot access the space. She knows that these young children cannot manage in a crowded space, so she takes charge of access to the play. She has decided the space can only accommodate two children, and so she turns away a third child trying to enter. When there is just one child behind the curtain, that child may choose whether or not another joins. Malcolm wants to enter, but Annie says, "No," so the teacher tells Malcolm he needs to wait. A moment later, when Malcolm is busy with something on the shelf, Alexander asks to join Annie, and Annie says, "Yes." When Malcolm's timing is off a second time, the teacher takes him into her lap to help him accept the message. These young toddlers are living in the moment, so the teacher does not impose an adult sense of fairness by requiring Alexander to wait until Malcolm has a turn, but instead allows Alexander to enter. We see that the next time Malcolm is ready, he is able to have a turn.

We also see a child toddle through the scene with gloves on his hands, oblivious to the peekaboo game (which is a great game for toddlers who are trying to understand how people appear and disappear in their lives).

It's easy to see how the sensory experience of the gloves is the entire focus of his learning at that moment.

Throughout the segment, the teacher describes the many things she sees going on around her, building the children's receptive vocabulary and minimizing the children's confusion.

PICKING LEAVES

Notice the pace in this section. The teacher's pace matches the children's pace, because she values a relaxed, peaceful learning environment in which the children can follow their own interests. The teacher continues narrating the children's activities. The "leaf through the fence" game is a variation on peekaboo. The teacher also models appropriate interactions as she asks "For me?" and awaits the child's action, and then responds with "Thank you." After Max pushes a leaf through the fence, he turns and points at the bush. The teacher supplies the words to go with his action: "More? You want to get more?" She also notices his reluctance to walk closer to the cameraman, and so she strolls along with him. Children do not always need adult attention as they experiment with the world around them, but in toddler groups with small ratios, children get a personal response often enough to know the teacher is interested in them as individuals.

SNACK TIME

Food is not just about filling the children's stomachs, but also about teaching them language and etiquette—at a very basic level, of course! These young one-year-olds are sitting at the table, having already learned that while the low chairs allow them to stand up and walk away at any time, the teachers keep food at the table. This is a lesson in independent decision making for these young toddlers. The freedom to make a choice is coupled with predictable consequences, so the child can make an informed choice: if he stands up, he must stop eating; if he sits, he may continue to eat.

Many adults fail to recognize how competent a toddler can be. After a few gentle reminders from a teacher, even these toddlers with little self-control will rarely stand up until they are finished eating! The teacher managing the snack encourages the children to use whatever language they have to ask for more, rather than simply passing out food. Whether they say "Naah," "Muh," or "Nana," she extends the language in her response, "More nana? You want more nana?" Sometimes she speaks in the child's voice, modeling, "I want more nana," or she tells the children they can ask the other teacher for toast, saying, "You can say 'Kim, I want more toast.'" A student intern observes in the background, allowing the children to get to know her without interacting with them. As the children finish at the table, the teacher takes a small group outside. A separate group that was outside moves inside.

Just as adults can feel overwhelmed living in the busy impulsive life of the toddler, toddlers can feel worried by the unpredictability of other children. For this reason, the teachers move the children in small groups, which keeps daily life comfortable and manageable and helps the children feel independent and competent. The teachers keep their focus on the children they are transitioning, but they are also in communication with each other about their plans.

Two-Year-Olds

The focus on supporting the development of autonomy in the young two-year-olds is reflected in their classroom setup. Nearly all the equipment is set up for solitary or parallel play (see appendix D), which children at this developmental level can manage. The number of toys available at one time is limited, to help the children focus and choose without being overwhelmed by too many choices. As children are introduced to new play materials, they also learn the routines for using them: how to choose something off the shelf, how to use the material appropriately, and how to return it to its storage spot. Along with keeping materials orderly, routines help children learn how to recognize when a toy is available (when it's on the shelf) or unavailable (when someone else has taken it to a table), and how to sequence by beginning, doing, and ending an activity. All these lessons and supports from the careful arrangement of the classroom environment intentionally facilitate children's understanding of autonomy—the key developmental issue for this age group.

ALEX'S FIRST PAINTING

Alex has just joined the young twos' group and is learning the routines. When the scene opens, he has gone to take an apron from the hook, knowing that is the first step in painting. Then he stands with the apron, not sure what comes next, so the teacher steps in and reminds him how to put it over his head, assisting as needed. Then Alex picks up the paintbrush, again having a general sense of what comes next but not quite remembering the details. The teacher reminds him, both verbally and with physical direction, to pick up the entire cup of paint and carry it to the easel. The teacher works intensively to teach routines as a new child begins in a group, knowing that learning the routines will allow the child to more quickly manage his play independently, which both builds the child's sense of competence and frees the teacher's time to help children in other areas.

Learning routines is particularly appealing to children at this developmental stage, and mastery feeds their growing sense of independence, so the teachers begin teaching routines that will carry through the next three years of their enrollment at the center, even as their play becomes more and more sophisticated. The teacher knows these preverbal children need to receive information both physically and verbally; the physical direction meets the current level of development, while the words accompanying the physical actions begin to build vocabulary for the child's emerging verbal development.

"NO APRON!"

Cabral, new to the group, wants to paint. The teacher steps in to remind him that he needs an apron for painting. She tries many strategies to invite him to put on an apron, with him steadily responding "No" to each. Finally, he walks away from the easel and decides to play with water in the sink. Once again, the apron becomes an issue. The teacher says, "You can tell me when you're ready," and then she stays nearby with an apron in her hand, ready to either help him put the apron on or to again restate that he needs an apron if he approaches the water without it. Finally he says, "I ready," and she repeats, "You're ready!" and helps him put the apron on as he lifts his arms. This teacher places a priority on teaching the children routines, for the reasons outlined above, and is comfortable holding her position even though it disappoints a child who is stopped from playing where he would like to play. In a friendly and supportive way, she continues to restate the requirement that he wear an apron, knowing that his desire to participate in the activity will eventually convince him to wear it. She also knows that his momentary unhappiness is inconsequential in the greater scheme of his growth. The confidence he will gain as he learns competence, independence, and success as part of a group far outweighs the difficulty he may experience this one morning.

PUTTING THINGS AWAY

These young twos may each have their own small tray with paste and collage materials to carry to the table. When Paige finishes her pasting and begins to walk away, leaving the tray on the table, the teacher reminds her to clean up, saying, "I see that you forgot." That is both a true statement and a friendly way to remind a child that there's some cleanup to do. The cleanup is always the last part of a play routine. As Paige casually picks up the tray, the paste drops to the floor. The teacher makes no comment, seeing that Paige has also noticed and will pick it up and continue to the shelf. When Paige again begins to leave, the teacher reminds her of the chair. With cleanup complete, the teacher says, "Thank you, Paige," modeling the polite language people use when they appreciate something another person has done.

MATEO'S BIRTHDAY PARTY

These four toddlers are each absorbed in their own activities at the same table. Leo finishes his activity and wants to join Roxie with her "birthday party" (pegs in a pegboard inspired her to sing "Happy Birthday" to Mateo), but Roxie knows that she does not have to share her tray of table toys. The teacher wants to find a way the two children can share an activity, so he suggests that the children move to the house area, where they can make another kind of birthday party. He begins looking for plates in the toy refrigerator, modeling for these children, who are just beginning to pretend, how to find the things you need to have a party.

Roxie then brings the teacher a kimono, wanting his help to put it on. The teacher reminds her that she knows how to do it, "just like you put on your jacket." Mateo puts his shirt on the same way. The teacher continues to facilitate the play, knowing these children will need a lot of support from him to be able to succeed in these complicated social interactions.

"WHOSE PLATE?"

Mateo grabs Leo's plate. The teacher puts his hand in to remind Mateo to keep his hands back, and prompts Leo to say "I'm still using this plate." When the teacher reminds Mateo that he can look for another plate, Mateo takes the other plate on the table, saying, "I'm still using this plate." Leo watches Mateo looking for more things to put in his bag, and quietly gathers a pitcher and teapot close to himself. When Mateo takes the lid off the teapot, the teacher again reminds him, "Ask Leo if you can use the top." Mateo asks, "Can I use the top?" and Leo shakes his head no. The teacher refocuses Mateo, saying, "You've got a lot of dishes inside your bag, too, Mateo. What are you going to do with all those dishes?"

This is classic twos' action and reaction. The need to understand who "owns" what can easily derail children's play. In this case, the children became more interested in knowing how many dishes they could each possess than they were in cooking. The teacher's question "What are you going to do with all those dishes?" reminds Mateo and Leo that they actually were in the middle of cooking play, allowing them to resume the more productive play they were originally engaged in.

ROCKING OUR BABIES

This is a nice illustration of parallel play, with the two children really enjoying the experience of being "together" while not actually playing together. Roxie, the older child in the pair, is outgrowing the egocentrism of a young two-year-old and becoming more interested in social play, so she gives a phone to Alex so he can match her in every way.

FARMER IN THE DELL

This is what literacy is about during toddlerhood—making stories interesting and engaging (song stories can often help focus very young children hearing stories in a group setting). Through years of story times, the children will begin to study the mysteries of literacy—why is it that every time someone reads that book, they say the same words?—and will want to learn what the adult knows. After the teacher sings "The Farmer in the Dell," we see a group of children outside in the afternoon looking at the book and singing the song, which tells us they've already made a preliteracy connection.

Three-Year-Olds

As children complete their toddler years, they are increasingly interested in independence. The teacher sets up the threes' classroom to support these desires, both in self-care routines and in play. As all development involves "letting go" of one's younger self as well as moving into new realms of exploration, the dramatic play equipment is designed to allow children to play the part of babies, to explore letting go of that baby role, and to change perspective. At the same time, other play choices in the room are growing more complex and more plentiful, reflecting children's more sophisticated abilities to choose and to focus on one activity in the midst of many. Supporting choices in the midst of plenty requires orderly presentation of toys. While there are still opportunities for solitary and parallel play, the classroom is designed to accommodate more associative play as the children enter the social years of preschool. As we see, however, these early attempts at playing together require a teacher's full attention and support in order to be successful.

THE ACCIDENT

The teacher and Larissa are in the process of changing Larissa's soiled underpants. While the teacher needs to manage the cleaning process for the sake of hygiene, she is now ready to return management to Larissa. They go to Larissa's cubby, which is conveniently located right outside the bathroom door, to look for clean clothes. The teacher prompts Larissa to look for underpants. When Larissa decides she also wants to change her socks, the teacher gives her the information that her socks are clean, but when Larissa insists she wants to change them anyway, the teacher acknowledges that and leaves the decision to Larissa. The teacher's goal is to help Larissa feel competent in dressing herself when she needs to change her clothes. Changing her socks will give her more practice dressing, and, more important, will communicate that the teacher is really leaving Larissa in charge of this project. This sense of independent competence is key to success in toilet learning.

Notice how the teacher encourages Larissa to dress herself, and then reflects Larissa's proud "I did it!" with "You did it!" She then reminds Larissa of all she knows how to do. Good teachers keep their focus on helping a child develop mastery, even when engaged in less pleasant jobs such as changing soiled pants. The focus stays on moving the child along her learning trajectory in the most constructive way possible. Here, the teacher's loving, supportive presence communicates what a fine big girl she sees Larissa becoming. In turn, Larissa sees herself as a competent, cared-for learner, rather than as a child who was bad or who made a mistake that displeased the person she needs and depends on as her safe base.

"I WANT TO PLAY"

As Audrey sits at the Duplo table and Tali pulls out the other chair, Madeleine scoots into Tali's chair. As soon as the teacher points out that Tali was getting ready to sit there, Madeleine bursts out crying and lies down on a blanket. The teacher asks Tali to tell Madeleine when he is finished, but when Madeleine sees the Duplo table open, she's no longer interested. The teacher realizes that what Madeleine really wants is to play with Audrey, rather than with any particular toy. Notice how Madeleine just cries when the teacher talks about having a turn with the Duplos, but once the teacher says, "I think you want to play with Audrey," Madeleine starts to respond with words. This is a good indication that the teacher is on the right track. Madeleine was crying because she was not able to say what was wrong and she needed the teacher to help her figure out how to express it.

When the teacher helps Madeleine think about how to tell Audrey she'd like to play with her, Audrey agrees to do so. This is a great example of typical three-year-olds trying to be social and not quite knowing how to make it work. Madeleine is smart and sensitive and she knows what she wants, but she's not quite sure how to get it. Crying like this is almost a reflex. Children may develop a habit of a crying response when things don't go the way they hope if crying has always been effective in gaining the help of a sensitive, loving parent. Children at this stage of development often react faster than they are able to verbalize. Crying is a less mature and less effective form of social communication, but it is tried-and-true!

Madeleine needs help to get what she wants so she can have a socially successful interaction with another child. Her teacher helps her by

- respecting her learning process and allowing her to be upset and see that crying doesn't work, rather than by shaming her or trying to change her behavior

- not responding to the crying, which would reinforce an immature habit
- slowing the action down so Madeleine can follow and understand what happened (Tali was sitting, you came and sat in his chair, when he's done you can have a turn)
- interpreting what Madeleine wants into words, and then saying those words, so Madeleine can use them to have social success with Audrey.

"I DON'T LIKE THAT!"

When young two-year-olds learn "power words," a key phrase is "I don't like that!" As the children get older, their teachers want to help them become more specific about what they don't like and model for them how to say it in a friendlier voice. Children at this age are ready to begin to understand the reciprocity in their relationships and to take responsibility for their part of the relationship by clearly communicating their needs.

Manny was upset because Amir put sand on his shirt. The teacher wants to be sure that Amir hears Manny's objection. From Amir's perspective, he was busy playing, and when Manny got in the way, he put sand on him and that made Manny leave—mission accomplished! The teacher knows that it is her job to help Amir develop a broader perspective, to learn that he can use words to tell someone he's in the way, rather than dump sand on him. After Manny gives his message and leaves, the teacher persists in the conversation with Amir until he acknowledges her.

Newly verbal children are better at saying what they need than listening to others. By insisting that Amir make eye contact with her, the teacher makes sure that he tunes in to her words. She is not angry or scolding, but just giving matter-of-fact information so Amir can respond accordingly if something like this happens again. After saying "OK," Amir returns to his play, saying, "This is a teapot!" The teacher responds, making sure that he knows she will listen to what's important to him, too, and that they can continue to build a trusting relationship.

NAPTIME ROUTINES

Notice how independently the children manage themselves as they move toward their cots for naptime. Some choose a stuffed animal from the classroom collection, while others have brought something special from home. Those who use pacifiers know where to find them. The teacher knows which children still need help to regulate themselves for sleep, and she thus stations herself nearby. She reminds Kenji that "playing with your fingers makes it take a long time to go to sleep," then wordlessly holds his hand to help him relax. One little girl puts her hand on her eyes to help cut down on stimulation; when she removes her hands, she can keep her eyes closed. The teacher is calm, relaxed, and present. She does not talk to the children much, but they know she is paying attention and is there to help them if they can't manage themselves.

IN THE PLAYHOUSE

Haley objects to Arianna taking her doll out of the high chair and climbing in. The teacher clarifies the situation by reminding Arianna that when she goes away, the other children will think she's finished (a common protocol at this school), but also reflecting Haley's interest in using the high chair for her doll. The teacher knows that while Arianna has technically relinquished the chair by going away from it, she is impulsive and most likely was not thinking she was done when she left the high chair. There is no need to be harsh about enforcing a rule. The teacher knows that since she has pointed out the rule, Arianna's attention has been drawn to her behavior and, when Arianna climbs out again, the teacher is ready to make sure she is finished and then to remind her to let Haley know it's her turn to use the high chair. Through her actions, the teacher has shown both girls that she is fair, consistent, and friendly and that she is there to help them.

As Haley puts her doll in the high chair, Arianna climbs onto the doll's changing table and pretends to go to sleep. The teacher asks Arianna if she needs someone to pat her. Arianna asks for a blanket. Then the teacher asks if Haley wants to pat Arianna, trying to facilitate some interaction for these children playing in parallel, but Haley is still more interested in playing with her doll. The teacher puts the blanket over Arianna and pretends to pat for a moment. Responding to Haley's smile of amusement at seeing the teacher pretending with Arianna, the teacher models a little play for Haley. Ben comes over with the toy radio, saying he can't do it. Arianna (a very competent baby!) grabs the radio.

Notice that the doll furniture in the dramatic play area is sturdy enough for the children to use, allowing them to take the role of the baby at a very concrete level. These very young threes are just beginning to develop empathy for others by taking roles in pretend play. The teacher stays nearby to facilitate, as the children are not very able at communicating their desires to each other or at controlling their impulses. While the teacher does not "play" with the children, she does help them play by teaching them socially desirable behavior and constructive language.

Four-Year-Olds

Older preschool children are beginning to think more symbolically, allowing them to use equipment in more abstract ways. Whereas three-year-olds need more realistic props to support their play, four-year-olds are able to pretend just about anything. Their room therefore has more open-ended, flexible materials and fewer toys meant for one type of use. A block can be a telephone, a plate of spaghetti, or a part of a structure. The classroom becomes a blank canvas that can be arranged by the children to suit their play. Because they have internalized all the rules, they are now able to successfully adapt them to use materials in innovative ways. The teacher's job at this point also becomes more complex, as she is required less often to enforce rules but more often to think critically about whether the children's plans are likely to succeed or if they may require some tempering input from her. In the midst of ever-expanding play, the teacher's thoughtful limit setting and direction ensures that all the children will have access to clear and separate play spaces at the same time that children are working with materials from many parts of the room.

BEGINNING THE DAY

With a brief conversation, the teachers plan their morning transition and group the children for optimal success before the children settle in to play in the classroom. Some specific children are selected for the first group, but the receiving teacher also asks for "whoever else is ready," which means the yard teacher will look for children who are completing an activity. Those children who are still engaged in play will have a chance to wrap up their activity and then enter with the next group. As each child enters the gate, the receiving teacher uses her arm to slow the child's entrance, greets each one individually, and gives him or her a message about the morning's plan. Having the children enter in small groups helps the children start their day in a calm, relaxed manner.

NO FRIENDS

This clip is ultimately about respect: respecting the right of two children to choose to play together without having to include a third child if they don't want to, and respecting the fact that a child who is excluded may feel sad. As children get older and their verbal skills improve, their social skills also will improve and they'll learn to manage their feelings and other children better. This clip shows the beginnings of that social learning.

The teacher approaches a group of three girls, one of whom is crying. She asks them what is happening, not because she doesn't know but because it will help the girls verbalize their troubles and it will help the teacher understand the girls' perspective. The teacher restates and expands Kira's limited explanation, so that there's a common set of facts for everyone to work with: two girls want to play by themselves, but a third girl also wants to play there and is sad to be excluded. The teacher helps give words to Abby's feelings, but also acknowledges the legitimacy of two children wanting to play by themselves. She uses the shoe discussion as a face-saving way for Abby to move away from the area without having to directly address the conflict anymore.

When Abby sits nearby, insisting she wants to play only with the girls who have excluded her, the teacher quietly empathizes with her and offers some alternatives. Abby turns away from the teacher, her body language saying, "I don't want to hear what you're saying," but the teacher continues to offer her support, concluding with the message that if she would like to sit and be sad for a while, that would be fine. It's important for Abby to know that it's all right to feel what she feels. The teacher moves away but keeps her eye on Abby, and she returns when she sees Abby stand up and look ready to try playing somewhere else. Though Abby doesn't like it, when she sees the teacher protecting and supporting the two children playing together, Abby knows that she too will be protected and supported when she wants to play with just one friend.

SILLY POEMS

Social fours tend to be silly and to love nonsense words, rhyming, and chanting. They love being together and laughing together. The teacher reads the first poem, Spike Milligan's "On the Ning Nang Nong," straight through, not pausing for interruptions. She has selected this poem for its rhythm, rhyme, and silly words; she knows its rich language experience would be diminished by interruptions.

This is a delightful poem for fours, who love the wordplay and get the joke because they're old enough and confident enough in their understanding of the world to know that trees don't go "ping" and monkeys don't say "boo."

The teacher next reads "An Alphabet," a poem by Edward Lear, which like an alphabet book proceeds from letter to letter. Again the teacher's goal is for the children to enjoy the sounds of the made-up words. Memorizing the alphabet and the letters is not the goal here; the teacher simply wants the children to enjoy the play of sounds and to build phonemic awareness, a key prereading skill. When the children spontaneously begin to respond by thinking about other J sounds and other rhymes for "nosies," it's clear that the teacher's goal is in tune with the children's level of development: they are ripe to receive and respond to wordplay. The teacher allows the discussion to evolve into one about alternative means of communication. This free-association thinking provides a great view into the mind of a preschooler.

THE BLOCK TOWER

Two children are building an amazing tower of blocks, but the teacher recognizes that it's unstable. He wants to be sure the play ends positively and that the harmony in the room is protected, so rather than let the play end with a big crash, injured children, and hurt feelings, he steps in and takes control of the play. Throughout the scene, the teacher's proactive stance keeps the experience positive. He helps the boys define a way to wrap up their play by saying he'll take their picture and then help them clean up. When Josh doesn't respond to the teacher's words, the teacher moves closer and puts his hand on Josh to help Josh know that he's expected to attend to the teacher's words. This toddler technique is still helpful for an older child when the child's attention is elsewhere.

After taking a photo, the teacher steps in to lower the shakiest part of the structure and to help the children clean up. He does not help by picking up blocks, but rather by asking Josh to pick up one kind of block and Grant to pick up another kind. While cleaning up the big pile could easily have seemed like an overwhelming task to the boys, the teacher helps them see the separate categories of blocks within the pile, which allows them to manage the job pretty independently. While the teacher continues to work with the whole group, his focus stays on the boys; he knows they can manage independently as long as they feel his presence, but if he moves too far away or breaks eye contact for too long, the boys may become overstimulated by the chaos, lose self-control, and become disruptive.

Five-Year-Olds

All the children in this clip are within months of kindergarten entrance. Like all the classrooms in a preschool, the fives' classroom is set up with plenty of opportunity for social play: a dollhouse, block areas, and lots of large-motor outdoor play. In this clip, the puzzle area and table activities are highlighted to show the maturation in a five-year-old's thinking. But it's important to know that the children continue to need a classroom that offers a broad array of activities. Each child you see has independently chosen his or her activity. The teacher knows both what the children are interested in and what they should be developmentally ready to learn, so for the children the classroom setup is appealing, interesting, and full of variety.

EXPLORING MATH CONCEPTS

Notice the concentration and focus as Hanif works on a very difficult puzzle. You see it again as Henry and Jack count money in the toy cash register and match coins to the stickers on the paper plates; as Kai creates a pattern with wooden pegs; and as Jack builds symmetric patterns with the pattern blocks. All these activities portray spontaneous academic play that the children have chosen because of their readiness to learn. The children are relaxed and happy, knowing they can come and go as they please and can choose what they like to do. The children wiggle and talk while concentrating hard on their self-initiated tasks, which they may or may not complete. When they're done with their task, they can run to the yard to swing or climb and release the tension such concentration has created.

Kira and Maggie have been building a large block house. Deep inside, they added a small block house for the little people. First they dump the basket of people, and then they sort them into groups to choose just the right people.

EXPLORING PRINT

Just as math skills are being engaged around the classroom, so are reading and writing skills. Laura and Kira make up a game to put an alligator alphabet puzzle together. Alix and Selihome move from looking at books to the writing table, where Selihome copies Alix's name. Laura, who was originally outside riding a bike, comes inside and goes to the art table. First she draws a design on the green paper, then cuts it out and glues it on her book. Next she writes her name and her sister's name on the book. She finishes by copying the letters from the EXIT sign over the door!

When Henry decides to write a book for his brother Manny, he traces a star on a piece of paper. Next he asks for help to make the letter M (note how subtly the teacher points to the next letter—"a"—she wants him to feel ownership of the project). Last of all, Henry gets a stencil for the number 3, Manny's age. Jess comes to the table where Henry is and gets busy writing words for feelings. Each page has one word, which he illustrates with a drawing about that feeling. (Often, the first books children make have only a picture on the cover.) The children "signing in" at the ticket booth show how integrated play and writing becomes.

THE FISH STORE

The last part of this clip illustrates cooperative play. That day the children sang "Molly Malone," an old Irish song attributed to James Yorkston and first recorded in the nineteenth century. After a discussion about the cockles and mussels and fishmongers mentioned in the song, the boys in this clip became taken with the idea of "fishmongers." Once outside, they begin to fill up buckets with "fish" (sand) and to sell them from the jungle gym. When they decide the fish store needs more sand shark, crab, and trout, the boys pull the big green bucket over and tie it to the jungle gym so they can fill it and haul sand up to the containers. The teacher's goal is to help the children have a successful, cooperative play experience, so she supports the play, staying near and sometimes suggesting ways the children can keep the play successful and positive. She knows play is fun when it takes ingenuity and has challenges, so she lets these big boys struggle, use their muscles, and experience some risk as they learn to work together in a large group.

A Philosophy of Respect: Ten Principles of Caregiving

The following principles are taken from Janet Gonzalez-Mena and Dianne Widmeyer Eyer's book *Infants, Toddlers, and Caregivers* (2000). The parenthetical text contains our summary of each of the principles.

1. Involve infants and toddlers in things that concern them. (Don't work around them or distract them in order to get the job done faster.)

2. Invest in quality time. (Time when you are totally available to individual infants and toddlers. Don't settle for supervising groups without focusing, more than just briefly, on individual children.)

3. Learn each child's unique ways of communicating and teach them yours. (Don't underestimate children's ability to communicate even though their verbal language skills may be nonexistent or minimal. Their modes of communication may include cries, words, movements, gestures, facial expressions, and/or body positions.)

4. Invest in time and energy to build a total person. (Concentrate on the "whole child." Don't focus on cognitive development alone or look at it as separate from total development.)

5. Respect infants and toddlers as worthy people. (Don't treat them as objects or cute little empty-headed people to be manipulated.)

6. Be honest about your feelings. (Around infants and toddlers, don't pretend to feel something that you don't, or not to feel something that you do.)

7. Model the behavior you want to teach. (Don't preach.)

8. Recognize problems as learning opportunities and let infants and toddlers try to solve their own. (Don't rescue them, constantly make life easy for them, or try to protect them from all problems.)

9. Build security by teaching trust. (Don't teach distrust by being undependable or often inconsistent.)

10. Be concerned about the quality of development in each stage. (Don't rush infants and toddlers to reach developmental milestones.)

Social/Emotional Developmental Continuum

	Infant	Young Toddler	Older Toddler	Preschooler	Prekindergartener
Seeks trusted adults for companionship, affection, comfort, and support	Looks into adult eyes during nursing or bottle feeding. Responds to adult soothing. Recognizes and reaches out to familiar adults.	Seeks to remain near familiar adults. Returns to familiar adults for comfort, for help, and to participate in simple games. Shows distress around unfamiliar people. Imitates actions of familiar people.	Requests adult help and attention. Begins to participate in caregiving routines and simple games. Uses a transitional object to symbolically keep adult close. Alternates between clinging to and resisting adult.	Looks to adults as resources and role models. Can separate from adult without distress.	Enjoys working and playing with adults. Seeks adult help and support when needed.
Examples	Stops crying when picked up and rocked by adult. Holds arms out to mother at the end of the day.	Crawls to follow adult around room. Goes back and forth between exploring environment and sitting on adult's lap. Plays peek-a-boo with adult. Turns head away from visitor. Tries to take sunglasses from adult and put on own face.	Calls "Help me" when trying to climb onto a high stool. Wipes face with paper towel given by adult after meal. Plays chase game with adult. Carries blankie or photo of family around as comfort item during stressful times. Pulls away and says, "No" one moment, then runs back for hugs and affection the next.	Mimics family members in home living center. Asks to help provider push snack cart back to kitchen. Kisses provider's finger when hurt in the door. Hugs Daddy good-bye in the morning and goes off to find playmate.	Comes over to help provider move tables over for dancing activity. Asks provider to fetch more blue paint for project. Asks provider to play Candy Land with him. Comes to provider for bandage when hurt in play yard.

From Common Psychological Disorders in Young Children: A Handbook for Child Care Professionals, *by Jenna Bilmes and Tara Welker, PhD (St. Paul: Redleaf Press, 2006).*
© 2006 by Jenna Bilmes and Tara Welker. Reprinted with permission of the authors.

	Infant	Young Toddler	Older Toddler	Preschooler	Prekindergar-tener
Looks to others for companionship, connection, and community	Searches for faces. Explores faces and bodies of others. Watches and responds to other children. Is interested in being with others.	Shows interest in other children at play. Participates in sustained play near other children with minimal interactions.	Seeks company during play. Plays with one or two favored children. For a short time, sustains play with another child with common themes. Begins to participate in routines with other children.	Enters ongoing play with one or more children, integrating easily into the play. Engages in social games and pretend play with others.	Identifies a child as a best friend and is identified in return. Leads or participates in coordinated play with others. Identifies self as a member of a group.
Examples	Turns head to follow movements of older child. Reaches out to touch face of nearby baby.	Watches children crawling up loft steps. Plays fill and dump game next to a child looking at a book.	Goes to block and car area where others are playing. "Drives" cars with special buddy most days at choice time. Runs to join activity table when sees provider take out a cooking project.	Watches children making rivers in sand and begins to help. Goes to children at the sensory table and asks, "What are you doing?" Pretends to be the pet cat in the home living area.	"I'll be the mommy and you be the baby." Builds a big city with others in the construction area. "I'm a sunshine kid."

From Common Psychological Disorders in Young Children: A Handbook for Child Care Professionals, *by Jenna Bilmes and Tara Welker, PhD (St. Paul: Redleaf Press, 2006). © 2006 by Jenna Bilmes and Tara Welker. Reprinted with permission of the authors.*

	Infant	Young Toddler	Older Toddler	Preschooler	Pre-kindergartener
Learns to regulate behavior, emotions, and attention	Develops eating and sleeping patterns. Shows emotions with body. Begins to find strategies to self-soothe. Responds to attempts of adults to soothe her. Begins to show interest in sights and sounds.	Uses adults to co-regulate. Uses transitional objects to manage separation. Comforts self by seeking a specific person or special object. Gets involved, but is easily distracted.	Toilet learning. Follows simple routines with reminders. Responds to and tests limits. Gets distracted but returns to task.	Follows established routines. Can adjust behavior based on setting and situation. Regulates behavior with self-talk. Relies on adult structured processes for turn taking, waiting, and sharing. Can concentrate on a task.	Anticipates and participates in daily routines, transitions, and activities. Accepts changes in daily routines and schedules. Can regulate own behavior/emotions/attention using learned techniques. Identifies emotional triggers for self and others. Can do two things at once.
Examples	Settles into two naps a day, one in the morning and one after lunch. Cries and curls up arms and legs when hungry. Sucks fingers to relax into sleep. Stops crying when rocked by an adult. Watches mobile move in the wind. Turns head to voices.	Reaches for object and looks at adult for approval before continuing on. Carries Tata's purse around when she misses home. Plays with toy drum but drops it immediately when he sees another interesting activity.	Begins toilet learning. With adult reminder, washes hands before snack. Runs away when called to come inside. Looks up from water table when hears kids laughing, but returns to his play.	Runs outside, but, with reminders, walks in the hallway. Says to self, "Flush the toilet," after using bathroom. With adult prompting, lets another child have a turn on the swing. Continues to work on art project even when other activities are going on around her.	Comes in from outdoor time and sits right down in the circle area for story time without prompting. Manages field trip to library without falling apart. Takes turns, shares, waits, and "uses words" if previously taught and modeled by others. Says, "LaHana is crying because nobody will give her a turn." Can eat lunch and carry on conversation at the same time.

From Common Psychological Disorders in Young Children: A Handbook for Child Care Professionals, *by Jenna Bilmes and Tara Welker, PhD (St. Paul: Redleaf Press, 2006). © 2006 by Jenna Bilmes and Tara Welker. Reprinted with permission of the authors.*

	Infant	Young Toddler	Older Toddler	Preschooler	Prekindergar-tener
Develops communication and social skills to interact with others	Smiles and makes sounds of pleasure when others are around. Cries to communicate needs. Responds to social play with babbling.	Follows one-step instructions for familiar tasks. Expresses basic needs, wants, and feelings through simple actions and crying. Understands simple words and phrases.	Uses basic language to attempt to communicate with others. Begins symbolic play. Uses physical behavior when he lacks social language.	Follows two-step instructions for familiar tasks. Uses language in more sophisticated ways to describe feelings and to tell a story with a beginning, middle, and end.	Follows three-step instructions for unfamiliar tasks. Understands "how" and "why" language. Can describe feelings and what caused them (emotional cause and effect). Has extended conversations sharing emotions, ideas, and information.
Examples	Smiles in response to adult smile. Cries when diaper is soiled. Babbles back in response to somebody talking or playing with her.	Waves bye-bye when prompted. Holds up cup to get more milk. Cries or fusses when hungry or overtired. Holds arms up when adult says, "Carry you?"	Says, "More milk" or "No naptime" or "You read this." Pretends a block is a cracker and pretends to eat it. Hits or bites to communicate with another child.	Follows directions when told "Wash your hands, then find a seat at the cooking table." Says, "I want to paint" or "My dog ranned away and he didn't come back and my brother he tried to find it."	Follows directions when told "Come get your body traced, then paint your face on it, and write your name on the page." Says, "My brother cried because the dog got lost." Talks with others at the snack table about a movie they all saw.

From Common Psychological Disorders in Young Children: A Handbook for Child Care Professionals, *by Jenna Bilmes and Tara Welker, PhD (St. Paul: Redleaf Press, 2006). © 2006 by Jenna Bilmes and Tara Welker. Reprinted with permission of the authors.*

	Infant	Young Toddler	Older Toddler	Preschooler	Prekindergartener
Recognizes that she can do things, make things happen, and solve problems (self-efficacy)	Tries communicating with others through noises and body language. Explores by doing the same thing over and over again.	Figures out how to solve problems without considering the effect on others. Seeks adult help to solve problems.	Seeks adult attention to get positive feedback or help. Insists on doing things by himself. Explores physical cause and effect.	Asserts needs and wants without hurting or violating others. Completes multi-step tasks without adult help. Uses learned social skills for sharing space and stuff.	Attempts several ways to do something complex if one way doesn't work. Begins to create original solutions to problems.
Examples	Lets others know that he wants to be picked up or played with. Turns head away when done feeding. Kicks at a mobile hung overhead.	Bangs an empty bowl on the table to get more cereal. Sits on another child to be closer to a book. Drops a shoe on the adult's lap to get help putting it on.	Calls, "Look" when climbs steps up the slide. Pushes adult hand away when trying to zip jacket. Shouts, "Me do it," when adult tries to help. Flushes toilet over and over to see what happens. Turns water on in sink and holds hand over the drain to see what happens.	Says, "My turn" to a child on the swing. Cuts out pictures and glues them onto the pages of a self-made book. Takes turns throwing the ball in the basket.	Tries a number of ways to tape two boxes together to make a dog house. Says, "I know! How about we make some more cars out of the Legos?"

	Infant	Young Toddler	Older Toddler	Preschooler	Prekindergar-tener
Develops an understanding of self and relationship to others	Reacts to facial expressions. Communicates needs through body language, crying.	Recognizes self and familiar people. Changes behavior in reaction to another's emotions.	Differentiates self from caregivers—demonstrates ambivalence of wanting to be connected and separate. Expresses ideas about self and connection to others. Is aware of and reacts to others' feelings.	Follows adult guidance about sharing space and stuff. Responds to peer assertion of needs or wants.	Uses words or actions to respond with caring to others' emotions. Can predict how another might react in a given situation. Tries to make amends when has wronged another.
Examples	Smiles and coos in response to others. Cries when hungry or tired.	Recognizes self in mirror. Points to photo of grandma and says, "Nana." Laughs and claps when another child laughs and claps.	Says, "No" and runs away when called. Then runs back weeping and asking to be picked up. Runs to hug older brother in the preschool room, calling him by name. Sees child crying and goes to adult saying, "Reena crying."	With adult prompting, moves over at circle time to let another child sit down. With adult reminder, passes the bowl of potatoes to next child at lunch. Lets another child join in at home living center when child asks, "Can I play with you?"	Says, "Let me see your owie. Does it hurt?" When provider asks about how the little pig might feel when the wolf is chasing him, says, "He gets scared." Says, "Sorry," when accidentally steps on another child's hand.

From Common Psychological Disorders in Young Children: A Handbook for Child Care Professionals, *by Jenna Bilmes and Tara Welker, PhD (St. Paul: Redleaf Press, 2006). © 2006 by Jenna Bilmes and Tara Welker. Reprinted with permission of the authors.*

Stages of Social Play

In 1932, Mildred Parten classified play into stages that help teachers understand the normal developmental progression of social play. Keeping these stages in mind shapes a teacher's expectations for the children's play: she sets up play areas based on the kind of play the children can manage successfully with just a little help from the teacher. While each age is associated with a stage, most children will exhibit several stages in a day's play. We classify stages of play as follows:

Onlooker Behavior: Play evolves through watching and copying, first watching grown-ups and then other children. Onlooker behavior is present in every stage of play; many children and adults like to watch before they join a group.

Solitary Play: Children play in the same area with minimal awareness of others. Their play is totally focused on their own interests or the adults nearby.

Parallel Play: In parallel play, children play side by side with similar toys; the nearness and similarity are the most important parts. In parallel play, children do not usually share toys or ideas; the social aspect comes from being near each other and the pleasure they take in their similarity, happily copying and building on each other's ideas.

Associative Play: In associative play, children seem to play together, but the roles the children adopt are not the result of any group agreement. Children in this stage of associative play might have a family consisting of a mom, a waitress, and a cat—the players being more interested in who they want to be as individuals than in the theme of "playing house." They will quit the play or cry or make other demands before they will take a role someone else assigns.

Cooperative Play: Cooperative play can be recognized when children assign and accept roles matched to a theme, such as when everyone is a firefighter going to the fire, an ambulance driver accompanying the fire truck, or a victim of the fire. Being part of the team is more important than holding the ladder or the hose, being first at the fire, or playing the first-choice role.

Games without Rules: After children begin cooperative play, they move into a stage called *games without rules.* Like associative play, it can be confusing to adults. Play partners either make up games and change the rules every chance they get, or they play existing games but change the rules to suit themselves. During this stage, rules are perceived as something to make other people do things, but not as something to apply to oneself. This play stage is creative, fluid, and fanciful, exemplified by the croquet game in *Alice in Wonderland*.

Games with Rules: The last stage of play is called *games with rules*. Achieving this stage allows children to manage games such as kick-ball, four-square, and T-ball. As in cooperative play, the team is more important than the individual. At about age seven, children come to accept consistent rules as being "good for the game."

Kindergarten Readiness

A summary of the report from the National Education Goals Panel (1997)

I. PHYSICAL WELL-BEING AND MOTOR DEVELOPMENT
A healthy, alert, and energetic child is able to give full attention to learning experiences and other tasks in the school setting.

    A. **Physical fitness and stamina** (sufficient exercise, minimal passive entertainment, good nutrition)

    B. **Sensorimotor skills** (vision, hearing, touch, kinesthesis, eye-hand coordination)

    C. **Gross motor skills** (balance, bodily coordination, running, large muscle groups)

    D. **Fine motor skills** (handling pencils, scissors, small objects with precision)

    E. **Oral motor skills** (related to feeding and speech)

    F. **Self-help skills** (feeding and dressing self, hygiene habits)

    G. **Health care/early diagnosis of any diseases or disabilities** (well-baby visits, early intervention as needed)

II. SOCIAL AND EMOTIONAL DEVELOPMENT
A child who has developed a positive sense of well-being will demonstrate the emotional security necessary for successful interactions with peers and teachers.

    A. **Emotional well-being**
        well-developed self-concept
        ability to express feelings
        bonded with caregivers
        sensitivity to the feelings of others, empathy, prosocial behavior

    B. **Social skills**
        bonding: a warm relationship with at least one adult
        ability to form reciprocal friendships in peer group
        cooperation with peers: ability to negotiate and compromise without being too submissive or too directive

III. APPROACHES TO LEARNING

Positive attitudes, habits, learning style, and motivation in early childhood will transfer to the elementary classroom.

Attitudes and learning styles that are conducive to learning are:
curiosity and openness to new ideas
initiative (ability to begin projects)
persistence (ability to carry them through)
attentiveness (ability to not be easily distracted)
creativity, imagination, and invention
reflection and interpretation (ability to put new learning to use)

IV. LANGUAGE DEVELOPMENT

The ability to interact and communicate effectively with adults and peers is essential for success in the elementary classroom.

A. Verbal language skills:
listening
speaking
social uses of language (expressing feelings, getting needs met, getting information, following social conventions)
vocabulary and concept development (includes spatial and temporal relations, sequence, causality, and meanings of words)
questioning (ability to ask who, what, why, when, where, and how questions)
creative uses of language (rhyming, word play, music, storytelling)

B. Emergent literacy:
print awareness (noticing environmental print)
storytelling and dramatic play
literature awareness (retelling familiar stories)
story sense (story structure, sequence, cause and effect)
writing process (pre-writing scribbles representing letters)

V. COGNITION AND GENERAL KNOWLEDGE

Children who are encouraged to explore, experience, and question the world around them in a play-based program are ready for the new, more structured learning experiences of elementary school.

A. **Physical knowledge** (understanding of the objects around them and how they behave)

B. **Logico-mathematical knowledge** (understanding relationships between objects, such as compare and contrast, measurement, mathematical operations, and problem solving)

C. **Socio-conventional knowledge** (understanding the conventions of their culture)

Sample Letter to Parents about Preschool Learning

Dear Parents:

Play-based, child-centered, developmental, whole child . . . all these preschool terms can seem like buzzwords with little relationship to getting children ready for kindergarten. You might wonder: "My backyard is play-based, and our whole house is child-centered these days—how do these words describe programs that will prepare my child to be successful in kindergarten and elementary school?"

The answer is based in the fact that the brains of preschoolers process differently from those of elementary-aged children. Young children gain information in unpredictable ways, and usually during play. When we say that children learn through play, we do not just mean that they learn no matter what they're doing. We mean that play is the very best way for preschool children to take in information and learn about things.

Most of us know adults who "think out loud." That is, when they are working out a new concept, they talk with people about it. They toss out preliminary thoughts and discuss them as a means of forming their final understanding of the topic. When children play, they are "thinking out loud" through their play. With their limited verbal ability and limited ability to think in the abstract, they cannot process all the thinking they are doing in their minds. They thus enact and reenact experiences and information they are trying to understand, which allows them to assimilate information in a meaningful and deep way.

Children may use the dramatic play area or small figures in the block area to study social dynamics and to try out the roles and feelings of other people in their lives. They may use the block area to understand math concepts, such as how two small blocks together form the same shape as one larger block. When they pretend that a block is a phone, they develop symbolic concepts that are the basis for reading and math, as written words and numerals are symbols for objects and things.

How does taking another person's perspective or understanding that two small items equal one large item prepare a child for kindergarten? What about letters, numbers, and colors? The world is so competitive and technological that one might think children can no longer afford to play, and had better instead hurry into academic learning. But while the world is changing very quickly, evolution takes millions of years—children today need the same childhood experiences their great-great grandma needed as a child. Children who select their own play activities learn how to explore and learn about something that interests them. They learn how to get along with other children. They learn that the teacher is their partner in learning. When their brains mature at age five or six, these qualities of self-respect and respect for others will allow them to be able to listen to and follow a teacher's directions.

Hurrying a child into academic instruction before her brain is mature enough to understand what is taught can make her feel both incompetent and less interested in learning. Although she may be able to recite information, she doesn't really comprehend it, so the "learning" is about pleasing an adult, without the satisfaction of understanding a new idea. Through play, children come to understand themselves, become interested in learning, and find pleasure as part of a social group. With these foundations in place, a child is ripe to learn whatever is presented in elementary school.

So the best early childhood program is one that not only *allows* your child to play, but that insists that he play. Let him learn about himself as a member of the world around him, and he will be ready to succeed in the most important thing that comes after preschool—life!

References

Als, H. et al. 1982. Manual for the assessment of preterm infants' behavior. In Theory and research in behavioral pediatrics, ed. H. E. Fitzgerald, B. M. Lester, and M. W. Yogman. Vol. 1. New York: Plenum Press.

Ames, Louise Bates, and Frances L. Ilg. 1976. Your three-year-old: Friend or enemy? New York: Dell.

———. 1976. Your two-year-old: Terrible or tender? New York: Dell.

Ames, Louise Bates, Frances L. Ilg, and Carol Chase Haber. 1982. Your one-year-old: Fun-loving and fussy. New York: Dell.

Biber, Barbara. 1948. "How do we know a good teacher?" *Childhood Education* 24 (6): 281–85.

Bloom, Paula Jorde. 1997. A great place to work: Improving conditions for staff in young children's programs. Washington, DC: NAEYC.

Dr. Seuss. 1960. Green eggs and ham. New York: Random House.

Gesell, Arnold. 1943. Infant and child in the culture of today: The guidance of development in home and nursery school. New York: Harper and Brothers.

Goleman, Daniel. 1995. Emotional intelligence. New York: Bantam Books.

Gonzalez-Mena, Janet, and Dianne Widmeyer Eyer. 2000. Infants, toddlers, and caregivers. 5th ed. New York: McGraw-Hill.

Gopnik, Alison, Andrew Meltzoff, and Patricia Kuhl. 1999. The scientist in the crib: Minds, brains, and how children learn. New York: William Morrow & Company.

Greenman, Jim. 1998. Places for childhoods: Making quality happen in the real world. Bellevue, WA: Exchange Press.

Healy, Jane. 1994. Your child's growing mind: Brain development and learning from birth to adolescence. New York: Doubleday.

Milligan, Spike. 1970. "On the Ning Nang Nong." In *Silly Verse for Kids.* London: Puffin Books.

Moats, Louisa C. 2001. "Overcoming the language gap." *American Educator* (summer). http://www.aft.org/pubs-reports/american_educator/summer2001/lang_gap_moats.html (accessed February 1, 2007).

Mooney, Garhart Mooney. 2000. Theories of childhood: An introduction to Dewey, Montessori, Erikson, Piaget, and Vygotsky. St. Paul, MN: Redleaf Press.

National Education Goals Panel. 1997. http://govinfo.library.unt.edu/negp/Reports/child-ea.htm (accessed February 20, 2007).

Parten, Mildred B. 1932. "Social Participation among Preschool Children." *Journal of Abnormal and Social Psychology* 27: 242–62.

Stevenson, Robert Louis. 1970. A child's garden of verses. New York: Avenel Books.

VandenBerg, Kathleen. 2004. Infant crying—issues and interventions. Talk presented at a Special Start Training Program 0–3 conference, June 11, 2004, in Sacramento, California.

VandenBerg, Kathleen, et al. 2003. Getting to know your baby: A developmental guide for community service providers and parents of NICU graduates. Oakland, CA: Special Start Training Program. http://www.mills.edu/specialstart/materials.html.

Index

and story time, 73–74

and substitute teachers, 66

toys for, 63–64

and transitions, 67–68

trust building with, 76–77

and unexpected changes in routine, 81

verbalization process, 76

verbalization process with, 76

worldview of, 66

toileting accidents, 128, 246–247

toilet learning

approaches to, 119–120

in full-day child care, 13

and independence, 116–118, 122–123

readiness for, 119

self-awareness and, 118–119

with three-year-olds, 106–107

toys for infants and toddlers, 63–64, 238

training, in relationship framework, 215–217

transitional moments in learning, 23–24

transitions

overview, 195

into child care, 9

from child care environment to home, 160–161

and children as individuals, 195–196

end-of-day, 129, 160–161

hints and techniques, 196

from home to child care environment, for toddlers, 67–68

infants and, 41–42

navigating, with two-year-olds, 90, 93–94

from outdoors to indoors, 138–139, 196–197

siblings, from home to child care environment, 136–137

substitute teachers and, 75–76

three-year-olds and, 110–111

trauma, and development trajectory, 183

trust building, 9, 74, 76–77

two-year-olds

behavior problem prevention with, 102

and biting, 101, 103–104

brain development of, 88–91

circle time with, 27–29

DVD vignettes, 242–245

and emotions, 97–99

goals for, 60, 87

and language development, 96–99

lunch time with, 93–94

naptime with, 94

and ownership concept, 93, 103–104

play extension with, 88

power words, 97–98

self-regulation by, 99–100

social development of, 94–95

and social misunderstandings, 96

story time with, 93

and tantrums, 99–100

teachers as translators for, 98

transitions with, 90

U

unexpected changes in routine, 61–62, 76, 81

unexpected sensations, preparation for, 81

V

verbalization process, 41–43, 76, 131

See also language modeling

visual dexterity, 174–175

vocabulary, five-year-olds and, 167, 170

Vygotsky, Lev, 21, 23–24

W

Wagner, Lovisa, 25

Waldorf schools, 22–23

walking, toddlers and, 63–64

word knowledge, 170

wordplay, 169–170

worldview, of toddlers, 66

Z

zoologists, compared to education providers, 3

Other Resources from Redleaf Press